DECONSTRUCTING ORGANIZED CRIME

D1564983

DECONSTRUCTING ORGANIZED CRIME

An Historical and Theoretical Study

Joseph L. Albini *and*
Jeffrey Scott McIllwain

McFarland & Company, Inc., Publishers
Jefferson, North Carolina, and London

LIBRARY OF CONGRESS CATALOGUING-IN-PUBLICATION DATA

Albini, Joseph L.
   Deconstructing organized crime : an historical and
theoretical study / Joseph L. Albini and Jeffrey Scott McIllwain.
      p.   cm.
   Includes bibliographical references and index.

   ISBN 978-0-7864-6580-4
   softcover : acid free paper

   1. Organized crime — History.   I. McIllwain, Jeffrey
Scott, 1969–   II. Title.
   HV6441.A393 2012
   364.10609 — dc23   2012032462

BRITISH LIBRARY CATALOGUING DATA ARE AVAILABLE

Front cover images © 2012 Shutterstock

Manufactured in the United States of America

McFarland & Company, Inc., Publishers
   Box 611, Jefferson, North Carolina 28640
      www.mcfarlandpub.com

With fond memories and love to my sister Rose who, during her lifetime, was both a mother and a sister to me.

—Joseph Albini

To these faithful departed who passed during the writing of this book: my father, Dennis McIllwain; my grandparents, Enrique and Alice Estrada; my aunts, Shirley Strommen and Melba Andrews; my friends Tim Kramer and Cpl. David McCormick (US Army, Battle of Sadr City); my teacher, Dr. Tom Bernard; my student and friend, 1st Lt. Joshua Palmer (USMC, 1st Battle of Fallujah).

—Jeffrey McIllwain

Table of Contents

Preface

The process of coming together to write this book was a protracted but ultimately rewarding one. We first met during Jeff's first research paper presentation at an Academy of Criminal Justice Sciences Conference in March of 1995. Jeff was a second year Ph.D. student studying under Joe's friend and fellow organized crime scholar, Alan Block, at the Pennsylvania State University. Joe came specifically to hear Jeff's paper on the history of Chinese organized crime in the United States and he took the time to introduce himself at the end of the presentation. We then spent the next two hours sitting on a couch in the conference hall lobby getting to know each other and our current research interests. Needless to say, Jeff was extremely happy to have a scholar of Joe's professional stature take the time to welcome him in to the fraternity of organized crime scholars (no secret oaths were provided so Jeff is still not sure if his membership holds).

Years later Jeff was humbled when Joe approached him to help develop this manuscript. Joe had written over 1,000 pages reflecting on organized crime, the object of his scholarly affection for five decades, and he wanted help providing it with more focus and adding additional perspective and substance to areas he felt were lacking. This manuscript was the capstone of his long career and he wanted to make sure his ideas about important topics in the historiography and current scholarship in the field were provided to his peers. Based on our many conversations over the years, we knew that our ideas had little divergence so partnering was an easy thing to do.

The manuscript took shape over the next few years and it finally came to a point where Joe feels it represents what he wants to say and how he wants to say it. Joe did not want it to take the form of a textbook, nor did he want it to be a comprehensive trade book. He wanted it to read as if we were having a conversation with the thousands of students and profes-

1

sionals we have been honored to teach over the decades. He wanted readers to learn about organized crime as a process, not just as a series of crime families and sensationalistic gangsters and crimes. He wanted to equip the reader with the perspectives and the tools to analyze organized crime in the past, present and future. Finally, he wanted to deconstruct the "Mafia Mystique" mythology that continues to have a hold in some corners. Hopefully, we achieved these objectives.

Joe wishes to acknowledge and thank Benjamin Dandridge of the Clark County Library in Las Vegas for his kind help in assisting him in the use of the computer throughout the writing of this work. His vast knowledge of computers made the author's task of completing the manuscript both a learning experience and an efficient mode for completing the project. As this work necessitated the obtaining of a large amount of historical material, this task was made less stressful through the skilled help of Suzanne Segal, Donna Sword, Darrell L. Craft, Lenny Souza and James Caal of the library staff of the Clark County Library in Las Vegas. He thanks them for their help.

For their help in understanding the complex phenomenon of the fall of the Soviet Union and the development of Russian organized crime, Joe is deeply indebted to his Russian colleagues, Col. Professor Victor Shabalin, Gen. Professor Valery Kutushev and Lt. Col. Professor Vladimer Moiseev. He also thanks them for their warmth and friendship. In this endeavor, a special note of thanks goes to his former student and now colleague, Dr. R. E. Rogers, an avid student of Russian culture and history who provided him with the contacts in Russia which resulted in his engaging in the study of this fascinating phenomenon. Finally, Joe wishes to thank all the casino card dealers, far too many to mention by name, who so willingly and enthusiastically provided him with an insightful view of the history and nature of gambling and organized crime in Las Vegas.

Jeff would like to thank his fellow organized crime scholars Klaus von Lampe, Carlo Morselli, Jay Albanese, and Michael Woodiwiss for their friendship and inspiration over the years. Alan Block and his lovely wife Constance Weaver continue to inspire him in countless ways. Phil Jenkins taught Jeff to always question the conventional wisdom about any academic subject (even the most sacred to academics themselves) and his influences on Jeff's research, teaching and interests are immeasurable.

Jeff thanks his provost, Nancy Marlin; his deans, Barbara Gattas and

Stanley Maloy; the directors of San Diego State University's School of Public Affairs; Lou Rea and Stuart Henry; and his dear friend and co-director of the Graduate Program in Homeland Security, Eric Frost, for all of their support over the years. A special thanks to Hal McNair, Mark Raney and the rest of the faculty in the Operations Department of Joint Special Operations University for giving Jeff the opportunities to test out ideas in this book with those at the "tip of the lance" who operate in a very dangerous world. Jeff also thanks Pastor John Palka and the rest of his church family at Christ Lutheran Church in La Mesa, California for their love, friendship, and support these past three years. Finally, Jeff thanks his wife, Donna, and his children, Collin and Reagan (who were born during the writing of this manuscript, hence many of the aforementioned delays), for occasionally allowing him to research, write and edit when *Yo Gabba Gabba* or Legos were calling.

Thanks to Wendy Flick, Nancy Petre and Bryan Young for reading over drafts of the manuscript, SDSU's Julie O'Connor-Quinn and Nancy Flitcraft for administrative support and friendship, and to Julia Teweles, Sherith Pankratz, and the late Alan McClare and our anonymous reviewers who provided valuable comments and criticisms of our work.

Introduction

This work arrives at an appropriate time in the historical development of that exciting, yet complicated, phenomenon that has come to be called organized crime. Scholarly works have shown that the excitement generated by this term arose out of a mythical portrayal of its origins, both in Sicily and the United States, under its commonly used alias, the Mafia. These works have also demonstrated that it was primarily the creation of journalists who sought to excite and entertain their public and several American politicians who sought to bolster their careers by conducting investigations directed at exposing (and exaggerating) a threat to public welfare manifested by the Mafia (aka La Cosa Nostra). The public responded to the hybrid of fear, interest and excitement generated by these investigations with a fervor that resulted in the creation of blockbuster movies such as *The Godfather* and *Goodfellas* and dozens of books that dwelled on sordid stories of killings, betrayals, bloody underworld wars and biographies of gangsters, their wives and their molls. The most recent celebration came in the form of a television series called *The Sopranos* in which the public could now watch a sympathetic head of an Italian American crime family undergo psychoanalysis and feed ducks between acts of brutal violence. The Mafia, it seems, had finally come of age.

However, beginning in the late 1950s, the term "Mafia" and the entire concept itself came to be battered around in the halls of cultural and scientific definitions. Essentially, in this battering, the government exerted the most influence, having on its side the influence of a very distinguished criminologist named Donald Cressey. Together they viewed the Mafia as a secret society with rituals and a highly bureaucratic structure that included "bosses," "underbosses" and "soldiers." But soon, during the 1970s, a group of academic researchers began employing innovative research methods and interdisciplinary perspectives that exposed the actual *modus operandi* of the so-called Mafia groups. These studies revealed that rather than using rituals and being bureaucratic in structure, their group structure was based upon network models otherwise known as forms of patron-client relationships.

Among these revisionist scholars were the senior author of this manuscript, Joseph Albini, and Dwight Smith (sociologists); Francis Ianni, Elizabeth Reuss-Ianni and Henner Hess (anthropologists); Peter Reuter (economist); and Mark Haller and Alan Block (historians). Of this group, Albini can be considered *The Godfather* of revisionist organized crime research, with a fifty-year career producing innovative theoretical and empirical research on the subject, beginning under the tutelage of Donald Cressey himself. These revisionist authors helped lead the way in challenging the governmental (or bureaucratic) model of organized crime that viewed the Mafia as the sum-all criminal organization that had a monopoly of rackets in the United States and around the globe. In doing so, they inspired a second generation of revisionist scholars who broadened their work from various disciplinary and methodological perspectives. One of these scholars, Jeffrey McIllwain, is the second author of this book. McIllwain was a doctoral student of Alan Block's in the mid–1990s and has distinguished himself as a historical criminologist researching organized crime and by his pioneering work on the application of social network theory to the understanding of organized crime and the role and function of organized crime in warfare.

Now that *The Sopranos* have stopped singing, we find a nation that is at a loss to understand the real and valid essence of organized crime, especially as it relates to a decentralized and globalized post–9/11 world. The public is confused by the fact that one keeps hearing of the Mafia, but the reality of the nature of its existence simply can no longer be factually explained by the old mythological beliefs of the past. Organized crime has become global in nature and its transnational connections have become a real menace to the legal, political and economic institutions of the world. In recent years it is increasingly linked to terrorism and other forms of irregular warfare affecting the security and welfare of millions around the globe. Coupled with this reality, the American public has, over the past two decades, come to suspect the veracity of its own government due to highly publicized corruption scandals and the selective targeting of some organized crime groups over others and it has basically become cynical about the government's willingness and ability to reveal the truth about its own operations.

Given these current conditions, the purpose of this book is to reflect on key issues related to organized crime with the first goal of filling the void in this current state of confusion by determining how the confusion came about. It gives a detailed account of what Mafia really consisted of and a revealing and accurate historical account of how it originated and where the term "Mafia" itself came from. The book then provides new theoretical lenses through which to view organized crime and, along with dealing with other major issues involved in the study of organized crime, presents case studies of the unique nature of organized crime as manifested in select criminal enterprises and in the former Soviet Union and the city of Las Vegas. A final emphasis of this manuscript is directed toward the topic of globalization and its effect on contemporary organized crime. It presents an explanation of the meaning of globalization to transnational organized crime and how this affects the representation of contemporary organized crime networks. It also discusses the intersection of terrorist and other irregular warfare networks with organized crime networks in certain areas of the world.

ONE

The Mystique of the Mafia

In Italy for thirty years under the Borgias they had warfare, terror, murder, bloodshed — but they produced Michelangelo, Leonardo da Vinci, and the Renaissance. In Switzerland they had brotherly love, 500 years of democracy and peace, and what did that produce? The cuckoo clock. — Graham Greene, *The Third Man* (1949)

What is in a name? Many years ago, the great playwright William Shakespeare observed, "A rose by any other name would smell as sweet." Perhaps, within the same context of searching for that essential or essentials which makes a thing what it is, whether it is the smell of the rose or, perhaps its shape, or perhaps its color, we come to rely on the creation of a word, in this case, "rose," that captures that meaning in such a way that a rose will, indeed, be viewed universally as a rose, easily distinguishable and distinguished from all other things. One wishes that Cosa Nostra ("Our Thing"), the traditional name that has come to be used to define a specific criminal organization that first came into public view in the 1960s, would be as easy to distinguish from other words as is "the rose." A rose, with little argument, can be shown to be a rose. However, Cosa Nostra, with much argument, continues to be a word whose meaning and context have created controversy within the realm of the study of organized crime.

What is true of Cosa Nostra can also be applied to another word, "Mafia," that many believe is just a synonym for Cosa Nostra and describes the same organization, while others become defiant over such a comparison and argue that the two are totally separate and different criminal organizations. Yet, we would be missing a vital part of both the history of and the study of American organized crime if we simply were to take the stand that the Cosa Nostra and Mafia should simply be viewed as the creation of the overactive imaginations of American journalists and freelance writers who gave birth to both these terms during the second half of the 20th century. Both Mafia and Cosa Nostra have become part of the American language and of the history of organized crime in the United States. They have become part of governmental action in the form of task forces erected to ferret out their membership, of long and very involved trials that resulted in the imprisonment of many of their leaders, of gang wars that bloodied the streets of major American cities, of government investigations seeking to expose their existence and of an entire generation who has come to believe that they are real. Science cannot simply take such a topic and relegate it to the realm of fiction. It is too real. Such reality cannot be left to sit, unexamined and nebulous, within the dustbin of history because it is history, a history that has produced much drama and confusion. To simply deny the existence of these two organizations is to miss a very important element of the evolution of the controversial nature of the history of organized crime in America.

If the nature of organized crime is to be understood, then the nature of Mafia and Cosa Nostra must simultaneously be made evident. They are real and have become part of the mental reality of the average American's conception of organized crime in America. Let us examine the essence of that reality because it is just as vital a part of the understanding of American organized crime as the presence of criminal syndicates in the towns and cities of the U.S. Let us turn now to a discussion of that reality and how it came into existence.

In order to bring into sharp focus the impact of the use of the words Mafia and Cosa Nostra in creating the mental images that they bring forth, let us do a simple experiment. Read the following sentence and then follow the directions. Say to yourself the word "Mafia." Close your eyes and let the images form freely. Now do the same for the words "Cosa Nostra." Finally, simply say to yourself the words "organized crime" and then "gangster" and let the images flow. There is no doubt that there are many different images that come to mind. Some might think of a tommy gun, a fedora, or an expensive pin-striped suit, while others may think of Al Capone's visage, piles of seized cocaine, Tony "Scarface" Montana spraying his Colombia assailants with bullets from his balcony, or Joe Pesci burying yet another body in a Martin Scorsese film.

This should not be surprising as it simply notes how effective the visual images created by the depiction of these subjects in movies and media influence our reality (Ruth 1996). This has become a major area of study known as communications research and indeed constitutes the study of how individuals and groups come to form their images of reality (Surette 2006). It is no different in reference to the study of organized crime. We must deal with how and why these images came into existence, yet we must remember that we are dealing with the scientific study of this phenomenon that we call organized crime. For his very helpful insight into this phenomenon, we turn immediately to the work of Dwight C. Smith (1990) who has made it possible to readily distinguish between the structure and function of organized crime in America by arguing that this structure and function emerged alongside another phenomenon to which Smith gives the appropriate name "the Mafia Mystique."

Dwight Smith always made a point of noting that he did not study organized crime per se, but instead studied how the image of the Mafia, not in terms of its structure and function but the image itself, came into existence in the U.S. Yet, although we agree with Smith, we still note that the mystique of which he speaks became so intertwined with the study of organized crime that the two have blended together in such a way that one cannot speak of one without simultaneously bringing forth an image of the other. Such are the two blended that it seems that they have and always will exist together despite and with all due respect to Smith's very convincing argument that they exist as two separate entities.

The knowledge of history and culture is vital to the discussion of the nature of organized crime in the United States. Likewise, the knowledge of the history and culture of mafia in Sicily is a key to understanding and rectifying the erroneous belief that a criminal cabal called the Mafia and Cosa Nostra were transplanted to American shores. The history of the involvement of other ethnic groups has equally been neglected in the Mafia and Cosa Nostra narratives by the noted and obvious absence of any mention of their involvement during the era in which such involvement was sufficiently evident to merit attention. The overzealous excitement of those caught up in the intrigue of the "Mafia Mystique" from the 1950s through the 1980s generated political, media and academic narratives that lent themselves towards generating a false, distorted, and incomplete assessment of organized crime in the United States.

Organized Crime: An American Way of Life

In order to understand the role and function of organized crime in America, one has to embrace the fact that organized crime in the United States is as American as apple pie, a fact that those who are victim of the Mafia Mystique may have trouble accepting for all of its implications. Much of the controversy that arose regarding the existence of Mafia and Cosa Nostra arose out of a nativist "alien conspiracy" premise which attempted to argue that organized crime was brought to the United States by Irish, Italian, and Jewish immigrants and that, until their arrival, Americans existed in a virginal state of innocence. Nativist fears exclaimed that these immigrants were akin to viruses, afflicting the innocent hearts, minds, and souls of the unsuspecting "American" citizen. The United States, it seems, has always attempted to keep itself clean of its most negative features by casting blame onto outsiders for its problems rather than looking into its history which readily reveals the fact that Americans of all backgrounds bring their problems upon themselves due to inherently systemic reasons.

Organized crime has been with us as a nation from the very day that Spanish conquistadors conquered and enslaved Native American peoples and the English, French and Dutch came with royal mercantilist sanctions to expropriate every bit of wealth they could from the colonized New World regardless of the human and environmental costs. Some of those who came indeed worked and sacrificed to create one of the most profound forms of republican democracy the world has ever witnessed. However, simultaneously existing alongside this democracy and as an unintended consequence of the freedoms, rights, and liberties preserved in the Constitution, the opportunities that formed a fertile seedbed for organized crime were created as well (Woodiwiss 2001). This is not to say that certain groups of organized criminals stowed away on the ships that brought pilgrims, colonists and slaves to the American colonies. Rather, the opportunity for organized crime to manifest itself in a multitude of ways is inherent to the laws, regulations, customs, folkways, and religious practices created by what is arguably the most diverse, pluralistic society ever created in the face of such unlimited natural resources open to private ownership. Organized crime, then, is a fundamental component of the social system that evolved into that complex entity known as American society.

Early Manifestations

The threads of organized crime originate in the very origins of the American colonies. For example, we must remember that the British, from whom the American revolutionaries won their freedom, employed force and the law to instill fear and control over the colonists while creating numerous lucrative opportunities for smuggling and piracy due to their oppressive mercantilist and tax-heavy policies. Indeed, many of today's headlines depicting terrorist or insurgent activity in various parts of the world would read like a page from an American colonial newspaper as the colonists, tired of British soldiers invading their homes without a warrant, publicly administering humiliating beatings to citizens and indiscriminately arresting and jailing colonists as they went about their daily chores, reacted by daily staging acts of rebellion consisting of throwing rocks at the British forces, stealing arms and supplies, burning down buildings, and attacking weapons depots (Breen 2010). As Barck and Lefler (1968:518) note, citizens upset with onerous British taxes and duties and the consequent arrest and repression of those smugglers who actively avoided paying them tormented the British troops daily in Boston by booing them as they marched in the streets and pelting them with snowballs, rotten eggs, and oyster shells. British authorities viewed these as acts of terror and rebellion.

Even before this form of rebellion emerged, organized crime had already made its appearance in the American colonies in the form of that exciting and colorful figure who became known in history as the pirate. In his very informative work on the subject, David Cordingly (1995) describes the legends that have come to surround the lives and times of such celebrated pirates as Sir Henry Morgan, Captain Kidd, Blackbeard, Jean Lafitte, and the female pirates Anne Bonny and Mary Read, as well as a host of others. These pirates were indeed fierce and menacing figures who suited the types of daring feats required for their hand-to-hand fighting as they attacked the captains and crews of ships whose goods they stole for sale in the colonies and other parts of the world. Along with such hardiness in battle these pirates had to daily face the survival of a brutal life at sea in which their living quarters were constantly cold and damp and demanding and fierce captains worked them from morning to night.

Our purpose here is not to dwell on the excitement of pirate stories and legends, but instead, to deal with the role that the pirate played in the history of organized crime in America. The pirate was a primary form of organized criminal in that he made goods such as gold, rum, sugar, tea, coffee, and silk available to the inhabitants of many of the American colonies. But what must be understood is the fact that merchants in the colonies were able to buy these goods from the pirate at a much lower price than if they purchased them through legal channels. Not only did these merchants buy these goods at a cheaper price, they also avoided having to pay the taxes and other costs that they would normally pay to meet the requirements of the English Trade and Navigation Laws that made it mandatory that the colonists conduct their business enterprises and trade through companies that shipped their goods only on English ships that sailed, originally, from England. However, in order for such a transaction to occur, it necessitated the cooperation of various government officials who offered political protection to these colonial merchants and the citizens who purchased their goods. In other words, the merchants and pirates paid large sums to government officials in order to provide legal protection that would allow for the safe and continuous importing, marketing and sale of the illicit goods.

According to Barck and Lefler (1968:517), one of our founding fathers, John Hancock himself, was accused of making a fortune as a merchant who secretly smuggled in and sold contraband goods (charges were eventually dropped). This system of cooperation between criminals, government officials, merchants and the citizens who purchased illegal goods constitutes a basic ingredient for one of the most prominent forms of American organized crime which we have come to call syndicated organized crime. We will define this form more clearly as our discussion continues, but, for the moment, we wish to note that this collaboration between citizens, government officials and organized criminals constitutes a standard modality for the existence of organized crime in America. This should be kept in mind as we engage in the further discussion of the nature, function and definition of organized crime itself. This form of collaboration has been with us from the time of our emergence as a nation and remains with us today. It must be understood that this collaboration is necessary to the very existence and continuous presence of syndicated organized crime in America and, as such, has become a part of the American social system and of American life itself.

Yet, although this reality is ever-present in even the most cursory analyses of the history of the United States, Americans have, it seems, developed a need to deny this reality. It seems that Americans have a need to view themselves as citizens of a very moral nation that seeks to avoid the appearance of sanctioning vice. The United States has developed the habit of immediately casting vitriol onto the foreign influences and groups, which it blames for communal and individual moral indiscretions. For example, the general reluctance of Americans to admit and confront their puritanical inhibitions, while simultaneously delving into vice and other criminal activities, is given credence by the behavior of the soldiers who engaged in the Civil War.

Once again in American history, we witness the existence of organized crime in the same form of syndicated crime that existed in the colonies. In the very appropriate title of his book, *The Story the Soldiers Wouldn't Tell*, Thomas P. Lowry (1994) reveals that the soldiers in both the Union and Confederate armies had a secret life, one that they tried to hide from their families and from posterity. The big lie was that they had not engaged in any form of sexual behavior during the war. In those few cases where soldiers did make mention of any sexual activity in letters, surviving relatives often destroyed the offending diaries, letters and memoirs. Hence, once again, puritanical Americans made certain that history would note that during the Civil War, neither the soldiers dressed in blue nor those dressed in gray had sex in any form or manner.

Thanks to Lowry's research, however, another reality emerges. Lowry presents evidence that shows that these soldiers indeed had available to them all manner of pornographic photographs and literature which they could purchase through the mail, that they memorized dirty jokes and poems and sang dirty songs as they sat around the campfires, and, most incriminating of all, that they used the services of the many prostitutes made available to them. Indeed, the vast amount of sexual activity that took place is evidenced further by the rapid spread of venereal disease transmitted by these prostitutes. The spread of these diseases reached epidemic proportions and, with no antibiotics available at the time, resulted in many soldiers developing painful and hideous scabs and blisters that accompanied the third stage of syphilis. Thousands of others died from these venereal diseases. Lowry's very informative work once again speaks to the need of Americans to hide their activities regarding their engaging in various forms of vice.

Yet, it is this interest in obtaining those goods and services that are defined as illegal or sinful in segments of the American public that helped set the stage for the emergence and growth of organized crime in America. For it is the role of the organized criminal to make these goods and services available to the public for a price while the criminal himself undertakes the risks of potential arrest and imprisonment and at the same time risking victimization at the hands of other criminals who are competing with him or her to make the same goods and services available. It comes as no surprise, then, that during the Civil War, criminal syndicates developed to provide prostitutes for the soldiers. Thus, as Herbert Asbury (1942:63–64) notes, in Chicago in 1865, Roger Plant, an Englishman from Yorkshire, constructed a resort consisting of several shacks where rooms and prostitutes could be rented, thus assuring privacy to soldiers who wished to engage in heterosexual or homosexual activity. It could be argued that Roger Plant was one of America's first well-known organized criminals in that, as Frederick Francis Cook (1910:159) points out, he not only provided these services but had a warning and escape service that protected his soldier clientele from being apprehended by military scouts which frequently patrolled the area in which the establishment was located. Plant also secured protection of his operation by making payments to the police in Chicago on a regular basis.

According to military historian Caleb Carr (2002:138–144), another type of organized crime that emerged at the end of the Civil War was inherent to the forms of state-sponsored terrorism systematically practiced in a rampage of vengeance, theft, plundering, and destruction that has come to be called "Sherman's March to the Sea." Carr speaks to the unnecessary use of force that General William Tecumseh Sherman allowed the Union soldiers to use against the helpless citizens of the South as a historical example of terrorism in America in its most caustic form: that of Americans killing non-combatant Americans. Carr carefully distinguishes between the amount of military force that was needed to bring the Confederate forces themselves to surrender and the amount of force and savageness that Sherman condoned and allowed his soldiers to vent toward the civilians in the South. It seems, as Carr notes, that Sherman unleashed his Union Army's terror on the South not so much as a strategy aimed toward achieving military victory, but rather as a consciously and purposefully directed campaign which allowed the retaliatory terror of his army to serve as a mechanism of punishment toward the South for starting the war and for creating and maintaining a vicious system of human slavery. Sherman himself said that he was at war with every man, woman and child in the South.

Carr emphasizes that this reign of terror, although it resulted in military victory for the North, unfortunately produced harm to the nation's future quest for post-war unification and peace. The residual anger and resentment felt by the average Southerner toward the North, anger resulting from having been subjected to starvation, murder, and the mass theft and destruction of property, caused the South to create its own terrorist and insurgent groups that engaged in organized criminal activities, groups like the Ku Klux Klan (Woodiwiss 2001:73–80). The Klan displaced its anger not on the Union Army that had just left the South but upon those helpless former slaves that were left behind (Carr 2002:141).

Carr (2002:143) goes further to note that, after the Civil War, several American commanders led by Sherman himself conducted wars of terror against North American Indian tribes, a point also established by Woodiwiss (2001). These wars had as their goal the outright extermination and annihilation of some of these tribes. The U.S. Army and government used as their tactics in these campaigns the breaking of treaties, the "ethnic cleansing" of entire territories, the wanton corruption of Indian agents, and the practice of specifically targeting non-combatant segments of the Native American population, even going so far as distributing among this population blankets laced with smallpox, a disease against which the Native Americans had no immunity (Carr 2002:144; Gwynne 2010). Tribal lands were seized as a result of this violence for the benefit of those interests seeking to exploit them for financial gain. In a sense, the Army acted as the "muscle" or "strong arm" of the mining, railroad and other interests that pulled the strings of many the politician and bureaucrat in Washington, D.C.

The Struggle to Define Organized Crime

We now turn to a discussion of the complexities involved in defining organized crime. The complexities emerge over the fact that different law enforcement agencies, diplomats, politicians, journalists, entertainers, scholars and average citizens each have come to define organized crime in terms of threat as viewed by their unique perspectives. Thus law enforcers view organized crime in terms of the laws of their respective jurisdictions while diplomats view organized crime in terms of the international implications presented when criminals cross borders in order to engage in criminal transactions. Politicians often view organized crime in terms of earning votes, either through demagoguing groups of "others" engaged in organized crime to gain political support or relying on said groups to turn out or suppress voting activities. Journalists and entertainers, be they true crime writers, filmmakers, or video game producers, emphasize the sensational to increase the bottom line. Scholars debate the nature and function of organized crime in their role as researchers and theorists, attempting to give it a heuristic basis for furthering a continuing dialogue with other scholars. The public typically develops its definition based upon the descriptions and images of the nature developed for it by the media. In short, most definitions of organized crime are functional to the goals and needs of those agencies and individuals who either study it or are required to deal with its political and legal implications.

For this reason, we should note at the outset of this discussion that, although we will try to examine the total parameters of what constitutes organized crime, and we will certainly introduce the reader to various definitions that have been offered and employed within the literature, we acknowledge that our definition most probably will not be viewed as definitive for the reasons already discussed. The reader should not interpret this difficulty as emerging only from the fact that those mentioned previously are restricted by the confines and obligations of their occupational roles to view organized crime within the goals of their occupations or discipline. Rather, it speaks to the complexity of the subject itself. Thus, it can be argued, the very concept of organized crime itself is flawed and its use should be avoided since it elicits several linguistic meanings and is not readily distinguishable from other forms of crime such as professional crime, gang crime, criminal networks, corporate crime and white collar crime (Salgo 1999:6). Still, it seems that, despite the difficulties inherent in its definition, the need for a definition itself must accompany every discussion in which the term is employed. Hence, rather than debate the difficulties inherent in the definition itself, let us now attempt to discuss those variables which constitute the essence of organized crime in hopes that out of an analysis of these features, we can come to an understanding of what makes organized crime different from other types of crime.

Many of the early definitions of organized crime that appeared during the 1950s and '60s and found in textbooks written by American criminologists were really not definitions at all, but rather attempts at identifying the various characteristics of the activities of those criminals engaging in what these writers viewed as a very broad spectrum of criminal enterprises. Mabel Elliot (1953:133–149), a prominent criminologist of that period, simply explained organized crime as an activity engaged in by professional criminals ranging in type from those who served as leaders or heads of illicit forms of enterprises such as narcotics trafficking to gamblers, swindlers, kidnappers, prostitutes, bootleggers, and counterfeiters. She went on to describe a "gangster" as one who will hire himself out to perform acts of violence for other racketeers who find such acts necessary in the continuous operation of their illicit enterprises.

Robert Caldwell (1965:133–158), another prominent criminologist of that era, also viewed organized crime as falling under the category of professional crime but distinguished the organized criminal from the professional by noting that the former involved a structure with centralization of authority, a fund of money, and a division of labor that required specialization of function among the participants while the latter consisted of professionals who stole purses, engaged in robberies, practiced counterfeiting and other types of forgeries, stole automobiles and fenced stolen goods. Caldwell did, however, make a very important distinction, one that will become prominent in our later discussion, when he noted that syndicated crime represented organized gang activity that involved making illicit goods and services available to customers who were willing to pay for them.

Barnes and Teeters (1959:19–24), who authored a very popular textbook in criminology, also spoke to the issue of syndicated crime, but differed from Caldwell, who saw syndicated crime as existing on a small and localized level; they instead defined it as consisting of an aggregate of organized criminals on a national level who used violence to control the enterprises that it chose to engage in. They distinguished this from racketeering, which they defined as enterprises using extortion to make money and any use of violence on the part of organized criminals was geared toward dealing with any potential threat of reprisals.

Interestingly, Taft and England (1964:184–194), the authors of another widely used textbook during this period, allude to defining syndicated crime without actually calling it syndicated crime by dividing organized crime into two categories: predatory and service-oriented. The former involves operations where theft, robbery, extortion, counterfeiting and pickpocketing are employed against victims while service-oriented means what others have called syndicated crime, that is, the criminals supply illicit goods and services for which there is a demand on the part of the public.

We cite these examples to illustrate the nebulousness and confusion that existed among many of the prominent criminologists writing during the 1950s and '60s when the topic of organized crime was rapidly becoming very popular and controversial. In order to bring some order to the debate, a number of definitions emerged from governmental and other sources. Ironically, they only confused matters more.

One of the earliest United States government attempts to define organized crime as a national phenomenon occurred in the conclusion of a Senate committee investigation during the early 1950s. As documented by historian William Howard Moore (1974), this committee had a special impact in that its hearings were televised during the early days of television when the images shown in black and white created a rather sinister portrayal of those witnesses who appeared before it. So, to further enhance the drama of the event, camera angles were frequently employed to add to the excitement. For example, during the testimony of several prominent witnesses, the camera would focus on the hands rather than the face of the witness as the hands moved nervously while the witness spoke. His nervousness obviously helped to create the impression that the witness was lying. This committee has come to be known by the name of the Senator who chaired it, Senator and presidential aspirant Estes Kefauver (D-TN). We here must note, as we will discuss later, that this committee created the background and gave rise to the images that were to manifest themselves later as the Mafia Mystique. Indeed, the definition reached during these hearings was not a definition per se, but instead a listing of the characteristics of organized crime, which were as follows:

1. That there existed in the United States a national crime syndicate which was called the Mafia.

2. That it controlled the most profitable rackets in the nation.
3. That its leadership was in the form of groups rather than individuals who controlled these rackets.
4. That it used as its major means of operating its enterprises, secrecy, violence, intimidation, political influence and bribery [President's Commission 1967:1].

Kefauver expanded on the findings of his committee in a book that he wrote one year later entitled *Crime in America* (1951). Here he emphasized the cultural origins of the Mafia as being a secret society that originated in Sicily and practiced a secret code known as "Omerta." It had now, according to Kefauver, come to and infected America.

The next major attempt at defining organized crime emerged from several conferences held between 1965 and 1966 at Oyster Bay, Long Island, New York. These conferences were significant in that they brought together policymakers, academics, law enforcement officials, lawyers, and other specialists in organized crime. It appears these conferences did not have a political agenda or motive but, instead, were serious attempts at defining organized crime in such a manner so the concept would have a more clarified meaning. The definition created for its final report, entitled *Combating Organized Crime* (1966:19), reads as follows:

> Organized crime is the product of a self-perpetuating criminal conspiracy to wring exorbitant profits from our society by any means — fair and foul, legal and illegal. Despite personnel changes, the conspiratorial entity continues. It is a malignant parasite that fattens on human weakness. It survives on fear and corruption. By one or another means, it obtains a high degree of immunity from the law. It is totalitarian in its organization. A way of life, it imposes rigid discipline on underlings who do the dirty work while the top men of organized crime are generally insulated from the criminal act and consequent danger of prosecution.

Unfortunately, this definition suffers from a dramatic use of terms that, as was true of other definitions of that era, did not meet the original aspirations hoped for in a more neutral definition as originally intended by the conference organizers. Instead, the conference produced a definition that was essentially a listing of all-too-encompassing, politically charged characteristics (i.e., using rhetoric like "malignant parasite which fattens on human weakness") instead of a more heuristically usable one.

The continuance of the use of dramatic terms in defining organized crime is illustrated once again in the definition that emerged from one of the most celebrated Congressional investigations that took place in 1963, the McClellan hearings, so named for the Democratic senator from Arkansas who chaired the committee's investigation. These hearings will become prominent in our discussion later as it was during these hearings that the American public came to hear a new name for the Mafia and organized crime; mainly, La Cosa Nostra. Here we wish to note the definition reached by this committee was reported in the 1967 *Task Force Report* of the President's Commission on Law Enforcement and Administration of Justice (1967:1). Once again it was not a definition per se, but a listing of the characteristics:

1. Organized crime consists of a society that operates outside the control of the American government or its citizens.
2. The society involves thousands of criminals working within structures as large as any corporation but subjected to laws more rigidly enforced than those of any legitimate government.
3. Its major enterprises include offering illicit goods and services such as gambling, narcotics, loan sharking and other vices to the American public.
4. It secures protection for its enterprises by corrupting public officials.
5. These criminals use secrecy to hide their basic modes of operation and, above all, these criminals strive for money and power.

Once again we see the dramatic but ambiguous language come through in the descriptions of these characteristics.

We could continue citing other definitions, but the point has been made. Each definition has its own limitations in that its parameters are either too broad or too narrow in their inclusion and explanation of the various types of organized crime, thus leaving the definition of organized crime itself in a state of ambiguity. In a very thought-provoking essay on the topic, Michael D. Maltz (1994:34–35) notes some important elements of this confusion. He makes a very important distinction when he suggests that organized crime needs to be viewed both in terms of the structure of groups and the actions of groups. Thus, he asks a significant question when he asks if the nature of organized crime consists of "an act or a group." Maltz mirrors our line of thinking when he notes that organized crime includes both acts and groups. However, he makes his most impressive argument when he notes a reality that lies at the root of the difficulties encountered when attempts are made to create a definition with which everyone can agree while including within that definition the entire range of possible organized criminal activities and the entire range of the differences in the complexities of the structures of the groups involved in it.

As we now move forward toward an analysis of the definitions of organized crime with the goal of offering some coordinated meaning or basis for agreement for researchers and others dealing with its reality, we should first clarify the problems encountered by the use of the terms "Mafia" and "Cosa Nostra." After all, these terms constitute a vital part of the history and the efforts involved in the long process of attempting to define organized crime to the point where they have become synonymous with organized crime to many. As we noted in our discussion of definitions, both the Mafia and Cosa Nostra emerged from the findings of governmental commissions. When these findings were presented, however, both terms became part of the discussion and debate concerning the definition of organized crime that, as we have noted, already was riddled with problems of ambiguity. Still, there was a difference. These two forms of organized crime captured the imagination of the American public. They became accepted as truth and to attack them was viewed in some circles as being tantamount to being sacrilegious. Indeed, in a very captivating article on the subject, Gordon Hawkins (1969:24–51) noted that many of the arguments offered as proof for the existence of the Mafia were in fact similar to those offered as proof for the existence of God.

It needs to be emphasized, however, that there were two elements that made the findings regarding the Mafia and Cosa Nostra different. Yet these two elements also gave these two groups their element of intrigue. One element consisted of the revelation of the existence of a nationwide crime syndicate. The second was the revelation that this national crime syndicate emerged from the efforts of a sinister criminal conspiracy of foreigners who brought this form of crime to America's shores.

Both of these conclusions were attacked at the time by critics who argued that they were claims supported only within the confines of the governmental committee's assumptions rather than the presentation of any convincing data. Although more than six hundred witnesses had appeared before the Kefauver Committee, Daniel Bell (1962:139) voiced the most severe criticism of the hearings when he noted pointedly that the entire testimony of these witnesses had failed to reveal any real evidence of the existence of the Mafia. Yet, despite these criticisms, the conclusions of the Kefauver Committee captured the imagination of the American public and so they since have become part of any discussion regarding the definition of organized crime. This is irrespective of the basic fact nobody on these committees ever thought to inquire about the origin of the Mafia in the homeland of its birth, Sicily.

Two

The Mafia Belongs to Sicily

Those who maintain that the Mafia came to America seemingly lack an understanding of the nature of mafia in its place of origin, Sicily.* Unfortunately, Senator Kefauver and his staff did not have an adequate historical and cultural knowledge of the phenomenon that he was investigating; otherwise he never would have argued that it was transported to America. Why? Because mafia is a unique part of the history and social system of Sicily and, as such, could not be transported anywhere, let alone to the U.S., in any real fashion.

Rather than using culture and history as his source, in its place Kefauver resorted to the use (or shall we say, the misuse) of various Sicilian terms that he played into a dialogue of intrigue aimed at grasping the attention of the American public. We should note that the Kefauver hearings came at a time when America was recovering from World War II; emerging from a major recession; adjusting to new social roles of women, juveniles, and African Americans; fighting a war against Communism expansion in Korea; adjusting to life in a time of possible atomic extinction, and experiencing a Senator Joe McCarthy–fueled climate of fear of a possible nationwide Communist conspiracy bent on conquering the United States from within. The multiple appearances of mysterious objects in the sky the public called "flying saucers" and a hip-swiveling, youth-beguiling Elvis were icings on the cake. The American public was tense, buffeted by change, fear and angst during the early 1950s. It was looking for something that would create a diversion, something that would draw attention away from these real and imagined dangers. Thanks to the emergence of television and

---

*The word mafia is not capitalized here as it does not refer to a specific organization. As was the case in U.S. Congressional committees, it is capitalized as Mafia when used to denote a specific criminal organization.

presumptive presidential candidate Senator Kefauver, the Mafia became that diversion.

According to historian William Howard Moore (1974), the hearings created another diversion, this one a bit more politically partisan in nature. Moore argues that given that Kefauver was a loyal supporter of the Democratic Party and seeking its nomination for the presidency, he used the hearings to create a smokescreen to draw attention away from the problems of the Truman administration and the Democratic political machines across the nation. By becoming an instrument of reform, he could also conveniently boost his candidacy for the Democratic nomination for president. Whether they were successful diversions or not is not relevant to our discussion, however. What is important here is that this need for diversions created a basic misunderstanding of the nature of organized crime in both the United States and Sicily.

Along with the Kefauver hearings, a book written by journalist Ed Reid in 1952, shortly after the hearings, gave a version of Mafia's origin, based upon a legend that captured the imagination of the American public. He presented a legend that was simple to understand and, above all, was filled with excitement. The problem was one that is always associated with the use of any legend to argue fact; that is, some of the elements contained in the legend can be verified while others cannot.

For instance, it is in this context that Ed Reid (1954:25) presented the "Legend of the Sicilian Vespers" and presented it as a legend but never offered any information as to the source. The legend contains an actual and significant occurrence in Sicilian history, a revolution during which the Sicilians in Palermo on March 30, 1282, rose up against the occupying forces of the French army. The instigation for the uprising, so the legend tells us, arose from an incident in which a drunken French soldier assaults a young girl who, along with her fiancé, had gone to a church in Palermo to make plans to be married. While her fiancé was inside the church making arrangements for the wedding, the soldier seized the girl. As she tried to escape, she tripped and fell, smashing her head against the church wall. She died instantaneously. When the young lad returned and saw his sweetheart dead, now seized by grief and anger, he yelled out the words, "Morte alla Francia" which translate into "Death to the French." Soon, Reid goes on to tell us, thousands of Sicilians took up the young man's cry adding to it the words, "Italia Anela" which translates as "is Italy's cry." Now the

24

crowds were yelling "Morte Alla Francia Italia Anela" or "Death to the French is Italy's Cry." Later, when the French began retaliating, the Sicilians formed a secret society to fight them and their password was taken from the very initials of the war cry that they had yelled in defiance of the French. Look at the initials of this war cry and what do they spell? M.A.F.I.A.

There is no question that this story or legend has all the ingredients for the making of a successful Hollywood movie. It has romance, it has violence and it makes for such an easy explanation of how the Mafia came into existence. Reid goes on then to explain that this secret organization helped the poor and extended help to the entire population of Sicily. Yet, suddenly, after Italy's unification in 1860, the Mafia turned on its own people, committing murder, extortion and other crimes against all classes. Reid never explains why this change took place. He merely notes that it did.

If one is seeking a very simple and short explanation of this phenomenon, one can readily understand why Reid's version is the version that most people would remember and cite when they speak about the origins of the Mafia. There is, however, the question of its authenticity. Does historical fact support or negate the veracity of the telling of this account? Let us examine the facts. One element is correct; there was a revolution called the Sicilian Vespers. It took place in Palermo on March 30, 1282. Later it spread to other cities in Sicily. It ended ultimately with the defeat of the French forces after which Sicily experienced a rare period of independence that lasted for about one hundred years. As to the story of the young boy and girl and her death at the hands of the drunken soldier serving as the instigating factor, there has never been any agreement among historians as to whether or not any one incident sparked the revolution. However, it here becomes necessary to evaluate Reid's legend in terms of the veracity of its other aspects.

Firstly, an examination of the definitive twenty-five volume work on Sicilian legends, tradition and folklore written by Giuseppe Pitre (1904:198–223) discusses eighteen legends regarding the Sicilian Vespers, none of which contain the version cited by Reid. Secondly, Reid's contention that a secret society named Mafia formed immediately after the Vespers to fight the retributions of the French makes no historical sense since the French forces suffered a terrible defeat. If anything, it was the French who became the victims of retribution, not the Sicilians. There certainly would have been no need then for Sicilians forming a secret society to fight the French, as the Sicilians were openly fighting and defeating the French all across the island. Finally, there is the nagging question raised by the use of the word, "Italia" in the war cry, as "Italia Anela" ("Italy's cry"). Sicilians have never viewed themselves as Italians. Certainly, they would not have done so in 1282 since Sicily then was not part of Italy and did not become such until the unification of Italy in 1860. Why then would the revolutionaries cry out, "Italia Anela"? Why not "Sicilia Anela"? But then the initials would not form the word M.A.F.I.A. Instead they would spell the word M.A. F. S. A. So, there goes the legend.

Patrons and Clients

The major disciplines from which we have gained the most useful knowledge about this phenomenon called mafia are history and anthropology. This is so because the roots of mafia lie in a history rocked with turbulence, distrust and constant change which lead the people of Sicily, very early in their history, to view life itself and particularly governments as being vehicles which primarily produce grief and suffering. Hence, fate, something which the average Sicilian defines as forces completely out of his control, but forces that are very real, becomes the determinant of an individual's success or failure. Thus, the only way to make it through life is to align oneself with someone whom fate has treated kindly and rewarded with power in hopes that, through them, they too will gain some semblance of power. This belief and practice becomes the basis for a major method by which Sicilians interact with one another. Anthropologists refer to this method as a system of patrons and clients.

Jeremy Boissivain (1966:18) describes a patron as any person who, because he occupies a position of power, can exert influence and thus be able to help and/or protect anyone that does not possess this type of power. A client, on the other hand, is the term used to define the person who receives help or protection and, in return, is expected to provide any goods or services he is able to provide for the patron. One can see that in such a system, as Boissivain notes, both clients and patrons find it expedient to help one another. So, too, it becomes the role of the client to help the patron retain his power in that, by so doing, the client will also retain his power.

What is inherent and interesting in this system is that no two functionaries are ever equal. The system is one in which life can quickly alter
a person's position of power. In other words, a patron may, if he loses his
position of power, become the client of his original client should that client
himself have managed, over time, to gain power. Of course, a patron, even
while he has the power of a patron, can serve as a client to another patron
who is more powerful than himself. Eric Wolf (1966:116–17) makes an
important distinction that serves to augment our description of the social
relationships found among those involved in the development of mafia in
Sicily when he notes that this system of patrons and clients operates for
both legal and illegal types of interactions. Hence, in either form, the
patron provides protection for the client while the client provides to his
patron valuable information to protect his social and personal welfare,
shows him respect and offers him his political support. The system works
in such a manner that the more clients a patron has, the more powerful he
becomes, as he can now demand favors from each of them (Hess, 1973).

Needless to say, a patron will try to develop client relationships that
represent individuals who occupy positions in different levels of society.
Clients also serve to gain power dependent upon how many patrons they
have, in that each can provide him with many forms of favors. The intricate
forms of this patronage system weave through all levels of Sicilian society.
The system is intricately bound into the life of every Sicilian. And it is as
serious as life itself for it consists of life itself in that it involves obligations
that can last for a lifetime. Thus, a client, once he receives a favor from a
patron, remains indebted to his patron for life. The patron, however, ends
his reign as a patron only if and when he loses his position of power. We
emphasize this system for, as we shall soon argue, the structure of mafia
in Sicily is not one based upon the existence of a secret society. Rather, it
is predicated upon a system of patron-client relationships that forms a
matrix of interactions that weaves itself through both legitimate and illegitimate sectors of Sicilian society itself.

A Culture of Secrecy?

It is unfortunate that Senator Kefauver and others misunderstood the
use of the Sicilian term *omertà* by referring to it as the oath of secrecy

which every member of the Mafia practices. Nothing could be further from a real understanding of this term. The term does not belong to the Mafia. Rather, it belongs to every Sicilian male. It is part of his culture's value system that helps him define himself as a man. He will die in order to abide by its rule. It gives him his pride. As for women, they will look up to him for, through his manifesting this form of behavior, women will gain the rewards, status and prestige which come with its practice and display. It makes a man feel strong. But it does not make him a member of the Mafia. Let us examine now how omerta came into existence.

The practice of omerta emerged as the result of a continuous series of invasions of the island of Sicily by foreign governments. Geographically speaking, Sicily has terrible real estate. It has been the center of the geopolitical and strategic machinations of great empires for three thousand years. One had to conquer Sicily first in order to invade Europe from Africa and vice versa. The same held true for those empires moving east to west and west to east. Sicilian history is a history of conquest and subjugation. First came the Phoenicians, who were followed by the Greeks and Carthaginians. Then came the Romans, followed by the Vandals, who in turn were followed by the Arabs and the Berbers. The Normans were the next to invade, followed by the Angevin French during whose rule the Sicilian Vespers took place. As we stated during our discussion of the Vespers, after the French were ousted, Sicily had about one hundred years of independence. However, this ended when the Spaniards invaded and they were followed later by the Bourbons. Then came the Nazis at the beginning of World War II followed by the Allied armies as this war was coming to an end.

Imagine the lives of the people of a country whose entire history was riddled by one invasion after another. These invaders took and demanded obedience and tribute in the form of goods, services and tax revenue from the Sicilians, but they gave nothing in return. They took, they pillaged and they went away, but they left the Sicilians with a truth that they have never forgotten: never trust any government. Consequently, every Sicilian has learned that he gains nothing from giving information to the agents of any government. At first this attitude was expressed toward agents from the governments of the foreign invaders. After Sicily was united with Italy in 1860, this attitude was expressed toward the agents of the Italian government and continues as a practice today. Because it involved not cooperating with any government agency, the practice evolved into another manner by which a man shows his manliness. This is the practice of not involving the law in the settling one's own disputes. Omerta came to incorporate the belief that a "real man" does not rely on the law but relies on himself to settle his own disputes. Rather than being a practice unique to mafia then, omerta must be understood as a Sicilian value and a practice found in all levels of Sicilian society.

Now one can readily understand why we said earlier that mafia, although conducting its activities in secrecy, did not have to rely on this practice in order to safeguard its activities from the law since it operated in a society where secrecy was inherent in the very daily actions and practices of the Sicilian citizens themselves. Indeed, when a case warrants an investigation where it is necessary to interview witnesses to a crime, particularly one committed in broad daylight with dozens of witnesses present, law enforcement agents in Sicily find their task overwhelming in that no one has seen anything. At times some witnesses will acknowledge that they heard something but never does this information lead to pointing toward a particular suspect. There is some evidence that, slowly, the practice of omerta has begun to show signs of disappearing. We will give illustrations of this in our later discussion. However, given its ingrained roots in Sicilian society, we believe that only a drastic change in values will bring about its total disappearance.

The Mafia as Method

Indeed, at its very core the concept of mafia is a complex subject and must be treated thoroughly so that the reality of what mafia in Sicily consists of can be explained as the complex phenomenon that it is. Indeed, one can argue that, perhaps, the reason that mafia has been given the trite yet exciting origins that journalists and the Kefauver and other governmental committees have given it resulted from attempts to simplify an otherwise exhaustive subject in hopes that, by calling attention only to those emotionally attractive and isolated elements of its entire history, a discussion of its complexity could be avoided. There is no question that this has indeed occurred as dozens of books and movies have appeared on the topic and audiences have been entertained, but there continues to exist a confusion as to what mafia really is.

Let us begin by stating what it is not. It is not and never has been a secret society. It does not have a bureaucratic structure consisting of specific, clearly defined positions such as "don," "boss," "underboss," "lieutenant" and other terms typically employed to describe its structure as found in the popular literature. This is evident in the works of a multitude of writers, among them Giuseppe Pitre (1889: 292), Cesare Bruno (1900:138), Douglas Sladen (1907:23), Michele Pantaleone (1966:34), Renato Candida (1964:10–11) and a host of others, which provide no evidence to support the popular notions that have become staples in much of the popular literature.

In discussing what mafia is, we must now give a description of syndicated crime. We will again, as we promised earlier, cover this in the coming discussion of our description of the types of organized crime. However, we here must offer the description in order to explain and evaluate the development of mafia in Sicily. Suffice it to say at this point in our discussion that syndicated crime consists of a form of organized crime that contains three basic and unique elements. These are:

1. A use of violence, intimidation or the threats of such as the basic method of operation for its enterprises;
2. The existence of a group or organization whose role it is to make available illicit goods and services to those segments of society that desire them; and
3. The ability of this group or organization to provide for those operating its illicit enterprises some form of political protection, either through direct payoffs to government officials or through endeavors to help political candidates achieve and/or retain their political positions and power.

The uniqueness of this form of crime is highlighted in the fact that syndicated crime, unlike other forms, necessitates interaction between those legitimate citizens who desire illicit goods and services and those who take the risk of making them available. Hence, such activities, whether they consist of illegal drug sales or prostitution, require that interaction take place between the buyer and seller. If these two can find each other, it stands to reason that law enforcement can also find them, thus the need on the part of the criminal for protection which creates an environment where law enforcement agents pretend not to witness the illegal activity itself. However, even with the provision for protection, the reality of this form of crime for both those who buy and/or sell these goods and services is such that protection, as a constant, cannot be absolutely guaranteed. Indeed, political power can change rapidly, and, even when protection is promised by those in power, disputes and competition within and between police forces and political adversaries can sometimes cause the protection to become erratic or suddenly non-existent. Consequently, both the buyer and seller stand the constant possible risk of being apprehended by the law.

Having given the attributes of syndicated crime, we can now move on to the discussion of the development of mafia in Sicily. As one reads the description of the elements which compose syndicated crime, one can readily come to understand that mafia is not only a form of organized crime, but it also consists of a method which can create the existence of this form of crime at any time and any place. Therefore, let us describe syndicated crime as both a mode of criminal enterprise and organization and as a method that brings its form of criminal activity into existence. In fact, much of the confusion regarding mafia, we believe, has been created because writers have been content to describe mafia only in terms of its existence as an organization or secret society that can be transported from one country to another. In reality, it is a method which can be employed in any social system that allows groups to put into effect the three elements which create its existence.

In our analysis of the factors that contributed to the development of mafia as a method in Sicily, we maintain that this development did not begin until after 1812, that is, after the breakdown of feudalism set into motion the appearance of three elements that allowed for its creation. The first element was the appearance of the *gabellotto*, a form of tax collector or excise man, and his role in the management on behalf of an absentee landlord of the second element, the *latifondo*, or the large landed estate that also came into existence after 1812. The third element necessary for the completion of the creation of mafia-political protection could not and did not become part of the method of mafia until the institution of universal suffrage by the Italian government, which gave Sicilians and Italians the right to vote in 1860 after unification of Italy.

During the era of feudalism prior to 1812, all land in Sicily was owned and managed by barons. These barons were powerful rulers and provided protection for their estate (barony) by hiring their own private guards, individuals skilled in the use of violence and adept at using weapons to protect not only the baron and his family but his livestock, crops, water supply, and the farmers and their families who worked his land. In reality, the end of feudalism did not radically change the feudal nature of the social class relationships in Sicily, as the system continued to function with a few rich landowners wielding power over a mass of farmers and peasants who depended upon them for their livelihood. It did, however, replace the old feudal relationship between serf and lord with one based upon a new system of land tenure. It is this system that became the breeding grounds for the development of modern mafia. With the end of feudalism, the barons no longer wanted to remain on the barony. The barony represented to them a boring lifestyle as compared to living in a major city like Palermo, which was rapidly becoming a lively cultural center with its frequent presentations of opera and theatre and attendant social scene. In reality, it was no longer necessary for the baron to live on the land as he could now turn the management of the barony over to an overseer who could carry out this function for him.

Consequently, the baron turned over the use of the land to an overseer who came to be known as a *gabellotto* (the word being derived from the Sicilian term *gabella*, which translates as "tax or duty in the form of a required payment"). All the baron asked in return was that the gabellotto pay him for the use of the land. In order to meet this obligation, the gabellotto rented out the use of the land to farmers or, in some cases, chose to sublet the land to another overseer known as a *sotto-gabellotto* (a secondary or sub-gabellotto). Like the gabellotto, the sotto-gabellotto, in order to be able to pay his tax or duty to the gabellotto, sublet his portion of the land to farmers who, in turn, would pay him for the use of the land. Typically all payments were made in the form of crops, with the farmer at harvest time giving a portion of his crops to the sotto-gabellotto, who in turn gave a part of his portion as payment to the gabellotto.

As we noted earlier, Sicilians view life as based upon fate. This especially held true for the Sicilian farmer, who lived a life of seemingly constant impending doom in the face of debt, drought, flood, pestilence, and injury. The farmer occupied the bottom position or rung on the ladder of this patronage system, yet the very foundation of its success or failure was placed in his hands. As such, this was a sharecropping system that, by its very nature, was meant to assure that the rich would become richer and the poor poorer. The farmer really had no chance for success in view of the fact that not only did he and his family have to work from dawn to dusk in order to cultivate the crops themselves, from his share of the profits was taken a portion that was used to pay for the seeds to be used during the next planting season, as well as a portion used to pay for the guards who were hired by the gabellotto.

Like the baron before him, the gabellotto had to hire guards to protect the equipment and livestock on the property, and to assure the safety of the gabellotto and the sotto-gabellotto, as well as that of all the other inhabitants now living on the newly formed latifondo or large landed estate. These guards, like those formerly hired by the barons, were hired based upon their known reputations for skilled use of violence. However, there was one major difference. The gabellotto was more prone to recruit his guards from the ranks of known criminals, particularly selecting those who had either recently managed to escape from prison or who, as "bandits," were being sought by the law for crimes for which they had not yet been tried or convicted by a court of law. These criminals would be more prone to faithfully fulfill the wishes of the gabellotto, for if they did not, the gabellotto could and would quickly turn them over to the legal authorities. It is important to note that these guards would later come to play an important role in the development of mafia.

The point that needs to be emphasized here is that the farmer stood, more so than the others in this system, to face utter despair in the event that the harvest failed to produce an abundance of crops. This was always a distinct possibility, given that the terrain, climate and weather in Sicily have never been known for their kindness to farmers. One drought could literally wipe out a farmer. The farmer would go into debt to the gabellotto for both his rent and tax as well as the cost of the seeds and supplies to be used in the next planting season. Once in debt, the uncertainty of his ability to fulfill his future obligations while simultaneously trying to pay off this debt presented him with the likelihood that life, most probably, would be bringing him closer to even more misfortune. This system lent itself to the exploitation of both fate and finances. Patrons and clients took on a very dichotomous dimension in that the multitude of farmers who had absolutely no power became the virtual slaves and clients of that all-powerful patron, the gabellotto.

The gabellotto continued to use his power as a patron to control the will and lives of all those under his authority. The peasant relied on him for his very livelihood and that of his family. The guards did everything to protect the gabellotto from harm as they, in turn, needed his protection. In the meantime, the baron was enjoying life in Palermo, not knowing that, before long, even he would become a victim of the gabellotto's increasing quest for more property and power. This quest began when several gabellotti began using their guards not defensively, but offensively; that is, they ordered their guards to attack the property of other gabellotti. These actions or raids, often conducted under the cover of darkness at night, consisted of stealing livestock, poisoning the water wells from which the inhabitants drew their water, poisoning the water troughs where the animals drank, destroying crops, damaging equipment and setting fire to the barns and/or houses on the targeted estate. In the event that the gabellotto who was victimized had a more skilled, daring and sophisticated army of guards, these could engage in a counterattack that not only would settle the score, but also discourage any further attacks. If not, the raids would continue until the defeated gabellotto would call it quits and put his property up for auction.

One can guess who would be ready to offer the highest bid for the land at the auction: the gabellotto who had the forces to overpower the others. Slowly, this gabellotto acquired more land and guards under his command and he proceeded to order attacks on other estates with the same goal of obtaining these properties at the next auction. Amassing more and more land and power, this gabellotto would eventually turn his sights toward an easier prey, the baron himself. Cleverly, as Michele Pantaleone (1966:26–29) explains, the gabellotto would initiate a covert terror campaign that included sending the baron threatening letters and purposefully shooting at him in order to convince him that someone was trying to kill him. All the while the baron never suspected that the gabellotto was behind these actions. Eventually, most of the barons who were targets of these types of terror tactics became so frightened that they decided to sell their land and leave Sicily. And who was only too willing to take the property off their hands? The gabellotti, of course, who orchestrated the terror campaign against them.

Thanks to these methods, the gabellotto became a new functionary in Sicilian society by the middle of the nineteenth century. His power lay in his skillful and violent acquisition of land. Along with him and because of his activities, he had amassed a band of private guards skilled in the use of violence and dedicated to the preservation of his power and his very well-being. He had managed to create a network and system of power described by Enzo D'Alessandro (1959:133) so pointedly and accurately as "L'industria della violenza" ("the industry of violence"). For here indeed was violence employed in a vast and effective manner. The gabellotto was now able to extend, for a price, the service of his protection to those farmers who were not part of his latifondo. These farmers knew his protection was needed and accepted it and paid for it despite the irony that the person that they were protecting themselves from was the gabellotto himself. And so, the gabellotto, toward whom fate had been so kind as to have turned him into a patron, now came to use that very patronage system to enslave those toward whom fate had not been so kind.

Soon the forces of fate made the gabellotto even more powerful. As the peasants became even more exploited, their frustration with their hopeless situation turned to revolt against the government. A peasant revolt occurred in 1812 and between 1820 and 1848 parts of Sicily ran red with the blood of soldiers and revolutionaries. It must be noted that the government found it difficult to control these uprisings as poor roads throughout Sicily made it difficult for the governmental forces to readily reach the areas of conflict and thus effectively and quickly quell such uprisings. However, the gabellotto with his army of guards could reach the areas of conflict and could crush the revolts quickly because he and his army of guards inhabited the regions where the peasants were staging these revolts. So, too, these guards were accustomed to maneuvering on the poor roads and were acquainted with the terrain as well as the revolutionaries. Therefore, the government came to view the gabellotto and his guards, as compared to its own army, as being a more cost-effective and efficient counterinsurgent force in the fight against peasant revolts.

The gabellotto was only too happy to oblige as he now became a client to the government by providing protection against what the government viewed as one of its most threatening problems, that of the potential increase in peasant revolts. The gabellotto did his job well as the revolts came to be suppressed and the gabellotto scored another point in his continuous quest for power, that of having now become a vital force and client which the government could use to further help keep the peasants under control. Actually, the gabellotto now had the peasants under his complete control when one considers that the peasant was obligated to him for his livelihood. The gabellotto could demand any contract, no matter how unfair and restrictive, concerning the use of his land and the peasant had to accept. If the peasant did not accept, he stood to go hungry or be killed.

Another service that the gabellotto was able to offer to political candidates was vote procurement. The peasant would have to vote for the candidate that the gabellotto chose to support. Of course, once in office, this candidate would have to return favors to the gabellotto, particularly if a protector was needed for any illegal activity engaged in by the gabellotto or any of his guards. The opportunity to assume this role came with the unification of Italy in 1860 when all Italians and Sicilians were granted universal suffrage and thus each was granted the right to vote. One vote is not much, but when someone can command the voting results on an entire landed estate or a vast number of estates, that is a form of power that most candidates would welcome.

It is this final development, built on centuries of evolving traditions, customs, and functions, that mafia as a method appeared in Sicily in 1860. The method began taking form historically in 1812 with the end of feudalism and had its first functionary emerge in the form of the gabellotto and his practice of partitioning the latifondo into various portions of land which he rented out to farmers. He now became a patron. As such he was able to hire private guards. With these developments emerged the first two of the three elements, as we described earlier, that constitute the system of syndicated crime: that is, (1) the ability to employ violence and (2) the establishment of a group of private guards trained in violence to carry out such acts. When the gabellotto provided for the government the service of suppressing peasant revolts, he not only gained total control over the peasants by the use of fear and intimidation but also became a client to the government by promising to continue to suppress any future peasant uprisings. With this control, after universal suffrage was granted in 1860, the gabellotto gained (3) the ability to provide himself with governmental protection by serving as a vote procurer for political candidates. Thus, mafia, as we define it, became an intractable part of Sicily's history and culture.

The Role of Violence

The role of the gabellotto takes on significance only if it is understood as one that involves the use of violence. As explained, circumstances allowed the gabellotto to amass control over the peasants by first becoming a patron by renting portions of his land to them and later, using his private guards, served to suppress their revolts through the use of violence which established him as a client who now served the needs of the government. Universal suffrage in 1860 then allowed him to exploit his power over the peasants by commanding their vote in order to obtain for himself the political protection of the candidate these votes helped place into office. It is this power that gave the gabellotto his new status. Yet his status must be understood amidst the other elements of Sicilian society, history and culture previously discussed.

However, let us re-examine them in their context as they now apply to mafia as a method. Firstly, omerta demanded that every Sicilian male settle his own disputes. He could not turn to the law. It also demanded that he never cooperate with or give information to the police. The patron-client system operated to place the client in a position of having to honor the requests of his patron, who served to control the client's welfare and livelihood. The government sought the gabellotto's help in serving as a powerful force that would and could keep the peasants from further revolt. Still, there is another element that can now be added to this picture. Although omerta demands that each male settle his own disputes, this does not mean that every man is in a position to do so. A weak client may simply not have the power to redress a wrong committed against him by himself. A professional, such as a physician or teacher, may not have the skills or weapons to use violence. Nonetheless, he must redress the wrong or suffer the fate of losing face among his fellow citizens. Thankfully for him, Sicilian values recognize that a wrong is a wrong and it does not matter who makes it right, so long as the wrong is redressed. It must be redressed in order for the victim who was wronged to regain his self-respect. Under such conditions, it was to the gabellotto that the victim turned.

Violence or the threat of it was made clear by the gabellotto. In some cases, a public apology would be sufficient. This may seem like a mild form of retribution until one understands how humiliating it is for a Sicilian to be forced to offer an apology in public. Anyone who has traveled through Sicily knows that, typically, the Sicilian is a very respectful and well-mannered individual who is quick to offer an apology should his behavior require such an apology. This type of apology, however, is not disturbing to the person who offers it as it is something that he does of his own free will. It is when he is forced against his will to make a public apology from a position of weakness, in a situation where and when he is threatened with harm if he does not do so, that he suffers the humiliation. By doing so he realizes, along with those who witness the public apology (care is taken to make certain that it takes place in a setting where the offended party and many of his friends and relatives are present), that he was forced to comply. By doing so he openly displays his position of weakness.

In any event, when the gabellotto succeeded in righting the wrong, the person for whom this service was provided became his client and would, in turn, for the rest of his life, be obligated to return any favor the gabellotto requested. One can see how, by providing this service, the gabellotto amassed clients at every level of society and himself came to transcend the legitimate and illegitimate segments of Sicilian society. This explains the power of the gabellotto in the Sicily of the 1860s.

Mafiosi and Mafioso

As one can readily conclude, mafia, when understood within this context, represents not a secret organization, but instead a system where powerful patrons came to control the lives and destinies of a multitude of clients. As such, then, after 1860, the gabellotto came to acquire the name "mafioso," derived, as we shall soon explain, from the word "mafiosi." His power was based upon land use and ownership. Indeed, his power continues to be based upon the value of land. This explains why the mafioso has continuously succeeded in blocking every effort the government has made to initiate any successful program of land reform. The mafioso tends to conduct his affairs in secret and in the process comes to learn secrets about those clients indebted to him, secrets which he can use to blackmail, if necessary, these clients into further subjugation. He does not belong to a secret society, nor does the term "Mafioso" represent a rank or position in a secret organization. Instead, it represents a position of power that the mafioso comes to wield as a result of the very system of patron-client relationships which is endemic to Sicilian society itself. It should be stressed that his need for the use of secrecy is minimized by the fact that the society in which he lives helps him keep his activities and actions secret. In a true sense, his secrets are guarded by the practice of omerta. And those who keep his secrets stand to be forever in his favor, which means they now become more powerful clients themselves.

The mafiosi also serve as patrons and clients to one another. Some come to be respected and viewed as being the most powerful in a given locale. This should not be interpreted as this person having attained this status by having been elected to such a position by other mafiosi during a secret voting session. Rather, it means that there exists a public awareness of this person's status as manifested by the power he has been able to amass and by his ability to persuade others into abiding by his dictates. It must be understood, if one is to truly understand mafia in Sicily, that power among mafiosi has never and is not now unilaterally or evenly distributed. If it were, one would see the same mafiosi continuously exerting the same amount of power in a continuous and unchanging flow of power. Instead, different situations make for different displays of power under various circumstances. Thus, a mafioso may own land situated strategically so as not to allow agents of the law to readily spot stolen livestock grazing on the land. Since there are many mafiosi who wish to move their stolen livestock, but must hide such movements from the law, this mafioso now has the power to allow these mafiosi to use his land. He becomes the patron and he is in control. However, if conditions should change so that an alternative route is discovered for moving the livestock more quickly, the owner or owners of the land encompassing this new route now become the patrons. They are in control. So, too, if a given commodity such as water is under the control of a mafioso, this person becomes a patron to all other mafiosi and citizens who have need for water. Thus, he is in control. What this is saying is that power changes with circumstances so as to generate a constantly changing system of power relationships.

Two major enterprises of the early mafiosi were those of extortion, cattle rustling, and the theft of other livestock. Roads improved and the economy began to grow and diversify as time went on, yet the role of the mafioso remained constant. He still wields his power from his ownership of land and his ability to serve as a patron with political protection for his enterprises (Blok 1969). Above all, his status continues to emanate from his ability to use violence. Slowly, his enterprises moved from those of stealing livestock to those associated with commercial businesses such as waste management, construction, and the control of equipment used in construction projects. As Pino Arlacchi (1986:94) notes, by 1982, mafiosi had amassed complete control over all construction projects in Palermo.

We need also to emphasize the importance of selling "protection" along with the growth of mafia involvement in commercial businesses. As Diego Gambetta (1993:2–3) notes, this enterprise arose as a result of the fear on the part of some Sicilian businessmen that they could not trust their competitors to conduct business transactions in a legal manner. In other words, they feared that their competitors could and would use sabotage or other criminal tactics to try to undermine the success of their business enterprises. Thus, to assure the success of their businesses, they bought the protection of mafia functionaries who would safeguard and protect their property and business interests. As such, Gambetta notes, the mafia in Sicily managed to develop this form of protection into a commodity, a commodity which, because it could guarantee protection and success to those who purchased it, allowed for the stimulation of business transactions between parties that otherwise would have been hesitant to engage in such transactions. As such, although it consisted of a criminal enterprise, this provision for protection, argues Gambetta, had the effect of serving to promote economic exchange and growth in the economy itself. As technology changed and the desires for illegal goods such as narcotics became worthwhile ventures, the mafioso turned his skills toward the establishment of the international networks necessary to make such goods available.

In her study of contemporary Sicilian and Italian organized crime, Letizia Paoli (1999) brings into focus a blending of the patron-client conceptualization with that of the structure found in brotherhoods. She is careful to note, however, that the groups she describes are not bureaucratically structured associations but, instead, consist of multifunctional ritual brotherhoods whose primary goal is one of cultivating and consolidating their local political power base. As a result of retaining power at the local level, Paoli argues, these groups have not developed the skills necessary to be successful players in the new globalized illegal world of commerce.

However, though that may be a general rule, there are notable exceptions, as well documented by journalist Roberto Saviano (2008) in his field research on the Gomorrah in Naples and its environs. He indirectly validates the thesis advanced by Paoli that local power is what it is all about when it comes to organized crime in Naples. However, he also implicitly advances a powerful corollary to this thesis: What happens when your local power base also happens to be one of the largest ports in the world, with extensive global trade networks going back to the ancient trade routes of Greece that were born in the 7th century B.C.? Many local power bases are, by their very nature, global ones, intrinsically intertwined with the very global networks that make legitimate global trade possible. Saviano provides many examples of such networks, chief among them the power bases in various segments of the garment industry for which Naples is universally revered.

In summarizing the contemporary role of the mafioso in Sicily, we do so by highlighting the findings of Henner Hess (1973), a sociologist who spent two years in Sicily examining police files, judicial proceedings, government documents and records of transactions regarding land ownership. Hess concluded from examining these data that the mafia did not consist of a secret society. Instead, the mafioso represents a power position in which he develops and maintains close network of relationships with a group of associates called a cosca (clan). Just as was true of the gabellotto, the modern mafioso employs the patronage system to align himself with a cosca of citizens, some law abiding and others criminal, who will do favors for him. He, in turn, continues to do favors for government officials and those respectable citizens who may be in need of his services.

As such, he remains a broker of violence. However, this ability and willingness to use violence has not resulted in his being viewed as an oppressive figure. Quite the contrary, he concludes. Hess emphasizes that, instead of being viewed as a fearful or oppressive figure, the mafioso instead reflects the image of one who is a mediator in the arena of social relationships. As such, he performs an important service in serving as the protector of the honor of victimized or offended citizens and can be called upon anytime to serve as a mediator between disputing parties. Hess makes clear a point which merits emphasis as we move toward ending our discussion of mafia in Sicily; mainly, the mafioso has developed his role in Sicilian society to the point where he is now viewed as an important and valuable functionary in Sicilian society itself. This then is the nature of mafia in

Sicily. What now needs to be explained is how the mafia came to derive its name.

The Play Is the Thing: I Mafiusi di la Vicaria

Giuseppe Pitre (1889:290), whom we mentioned earlier regarding the legend of the Sicilian Vespers, seems to offer the only plausible explanation for the emergence of the word mafia. He argues that it derived from its use as the title of a well-known play entitled *I Mafiusi di la Vicaria* written by Giuseppe Rizzotto and first produced in 1863. The play described the evil deeds, argot, and behaviors of prisoners in Palermo's largest prison, known as "La Vicaria." Given that the word "mafia" did not appear as part of the Sicilian language until after 1860, it seems plausible that the title of the play may have been the basis for the word taking on its contemporary meaning with its criminal connotations.

Although any absolute verification for its origin is lost in time, we can offer some arguments that seem to be in agreement with Pitre's hypothesis. Firstly, Gaetano Mosca (Vol. X:36) notes that the word does not appear in any Italian writings prior to the nineteenth century. Migliorini and Griffith (1966:439), in their study of the Italian language, argue that the words "mafia" and "Mafiosi" are of Sicilian origin and did not become part of the Italian language itself until after 1861. Since Rizzotto's play was first produced in 1863 and became extremely popular, having been performed 2000 times in twenty-three years, the use of the term "Mafiusi" in the title warrants the attention it receives from Pitre.

However, there is the problem that Pitre himself does not tell us what the term means. He assumes that because of the evil life portrayed and practices depicted by the characters in the play, the word "mafiosi" came to represent a synonym for evil acts and evil deeds committed by criminals in general. However, with all due respect for Pitre's thesis, we must also allow for the possibility that Rizzotto, being a playwright, took the opportunity to create a new term, "mafiosi," to describe the lifestyles and actions of his characters. All possibilities considered, the evidence, as nebulous as it is, does support the argument that the terms "mafia" and "Mafiosi" became, after the appearance of Rizzotto's play, part of the vocabulary of politicians and journalists and eventually, according to Pitre (1889: 291,

293), came to serve as synonyms for organized crime and organized criminal activities of all kinds.

Lingering Confusions Regarding the Nature of Mafia in Sicily

The literature continues to present conceptual issues and arguments regarding the definition and description of the current mafia in Sicily. Much of this emerges from the use of and confusion regarding the term "mafia" that became customary in Sicily after the appearance of Rizzotto's play in 1863. Indeed, we are willing to argue that the emphasis on secrecy and ritual that has become for many writers the identifying feature of mafia lies at the root of this confusion. A case in point is found in the history of those criminal associations known as *fratellanze* ("brotherhoods"), criminal organizations that came into existence during the reign of the Bourbons, whose rule began in 1738. Despite the belief, however, that they arose as a response to fighting the injustices of the Bourbon regime, the evidence reveals that this was an honorable but erroneous label attached to them by writers who wished to argue that they were mafia groups. Instead, the literature that describes their structure and purpose depicts them as criminal groups who committed crimes for their own financial gain. These groups took on rather interesting names, some of which they gave to themselves, while others, which had a derogatory connotation, were given to them by their enemies.

Some examples are noted by Candida (1964:12–13) who lists, among others, the *Code Piatte* ("flat tails"), the *Fontana Nuova* ("new fountain") and the *Stoppaglieri* ("cork stoppers"). Two authors, Montalbano (1953:168–182) and Lestingi (1884:452–463), offer the most authoritative and extensive accounts of these brotherhoods. Montalbano, in describing the "cork stoppers," notes that they lived for the welfare of one another, promising, in their oath of allegiance, never to reveal any of the brotherhood's secrets and to vindicate any offense committed against any of their members. As members, they shared the profits generated by their criminal activities. Their initiation ceremony consisted of the initiate's being made to stand before a paper image of a saint. The thumb of his right hand was pierced by a needle after which he was told to wet the image with his blood. He then recited an oath followed by his burning the image with a candle. The new member, now considered baptized, was referred to as a *compare*, the Italian and Sicilian title used to refer to those related through the religious sacrament of baptism.

Lestingi's description of *The Fratellanza* (the Brotherhood) is almost identical to that provided by Montalbano with the exception that, in the initiation, the forefinger of the initiate instead of the thumb was pierced and this finger was tied with a string to symbolize the unity among the members. So, too, after the paper image of the saint was burned, the initiate was instructed to scatter the ashes in the wind. This group differed significantly from other brotherhoods in its promise of providing for the family of a member in the event of his death or incarceration.

The main point that needs to be emphasized about these brotherhoods is that they all possessed the following similarities: they were structured as secret societies, the members swore allegiance to a chief, and they practiced elaborate initiation ceremonies. These brotherhoods constituted the characteristics commonly associated with mafia. However, these similarities, as a whole, stood in direct contrast to the structure of the patron-client nature of the power established by the *gabellotto* whom we argue became the most influential form of mafioso. These groups, although they practiced secrecy, were basically organized as gangs. The Fratellanza and the *Stoppaglieri*, for example, were organized in groups of ten, with each group being led by a *capo-decime* (head of the ten) with all the groups being under the leadership of a *capo-testa* (the head) who had liaisons with the heads of the gangs in other localities. Upon being initiated, the new member had to pay an initiation fee and each month thereafter was required to pay a given stipend to his the leader of his group.

Above all, in terms of our viewing mafia as a method, these groups, according to the literature, did not have the element of political protection from the law. As we indicated before, the mafioso, whose power originated as a gabellotto, was insulated from arrest throughout the development of his career by the cultural practice of omerta. However, his protection was further assured when he became a patron to the government and could surround himself with the patronage of judges and politicians whom he helped put into office. Perhaps this is why the mafioso as we describe him was not in need of the cover of secrecy, in contrast to the brotherhoods whose leadership spent a vast amount of time in creating secret ceremonies geared toward protecting them against prosecution by the legal authorities.

Today, the existence of brotherhoods or gangs that are composed of the descendents of these brotherhoods makes for the continuing confusion regarding the nature of mafia in Sicily. Diego Gambetta (1993:chaper 6) reflects this confusion when he presents the data from Sicilian historical reports and contemporary informants in Sicily as revealed in their testimony as witnesses in governmental investigations. The initiation ceremonies described in these reports and by these informants presented by Gambetta show that the finger of the initiate is still pierced and the blood is placed on a saint's image, which now consists of a card rather than a paper image. The initiate burns the card while swearing allegiance to obey the rules of the organization, passing the burning card from hand to hand to keep his fingers from being burned. Indeed, in the description of the wording of one of the ritual ceremonies dating back to 1884, the initiate indicates that as the burned ashes and blood cannot ever return to their original state, he "cannot leave the fratellanza" (Gambetta 1993:147). However, on the same page (147) that he describes this swearing of allegiance by a member to a brotherhood, Gambetta quotes from a ceremony revealed in the 1987 testimony of a government witness who, although similar to the one described for the brotherhood, does not include the swearing of allegiance to a brotherhood. Instead, he promises "to keep silent about the Cosa Nostra around outsiders." Yet, this same witness, as Gambetta notes, forgetting that he had just testified that the group to whom he swore allegiance was called "Cosa Nostra," contradicted himself by testifying that the mafia "is the organization of those who have taken the oath" (Gambetta, 1993:153).

Gambetta (1993:154) argues that whereas the mafia groups in Sicily have control over how they structure their enterprises and the content of their rituals, they do not have control over the name by which these groups are known. Thus, he states, they have come to be known primarily as the fratellanza, Cosa Nostra, Mafia and My Tradition, a term whose usage Gambetta (1993:138) attributes to the Italian American organized criminal Joe Bonanno. We note that what Gambetta has illustrated, and is also found in the work of Letizia Paoli (2003:chapter 1), is the continuing confusion that surrounds the nature of mafia, a confusion, as we argued earlier, that emerges from a lack of clarity in the use of terms by informants and writers. This usage has been further confused by an inadequate identification and comparison of the differing structures, criminal ventures, and methods employed by the various criminal groups that have come to be lumped together under the name of mafia. Once again we emphasize that mafia in Sicily is best understood not as a secret society, gang or association, but as a system of patron-client relationships that weaves itself through the legitimate and illegitimate segments of Sicilian society.

There is no question that the history of Sicily consists of a violent and confusing history. Yet, no matter how confusing, we are confidant that if Senator Kefauver and his colleagues had read their history and anthropology before appropriating a term they did not truly understand, they would have conceded that what they called "Mafia" was not actually "mafia" in its true sense. After all, mafia was a phenomenon that was wrapped within the cultural confines of Sicily's history and social, political, and economic structures. As a history that manifests a combination of unique variables, it is a unique social, political and economic system that belongs to Sicily and cannot be transported anywhere and survive outside of its natural state, let alone in Brooklyn, Chicago, and Newark.

Indeed, it can be further argued that it is a phenomenon unique to western Sicily and was never even transported to the eastern provinces of Sicily, let alone the United States. According to the hypothesis of Paulo Sylos-Labini (1961:94–95), the landed contracts that developed in eastern Sicily after the breakdown of feudalism consisted of tenure contracts where land was rented on a long-term basis. Under this system, the landlords were interested in developing the land and, rather than exploiting the profits of the farmers, instead contributed to the farmers' welfare by reinvesting part of their own profits back into the land. As such, this system, based upon cooperation rather than exploitation, eventually resulted in the emergence of an agricultural bourgeoisie. There is no doubt that Sylos-Labini's hypothesis regarding the differences between the types of landed contracts employed by eastern versus western landlords following the end of feudalism would help explain why today there are distinct economic and social differences between eastern and western Sicily. Of course there are even greater differences between Sicilian organized criminals in Sicily and those found in the United States.

THREE

Searching for "Our Thing"

The Kefauver Committee whet the appetite of Americans searching for the secret invaders who brought the evil virus of organized crime to the shores of America. Without producing any substantial proof of its existence and ignorant of its cultural and historical foundations back in Sicily, Kefauver nonetheless had ignited a fear that served to send Americans searching further for those foreign invaders who brought the Mafia to America. What must be understood about this era and belief was that it encompassed that most intriguing element which always has fascinated the American public — secrecy. Thanks to the attention and hype of the Kefauver Committee, Americans desperately sought to know all the secrets of the Mafia. The American people needed someone to shed light on the dark secrets of "Our Thing" in order to pierce the Mafia mystique. They needed an inside source who could tell those on the outside what really went on inside. This source finally appeared in 1963 and his name was Joseph Valachi.

Joe Valachi was sitting in prison while a young Attorney General, Robert Kennedy, brother of then-president John F. Kennedy, was preparing his own war against corrupt labor unions with his sights focused specifically on the then-president of the Teamsters Union, Jimmy Hoffa. Robert Kennedy had suspected corruption in the labor unions as early as 1956, but it was not until as chief counsel of the Senate Permanent Subcommittee on Investigations that he read, and was persuaded by, the anti-racketeering reports of Clark Mollenhoff, investigative reporter for the Des Moines, Iowa, *Register-Tribune* (Kennedy 1994:ix–x). It was at this point that a series of events led to one of the most celebrated investigations of organized crime. While Kennedy was focusing on labor unions, it came to his attention that a prisoner, convicted heroin trafficker Joseph Valachi, was fearful that fellow gangsters were going to kill him in Atlanta Federal Penitentiary and so he offered to become an informant against the Mafia in exchange for protection. By breaking the "code of silence" to save his own skin, Joseph Valachi made history as the central source of information in a major congressional investigation. Like the Kefauver hearings from a decade before, the McClellan hearings, named after the Chairman of the Committee and Hearings, Senator John McClellan (D-MD), dominated television and news media and transfixed the American public.

We should note at the outset of this discussion that these hearings, and particularly the evidence presented by Valachi, gave birth to vitriolic disagreements. These disagreements caused the formation of two camps of "believers" (those who agree with the findings and those that do not) and neither will accept or even listen to those who hold views opposite of their own and have probably produced more argument among scholars, law enforcement agents, journalists, and organized criminals themselves than any other set of criminological data. We base our arguments presented here upon a thorough review of the hearings themselves and an evaluation of the evidence presented during the hearings with outside data.

The Narrow Spotlight

The first thing that one recognizes is that the committee's findings are based on one primary source: Joseph Valachi. Those who hold Valachi as a sophisticated and knowledgeable informant must bear in mind that he was just that: one informant. That may sound odd, but, as we shall soon note, Joseph Albini (1971) was privileged to interview several informants for a study that was published as a book entitled *The American Mafia*. Each of these informants, who served different functions as participants in various types of organized criminal ventures, had their own unique versions in describing what organized crime consisted of, what term or terms they and their associates used to refer to the groups to which they belonged and their descriptions of how these groups were structured. A similar approach would have benefited the committee's investigation greatly. Consequently, it is unfortunate that the McClellan Committee presented only one informant and thus the committee obtained one interpretation. In other words, it had a remarkably small sample size given the immensity and complexity of the object of the investigation.

Many critics have argued that the government purposefully wanted Valachi's view presented because his view "fed into" the further building of the Mafia mystique. There is no doubt that it did. One has to admit that his looks and demeanor helped reify the stereotype of the mafioso that Kefauver had displayed to television viewers in 1950. Also, Valachi spoke with an accent and had many mannerisms similar to those of Kefauver's witnesses, thereby reinforcing an established "wise guy" gangster trope (Ruth 1996). His image thus created an experience of déjà vu that mentally helped television viewers to connect him in a long line to those foreign elements that supposedly brought the Mafia to the United States. Furthermore, this experience of déjà vu certainly helped strengthen the Mafia mystique.

John Scarne, a highly regarded expert on gambling who testified as an expert witness before the McClellan Committee, is one critic who made a case that Valachi's testimony was used with conspiratorial intent. As expressed by the title of his book *The Mafia Conspiracy* (Scarne 1976), Scarne maintains that Attorney General Robert Kennedy purposefully used the Valachi testimony to generate sensational headlines concerning the Mafia that would help his brother, President John Kennedy, in his bid for a second term. Already saddled with his father's ties to rum runners during Prohibition and alleged support by organized crime–backed unions in the previous election, President Kennedy was suffering a decline in popularity due to the fiasco resulting from the Bay of Pigs invasion of Cuba, a missile crisis that had brought the United States and Soviet Union to the brink of war, and the continuous daily disturbances created by civil rights demonstrations. Scarne (1976:189) argues that Robert Kennedy strengthened his brother's image by going to war against organized crime and creating some banner headlines that would put him in a more favorable public light and thereby assist his brother's re-election efforts. Scarne presents some very valid arguments to support his case, one in which he pointedly calls Robert Kennedy's and the government's creation of the Cosa Nostra a "hoax" (Scarne 1976:part 5).

As we view the McClellan Committee data, we, unlike Scarne, do not quite see conspiratorial motivation on the part of the Senate committee members and Valachi to purposefully deceive. Rather, we see evidence of a process that allowed the generation of testimony that was accepted at face value without being properly examined and critically questioned. It is our belief that if Valachi and the government tried to create a hoax, it would not have resulted in what we view as the contradictory findings that emerged from the hearings. It seems, instead, that the unspecified goal, yet hope of the committee, was to bank politically off the findings of the Kefauver hearings and revitalize what was already now a part of the American psyche, the Mafia mystique.

One is easily captivated when reading reports of the hearings. Watching them on television only serves to increase this captivation by building the drama in real time, as the Committee seemingly peeled layer after layer of secrets away from the Mafia. The coup de grâce of the hearings was, of course, Valachi. Here at last was someone who would reveal the secrets, to violate omerta and risk a sentence of death. Given their fascination with the Mafia mystique, how could Americans now resist? So they watched and they listened to this middle-school dropout, a drama of real life cops and gangsters brought home in black and white. The contradictions in his testimony were glaring, but we need to understand that the public wanted to believe every word he said. They had waited since before Prohibition for words from the inside. Secret oaths, violence, betrayals at every corner, corruption, power, murder, sex; they were all here. The government presented its evidence and where there were contradictions, it simply did not address them. Instead it presented the evidence in the form of summaries that brought together a series of random incidents for which no historical or other forms of proof were provided. It argued for a new name for a new criminal organization now called Cosa Nostra and yet simultaneously concluded that it could still be called the Mafia.

What must be understood, for research purposes and for the clarification of the understanding of the history of organized crime in the U.S., is that the major goal of the hearings was to further federalize the investigation and prosecution of organized crime. The federal government had to establish that organized crime was not just a local concern in order to achieve this. What appeared to be crews of local wise guys were actually the tips of a massive iceberg in the eyes of the government, a nationwide, indeed international, criminal organization systematically monopolizing criminal enterprises as diverse as gambling, prostitution, labor racketeering, narcotics trafficking, and contract murder. Robert Kennedy himself validated this belief when he warned the country, "If we do not, on a national scale, attack organized criminals with weapons and techniques as effective as their own, they will destroy us," noting further that "either we are going to be successful or they are going to have the country" (Kennedy 1994:x).

What Is in a Name?

One of the major issues that arose from Valachi's testimony was in regard to his use of the name Cosa Nostra to describe the organization to which he belonged. This simply does not translate easily into "Our Thing," nor have later translations such as "This Thing of Ours" resolved the issue. The problem is that any way one tries, the term is just too awkward to employ as a name for an organization. Perhaps the most accurate translation of "Cosa Nostra" is as "Our Concern," a term in which Italians engaged in a private conversation are sometimes prone to employ out of politeness to someone who wishes to join in the conversation. The topic of conversation is viewed as being of concern only to the individuals engaged in the conversation at the time. The practice involves politeness, not anything of a sinister nature. Above all, the use of the term Cosa Nostra in the Italian language does not mean that the conversation's content results in the participants in said conversation being referred to as a group belonging to a "Cosa Nostra." Its use simply is not applied to an organization in its native language.

According to Valachi, however, it can, and he did use it and the name has become a household term for organized crime involving Italians. Despite the many twists and turns to try to make it fit a given meaning, the result has been that the *Collins Mandadori Nuovo Dizionario Inglese* (1997:150) still translates Cosa Nostra from the Italian into English simply as Cosa Nostra. That is its most accurate translation. Still, one can argue that whatever term Valachi used, this would be the term that would describe his organization. After all, he was the informant and, as an informant, this is the term that he had to offer. It is unfortunate, as we said earlier, that the committee did not present more than one informant since we feel confident that others would have used different names.

Let us give a very cogent example. When Albini (1971) was conducting his research, a police source informed him about an investigation that was in progress regarding an individual involved in syndicated criminal activity. Of paramount interest to the investigators was the name and structure of the syndicate groups to which he belonged. They had never heard of Cosa Nostra. The investigators, however, were intrigued by the Italian term he used to describe his group and other groups that were, at the time, interacting with his group in syndicated criminal activities. The Italian term he used to describe his organization was "Catena."

At first, the term generated excitement because it was believed that it perhaps represented a new secret word. Instead, when a tape recording of the testimony was played for a translator familiar with the informant's dialect, the word translated simply as "chain." Once again supporting our earlier observation that each informant has his own way of describing his group, this informant chose to give it the name, Catena, describing it as a chain made up of many individuals or links that were joined together in cooperation with one another (a useful analogy when one considers social network–based perspectives on organized crime discussed later). We note this example to illustrate the possibility that, had this individual been called before the McClellan Committee in place of Valachi, today the public would be calling those who belong to Cosa Nostra by the name "La Catena." History is fickle like that.

After its use in the hearings, the term "Cosa Nostra" took on a life of its own. Valachi's term has become the term of choice evidently even for those involved in organized crime, since its use has become common among these criminals since then, an underworld version of life imitating art. After all, we should note that its use was not common at the time of Valachi's testimony, let alone before. Vincent Teresa (1973:24–25), himself a prominent organized criminal, reports that while Valachi was testifying, Raymond Patriarca, who was described as a New England "crime boss," was watching the hearings on television and asked his associates who were watching with him, "What the hell is Cosa Nostra?" and made other remarks making fun of Valachi's testimony itself. In his work written with Thomas Renner (Teresa and Renner, 1973b:95–96) describing his life in the mob, Teresa also noted that neither he nor his associates in Providence, Rhode Island, ever used the terms "Cosa Nostra" or "Mafia." Instead, they used several different titles. He noted that in Buffalo, it was called the "Arm" and in Chicago, the "Outfit." So, too, Joe Bonanno, noted as head of one of the prominent New York crime syndicates, in his autobiography (1983:164) indicated that he referred to his group as "My Tradition."

FBI agent William Roemer, who, as an agent, was involved in several investigations regarding organized crime, notes in his book that Joe Bonanno, when referring to other members of his group, spoke of them as being part of "Our Tradition" (Roemer 1990:5). We should also note that the term "Cosa Nostra" was not commonly used by the many underworld and upperworld informants that Albini (1971) interviewed for *The American Mafia*. Those few who used it indicated that they had adopted the term only after Valachi used it. After all, it was used on television and in a Senate hearing, so it must be true, right? They, instead, chose to use "the Mob," "the Boys," and "the Outfit," with "the Syndicate" serving as the most commonly used term.

An Inconvenient History

One of the most serious weaknesses of the McClellan hearings was its complete acceptance of Joseph Valachi's historical narrative of La Cosa Nostra in the United States without even the most rudimentary independent historical inquiry to validate his claims (i.e., searching newspapers to validate whether historical events even happened). For example, Valachi provided a first-person account of what he claimed was a major turning point in the history of organized crime in the United States, the Castellammarese War. The Castellammarese War is an event, said by Valachi, to have taken place between two rival factions, one, named after its main leader, Joe Masseria, and the other named for its leader, Salvatore Maranzano, who was, along with other members of his group, from the area from which the war took its name, Castellammare del Golfo (a town in Sicily). This war, which supposedly took place between 1930 and 1931, was viewed by Valachi and the Committee as the beginning of the origins of the Cosa Nostra and, thus, the spawning of a national organized criminal syndicate. However, the history of this war is, as Alan Block (1978) so devastatingly demonstrates, nearly void of historical fact and those events that factually did occur occurred for reasons very different than those ascribed by Valachi. Indeed, the Castellamarrese War is best viewed as mythology, not history, given it is filled with fables, exaggerations, and half-truths. This should come as no surprise given that Valachi was only a young teenager when this event occurred, a point the committee seems to have overlooked when he testified to events as if he was party to the decision-making of the power players.

Valachi's version of events expressed the belief that the leaders on both sides of this conflict, Maranzano and Masseria, were old, backward-looking bosses from Sicily. They were "Moustasche Petes," as they have now came to be labeled, who just did not want to accept the modern, corporatist blueprint for expanding and running organized crime as envisioned by a group of young, enterprising newcomers led by Charles Luciano, who felt restricted and constricted by the outmoded rules and ideas of these old-timers who were not even born in the United States. Since the Mustache Petes were impeding good old American progress in favor of Old Country ways, as the narrative goes, they had to be eliminated and replaced with a truly American organization, La Cosa Nostra.

Suffice it to say that it appears that this "war" was given greater significance than it actually deserved and became the foundation for further Mafia mythology. Indeed, one can argue that the war served as a backdrop of confusing incidences, rumors of a planned overnight execution of "Moustasche Petes" across the nation, and a host of other underworld stories, all generated to give credence to the belief that Charles "Lucky" Luciano managed, out of this mess, to create a nationwide criminal organization run like a corporation and restricted in membership only to Italians. This false history constitutes the basic historical evidence for the creation of Cosa Nostra.

It seems that Valachi and the government chose to concentrate on placing emphasis on an organization that was vividly distinct from any other organized criminal organization that existed before its existence was made known. Unfortunately, most of the facts as presented by Valachi and the Committee are just not true or are, at best, half-truths devoid of context. As such, they presented serious problems to those researchers who later attempted to confirm their veracity. Firstly, there was entirely too much attention paid to Italian gangsters to the exclusion of the role of Jewish colleagues in the war itself. As Rich Cohen (1998:chapter 3) describes the era, Jewish gangsters were cooperating with Italians in a variety of criminal ventures, including the war itself. Two functionaries, Charles "Lucky" Luciano and Meyer Lansky, friends from childhood, were closely allied in both ideas and actions regarding their future ventures in organized crime. Alan Block (1983) gives a detailed analysis of the role and power that Jewish criminals exerted in the development of organized crime's syndicate structures and criminal ventures in New York beginning in the 1930s. Yet, during the McClellan hearings, the role of the Jewish gangster is actively diminished in the light of Italian conspiracies.

Perhaps the best illustration of the role which mythological belief played in giving support to the importance of the Castellammarese War is found in the story of the Night of the Sicilian Vespers. Once again we encounter the use of the term "Sicilian Vespers" which, employed in this new context, again serves to generate an aura of mystery and intrigue. In this case, the story was told that, on September 11, 1931, which came to be known as "Purge Day," Luciano ordered the killing of "Mustache Petes" in cities across the nation. Valachi had mentioned these killings, but placed the total number killed at four or five individuals. Instead, as the story took hold, the number was raised from 30 to 90 and so on. There was only one problem. There was a desperate shortage of bodies to be found. Consequently, most researchers were satisfied with simply accepting the war as a creational myth.

However, two researchers, Humbert Nelli (1976) and Alan Block (1978), felt that such an important historical event warranted further investigation. So they went methodologically looking for the bodies. As skilled and creative researchers, they hypothesized that, if a purge had indeed taken place, they should be able to find newspaper obituaries and/or other accounts of these murders by examining the newspapers in the cities and during the time period where and when these murders had supposedly taken place. Certainly, they assumed, if a known criminal of importance was killed in a given city, the newspapers would surely report it. In the end, neither found any evidence that a purge had taken place. Oddly enough, their research-based findings were confirmed by Charles "Lucky" Luciano himself in his life story as told to Gosch and Hammer (1976:147–148). Luciano admitted that although one individual had been killed, a "purge," as such, never occurred. He attributed the creation of the story to the imagination of those who wrote about it and presented one of the most critical questions regarding its authenticity when he noted that, although the count of the number of bodies kept growing with each story, no one could ever come up "with the names of the guys that got knocked off."

Rich Cohen (1998:66) views the story and the fact that gangsters continue to tell it as being one that serves as an underworld Bible story. Like that of Noah and the Flood, Cohen concludes, it marks the end and destruction of one world and the birth of another. We agree. However, as is true of biblical stories, we must remember to ask whether or not this one really happened. It seems safe to conclude that the Castellammarese War, the historical foundation of the Mafia mystique, did not happen and simply relegate it to the realm of Cosa Nostra mythology.

Along with the Jewish organized criminals, another ethnic group that was completely overlooked in the McClellan hearings was the Chinese syndicates. In his very detailed study of the early history of Chinese organized crime in the United States, Jeffrey Scott McIllwain (1997, 2003) presents data and arguments that serve to counter the belief that contemporary Chinese organized crime represents a new or emerging form of this type of crime in America. Instead, he argues, by the late 1800s and early 1900s, Chinese syndicates, under the cover of benevolent associations called "tongs," existed as highly structured, national organizations operating within the multiethnic social system of organized crime encompassing other criminal networks composed of underworld and upperworld figures. Contrary to mistaken, yet popular, belief, McIllwain documents the fact that, over a century ago, Chinese organized crime had managed to infiltrate the political, economic and social arenas of not only the Chinese American community, but those of the larger American society itself. As such, it victimized Chinese and non–Chinese alike in criminal ventures that included, among others, labor racketeering, extortion, price fixing, prostitution, gambling, drug trafficking, and contract murder. Indeed, as noted by Dillon (1962) and Gong and Grant (1930), major, nationwide tong wars, in which hundreds of men were killed over the decades, occurred throughout the second half of the 19th and first half of the 20th centuries. Indeed, if one was looking for evidence of underworld "purges," one should begin by looking in the Chinatowns of old because at least the bodies were there, unlike the mythology attached to the Castellammarese War (Block 1978).

Consider also the history of organized crime in the American South. For example, fresh in the memory of any participant in the McClellan Committee would be the dramatic incidents originating in Phenix City, Alabama, becoming national news with election repercussions during the 1950s. Phenix City sat across state lines on the opposite side of the Chattahoochee River from Fort Benning, Georgia. Its entrenched red light district and illicit economy relied on the patronage of U.S. soldiers stationed at Fort Benning who came to Phenix City for booze, gambling, and prostitutes. The local political and law enforcement establishment protected and profited from these criminal enterprises, covering up violence directed towards drunken, rowdy, and cheated servicemen and any local reformers who chose to meddle in their affairs. As the reformers gained power, they eventually succeeded in getting one of their own elected as Alabama's Attorney General, only to have him gunned down and killed in the middle of the street in Phenix City before he could take office. This national embarrassment forced the governor's hand, declaring martial law and ordering the Alabama National Guard, led by World War II General Walter Hanna, to crack down on the organized crime in the Phenix City area. When reading Margaret Anne Barnes' (1999) definitive account of the events in Phenix City, one is struck by the fact not a single Italian is mentioned. Indeed, the Scots-Irish and English descendants of the Revolution and the Confederacy ruled with an iron fist as they did in other Southern states, a point surely not lost on Senate and House committees and leadership dominated by Southern politicians who knew better than to bite the hands that fed them.

Square Pegs, Round Holes

The structure presented by Valachi was one which referred to criminal syndicates as consisting of twenty-four families, each described as having a hierarchical structure consisting of a "boss" who controlled those functionaries beneath him and held the title of "underboss." These, in turn, commanded the "lieutenants" and, underneath them in rank, and holding the lowest position, were the "soldiers" or "button men." In contrast to other cities, each of which had only one family, New York had five. The membership in all the families was described as consisting exclusively of individuals of Italian and Sicilian descent. Overseeing the entire organization was a national "commission" whose number varied from time to time, but was always made up of the heads or "dons" of the most powerful families in the United States.

Although police officials from various police departments across the nation presented data in the form of charts describing the structure of the "family," families, or criminal syndicate or syndicates operating in their cities, these data, we feel, were marred by the fact that they were not independently generated. These police witnesses had been shown the Valachi material before they testified. It seems safe to assume from this that the police were being asked to present their material from within the model presented by Valachi. Several of these police officials indicated to Albini (1971) that they were frustrated by the government's request, arguing that they felt forced to fit their data to match the hierarchical model presented by Valachi.

These frustrations become apparent as one views the police data presented. For example, the Mafia organizational chart presented by Tampa officials does not have a "boss" at the top as designated in Valachi's description. Instead, a "top man" is listed with two underneath him also indicating positions of high rank. Descending from these upper-level positions are lines drawn to middle-level positions that bear no title. Occupying the lowest positions are those classified as "non-member associates" and "employee associates" (U.S. Senate 1963:part 1, exhibit 45).

Similarly, Detroit police witnesses, in presenting their chart, placed at the top "the dons" which represented a form of ruling counsel, not a "boss" in keeping with Valachi's description. Underneath them was not an "underboss" as listed by Valachi, but, instead, "the big men" who were above the "chiefs" of operating units, neither of these two levels being represented by the Valachi data (U.S. Senate 1963:part 3, exhibit E).

The Chicago chart varied most radically from Valachi's description in that it presented two groups instead of one; a "mafia type group" which, in contrast to Valachi's four levels, had only two levels — "bosses" and "lieutenants" — and another group designated as "non-member associates of the Chicago–Italian Organization." In the testimony, it was emphasized that the crime syndicate in Chicago consisted of Italians and non–Italians and that, along with its being called "Cosa Nostra," it was also referred to as "the mob," "the outfit" and "the Mafia" (U.S. Senate: 1963: part 2, exhibits 39, 40).

These obvious contradictions were not addressed. Instead, the McClellan hearings found and concluded that Valachi's data lent support to a belief in the existence of Cosa Nostra, an octopus-like entity with tentacles reaching across the United States and into the pockets of all honest citizens. If the simple, hierarchical Cosa Nostra assumption guiding the analyses of the data had been viewed as just one of the many interpretations borne out in the evidence, another more contextualized and accurate interpretation of organized crime in the United States may have evolved.

The Cressey Factor

The Valachi narrative and those of the McClellan Committee were given support in the writings of Donald Cressey, a prominent sociologist who served as a consultant to the 1967 President's Commission Task Force on Organized Crime. Although he gave credence and respectability to the data supporting a belief in Cosa Nostra in the Task Force Commission's Report of 1967 (President's Commission, 1967) his influence became more pronounced after the publication of his book *Theft of the Nation* (1969). The book became a best seller and numerous professors adopted it for use in criminology and sociology classes across the country.

Cressey's definition of organized crime equated it primarily with the Mafia and Cosa Nostra. But, along with data from the McClellan hearings, Cressey drew heavily from evidence obtained through government wiretaps and presented in the form of airtels (the FBI term for air mail messages sent through FBI channels). For Cressey, these wiretaps represented proof of the existence of a large, national, centralized organization that netted a vast income from its enterprises. In contrast, Murray Kempton (1969), using the same wiretap data, found that instead of netting a multimillion-dollar income from its operations in gambling enterprises and drug trafficking, its total net income amounted to no more than a few hundred dollars. So, too, in contrast to the belief that these criminals had now come to exert enormous avenues of power and influence in their communities, Kempton found instead in the telephone conversations, anger and frustration in their unsuccessful attempts at persuading employers to hire their relatives even in such menial occupations as janitors. Yet despite these findings by others in his source material used in *Theft of the Nation*, Cressey built on the Mafia mystique and captured the imagination of the nation.

The Apalachin Meeting

Another incident that has been widely argued as presenting undeniable proof for the existence of a national syndicate is that of a meeting of syndicate leaders in Apalachin, New York, on November 14, 1957. Once again, like the missing bodies involved in "Purge Day," the count of the number of individuals in attendance varies from account to account. In his book, Attorney General Robert Kennedy (1994:239) placed the number at fifty-eight. However, in his testimony during the McClellan hearings, Kennedy stated that "more than a hundred top racketeers" were present (U.S. Senate 1963:part 1, p. 6). Both Cressey (1969:57) and the *Task Force Report* (President's Commission 1967:11) placed the number at seventy-five. Although the number of attendees was in question, the more complex issue surrounded whether or not they represented a national gathering of organized criminals. In a listing derived from police data, Arthur L. Reuter, a former Investigation Commissioner from New York presented data that indicates that, of the 56 on his list, the bulk came from the New York–New Jersey area. The list also indicated that their major criminal enterprises and interests fell in the areas of narcotics, gambling and labor racketeering (Frasca 1963:130–140).

This certainly does not appear to lend credence to the belief that this was a meeting of a national organization. Besides, meetings have always been part of the history of organized criminal groups just as they have for any other groups, formal or informal, in the legitimate world. Such meetings are necessary in order to allow for participants to discuss their mutual business problems and issues concerning the operation of their various ventures. After World War II, syndicates in various parts of the country were developing interests in expanding old enterprises and creating new criminal ventures, many of which necessitated extending interaction and cooperation with groups in different geographic areas of the country. It was during this era of suburbanization and national highway proliferation that cities like Las Vegas became a favorite target of criminal investment and expansion. In our opinion, the Apalachin Meeting in 1957 represented the continuing need and practice of syndicate leaders to interact with one another for business purposes. In this case, we find syndicate functionaries primarily located in the New York–New Jersey area whose major interests involved narcotics, gambling, and labor racketeering.

We also find it telling that the meeting occurred in the context of massive change and turmoil in the labor movement. The recent formation of the AFL-CIO in December 1955, the high-profile assault on nationally syndicated, anti-communist and labor-racketeering columnist Victor Riesel (sulfuric acid was thrown in his face by a man hired by the Genovese crime family) in September 1956, and the ongoing, relentless press and Congressional scrutiny of corruption and racketeering during the mid- to late

1950s had labor racketeers under siege and would have easily justified meetings for those with stakes in the game.

Look Out! Here Comes the Boss!

Valachi and the McClellan Committee made special note of the importance and power of the "boss" in his unquestioned ability to rule over his underbosses, lieutenants and soldiers with an iron fist. Valachi told the committee that any failure to abide by the orders issued by a boss would land the violator in serious trouble, alluding to the certainty of swift and certain retribution. Again in immediate and direct contradiction to this observation, Valchi stated no one obeyed the rule laid down by Valachi's own boss, Frank Costello. In 1957, not only Costello, but other bosses, according to Valachi, laid down a rule so profound that Valachi impressively referred to it as "a law." This law clearly stated that no one was to deal in narcotics. That is impressive and should have impressed every underboss, lieutenant and soldier in each of these groups. Yet it was so impressive that nobody obeyed it. Why not? According to Valachi, there was just too much greed and too much money to be made. This assuredly does not lend credence to the power and reach of the boss.

We are not here trying to argue that bosses do not have power. They do. But their power, as we will discuss in the coming chapter, emanates not inherently from their position, but from the nature of their patron-client status and their ability to establish relationships with both their peers and underlings. These relationships are based not so much on fear but on mutual respect and the fulfilling of mutual goals and interests between them and those obligated to the boss and thus dependent upon him for the success of their own enterprises. Hence, their power is neither absolute nor completely fungible. Valachi made this clear when he noted that none of the underlings received a salary or other form of payment for their services from their boss. Instead, he noted that they received protection for their enterprises. This again notes the patron-client nature of the underling-boss relationship.

We should here also highlight the fact that when Valachi spoke of the various ranks (i.e., boss, underboss, lieutenants and soldiers) he never explained how one came to occupy these positions and the exact duties required by those who held these ranks. It appears that he simply intended to describe loosely defined relationships of power and authority rather than a system of formal positions in a rigidly structured hierarchy. As such, Valachi's description of his group, which displayed the characteristics of a loosely knit network of functionaries, was elevated by the findings of the committee into one that had all the attributes of a nationwide organization. We will argue that these attributes do not fit those of an organization per se and we will explain why they do not in the next chapter.

While on this subject, we should also clarify another area of confusion, the confusion regarding the alleged existence of a "Commission" made up of the bosses of the various Cosa Nostra families whose function was and is to settle disputes between groups. Again, a confusion of terms resulting from Valachi's unclear usage makes it appear that "consigliere" or "counselors" have always existed as part of the Cosa Nostra structure. The hearings themselves revealed that the practice of using counselors was the creation of Charles "Lucky" Luciano, a practice, we are told, geared toward protecting soldiers from the injustices perpetrated against them by their lieutenants (U. S. Senate 1963: part 1, p. 81).

Later, however, in his description of the role and effectiveness of these counselors as told to his biographer, Peter Maas (1968:117), Valachi stated that the original group of counselors consisted of one man from each of the New York families and one representing the Newark area and described as performing their protective role for the soldiers only during the Castellammarese War, a creation and unique product of the war itself. In the charts presented during the hearings, however, the five New York families are depicted as each having a "consigliere" position, one that is permanent and not one that existed only during the war.

The issue becomes more confused when, in the *Task Force Report*, we find that the position of consigliere is depicted in its charts of all the families. Thus, the position is not limited exclusively to the New York families, but instead becomes a position in all twenty-four families, nineteen of which were not located in the New York area and certainly were not part of the Castellammarese War. In this report, the consigliere is simply described as an individual who, acting "in a staff capacity," gives advice or counsel (President's Commission 1967:7). Creating still further confusion is the question regarding why these counselors were given so much importance in the first place, especially since Valachi himself made clear

to Maas that even among the New York families, the advice of these counselors was "as often as not ignored." This led Maas to conjecture that the
only purpose served in Luciano's creation was an attempt on Luciano's
part to bring "an aura of stability" to the period following the Castella-
marese War (Mass 1968:117–118).

There is a great deal of ambiguity remaining in the literature followed
by Valachi's description of the existence of a Commission. There is no
question, as argued by Rogovin and Martens (1989:11–14), that this literature includes evidence drawn from informants and other sources that
argue that a Commission of some sort in fact exists. The problem is that
it is difficult to determine how it functions when one examines, critically,
not this evidence, but the activities of the bosses and the families themselves
when viewed over time. The original composition of the Commission, we
are told, varied from nine to twelve members and consisted of the bosses
of the most powerful families (President's Commission: 1967:8). Yet what
is not given are the criteria employed for determining which families are
the most powerful. Thus, consistent with the original description of its
membership, Jimmy Fratianno (Demaris 1981:294), a very eloquent and
important government witness, noted that there were ten to twelve members on the Commission. However, by 1981, the Commission suddenly
had only six members, consisting of the bosses of the five New York families
and the boss of the Chicago family.

Admittedly, the literature is filled with all kinds of stories that frus-
tratingly try to explain why this happened. But, if it did happen, and there
is no reason to believe that it did not, then this serves to contradict the
belief that the Commission is made up of the heads of the most powerful
families. These issues would not be issues if there were a clear statement
or explanation of how the Commission came into existence. Unfortunately,
however, there is not. Instead, in the *Task Force Report* (President's Commission, 1967:8) we are simply told that the size of its membership varies
and that the members "do not regard each other as equals." So, too, we
are not given any knowledge as to how the members are selected. However,
we are told "the Commission is not a representative legislative assembly or
an elected judicial body." The *Task Force Report* emphasizes that the "Family members look to the Commission as the ultimate authority on organizational and jurisdictional disputes." Yet the conflicts between families
that have continued during the past thirty years do not give credence to

any successful acts of intervention on the part of the Commission. Not only have the members of the various Commissions over the past several decades not been able to settle disputes between families, the literature reveals some of the members of the Commission itself, in various struggles for power, began fighting each other.

An understanding of the Commission is inherently difficult due to the nebulousness of the procedure by which one becomes a boss of a family. Like the Commission, neither Valachi nor other informants have been able to clearly and effectively describe the process in which a member becomes a boss. Adding to the confusion is the informal manner by which families themselves come to acquire their names. Rich Cohen (1998:63–64) explains that each boss gave his name to the family over which he now ruled after Maranzano named the original bosses. Thus we had the Profaci family named after Joseph Profaci, the Bonanno family named after Joseph Bonanno, etc. However, as time passed, Cohen explains, bosses were killed or deported and the family names were changed. When Albert Anastasia was killed, his family became the Carlo Gambino family. When John Gotti took over its reign, it continued to be called the Gambino family. So, too, the family of Charles "Lucky" Luciano was known by his name until he was deported to Italy, after which it became known as the Frank Costello family. This family, however, became known later as the Vito Genovese family. Then, when Genovese was accused of murder and went into hiding, the name of this family again reverted back to the Costello family. When Genovese returned to New York, he found that Costello would not relinquish his power, so he planned a coup. Costello was shot but survived, after which he decided to surrender his power. Following the death of Genovese, the family leadership went to Vincent Gigante but remained the Genovese family.

As we examine this history presented by Cohen, we once again are struck by the lack of a formal structure as the names of the families and the power structure depicted in the changing and obtaining of the position of boss reflects one in which rules are not set up to outline how the boss will attain this position. Instead, we see a system in which killing, intrigue and power struggles decide who becomes the boss of a given family and, in turn, how the family gets its name. Such procedures do not describe a system of change in a manner consistent with those of formal organizations. Above all, this system does not speak well for the belief that the Commission settles disputes and serves as a governing body. The Commissioners themselves are seemingly fighting all the time with deadly consequence. That is no way to run a successful business.

The McClellan Hearings: Is There a National Crime Syndicate?

We believe we have presented sufficient information to argue that the structure and practices of the organization that Valachi described does not fit that of a formally structured organization. Instead, the evidence for such lies hidden in the massive confused and contradictory assumptions and conclusions of those who claim that they have demonstrated its existence, evidence that, on the other hand, actually shows that elaborate and extensive criminal networks existed, just not La Cosa Nostra. The confusion of the claimants remained as a result of the unclear usage of terms, the most unclear being those surrounding the use of the terms "Mafia" and "Cosa Nostra." Although an effort was made to argue that Cosa Nostra was a new organization, the conclusion on this issue rests with that individual who brought the McClellan hearings into existence, mainly Attorney General Robert Kennedy. When asked during the hearings to distinguish between the Mafia and Cosa Nostra, Kennedy replied, "It is Mafia. It is Cosa Nostra. There are other names for it, but it all refers to the same operation" (U.S. Senate 1963: part 1, p. 21). Buttressing Kennedy's position was that first voice from the inside, Joseph Valachi, and the alleged secrets of the Mafia mystique were now revealed.

In ending this discussion, we do so by noting one of the most striking contradictions of the McClellan Committee findings, one that could only be overlooked because of the myopia created by the Mafia mystique itself. This is noted by Raymond Michalowski (1985:370), who observes that the twenty-four families identified in the hearings cover only sixteen states yet organized crime activities are found in every city in the United States. We should now pause for a moment and reflect upon the power of the Mafia mystique. In creating this concept, Dwight Smith gave Americans cause to reflect upon the fact that life has a way of letting emotion overtake logic and in so doing, confuses the nature of reality and puts it on hold. Yet there is one attribute about reality that cannot be ignored. Eventually, it must be faced. So we move now to a discussion of how America attempted to deal with its new socially constructed reality that is Cosa Nostra.

The effects of the McClellan hearings were to have a substantial impact upon how Americans viewed organized crime. Once the name Cosa Nostra was defined as representing the nature of organized crime in the United States, the literature dedicated to organized crime was consumed with attempts on the part of writers to further elaborate on what was revealed in the hearings. Despite the fact that it was a novel, Mario Puzo's *The Godfather* (1969) added to the intrigue and excitement, since many believed that Puzo wrote the book as fiction in order to reveal its secrets without angering members of the Mafia. When the movie by the same name came out in 1972, audiences were enthralled by the fact that they could now identify the characters in the novel with those portrayed so vividly by the actors.

The Mafia mystique now had a visual portrayal of the stereotypes on the movie screen and an incestuous cycle began to develop. The mainstream media cited the government reports and the government reports cited the mainstream media. Film influenced and was influenced by both. Scholars based their studies on both and subsequent government and media reports relied on these scholars for guidance and catchy quotes. In an analysis of this literature, Mieczkowski and Albini (1987) found that, because the government, media, and scholars used each other's data as sources, they were destined to come to the same conclusions as each continued to present data that reinforced an incestuous belief in the existence of a national criminal organization. Mieczkowski and Albini emphasized in their study the fact that social scientists simply were helpless in their attempts to alter this belief. Academia seemed to give respect and credence to the fact that a renowned criminologist, Donald Cressey, supported the belief and, although there was a growing literature that contradicted the findings of the Cressey and governmental model, few writers in the area of criminology noted or challenged these contradictions. Indeed, the opposite was the case. As Galliher and Cain (1974) found in their study of criminology textbooks written during this era, the citations in the textbooks widely used at the time only offered documentation that supported a belief in the Mafia. So it comes as no surprise, then, that scholars began to notice the same and began to start asking critical questions of the dominant ideology. These questions came from a number of different scholarly disciplines and used a variety of research methodologies and collectively sparked a vibrant revisionist debate over the subject of organized crime.

FOUR

Revision

When the Mafia mystique was at its zenith, Joseph Albini published his book *The American Mafia* (1971). Albini's findings, as mentioned earlier, were based upon interviews with members of the underworld and interviews with detectives and investigators in police forces in the U.S. whose careers focused upon investigating and studying the nature of organized crime. Along with these interviews, he conducted an exhaustive review of the literature on mafia in Sicily, reading works both in English and Italian as well as the literature and documentary evidence pertaining to organized crime in America. This "pioneering study" (Albanese 1991b:206–207) was one of the first to employ empirically derived data to the problem of the Mafia in the American experience.

This study helped dispel a concern which researchers shared, one which had been Albini's concern during his research: that of the risk of becoming a victim of violence resulting from delving into the secretive nature of the information. Very early in the study, Albini cleared his research with a top investigator from the New York Police Department, Ralph Salerno, who assured him that he had nothing to fear. Indeed, Albini never confronted any reason for concern throughout the study. The fear, he came to realize, was born out of the mythologies surrounding the Mafia mystique. The informants that he interviewed did not seem to mind discussing their work, particularly since this gave them an opportunity to explain their enterprises in their own words.

Not only was this true of those whom Albini interviewed in the U.S., but, it was true also of those that he interviewed as part of a later study that he conducted in Great Britain (Albini 1986). In this study, which took place during 1972 and 1973, what Albini found interesting was that several of the Scottish and English informants themselves requested that he interview them. The reason for this, he came to realize after completing the study, was that, in Great Britain, since his book *American Mafia* had just been published and read by some of these informants, he was now viewed as a serious author. Hence, these informants felt that if Albini did not interview them it could give the impression that they were not important and did not merit interviews. To their horror, this could have possibly resulted in their losing face among their peers.

The use of informants in both these studies confirmed that drawing data from a number of sources, unlike the approach used in the McClellan hearings, allows researchers more extensive bases from which to draw conclusions. The publication of *The American Mafia* in 1971 was well received in academic circles. However, the general public and segments of the mainstream media were forced to confront the suspicion of Albini's revisionist assault on the widely embraced gospel that was the Mafia mystique. Indeed, the first question Albini was asked during his first television interview after the book appeared was "did the Mafia pay you to write this book?" Albini soon learned that a popular rumor had taken form that the Mafia had paid Mario Puzo to write a book portraying the existence of a Mafia while, simultaneously, Albini was paid to write a book arguing that there was no Mafia. By paying both of these authors to come to opposite conclusions, the logic of the rumor maintained, the Mafia would keep everyone confused.

Soon, other studies supporting Albini's description of the nature of syndicated crime in America made their appearance. As we noted in our discussion of mafia in Sicily, the fine work of anthropologists like Boissevain (1966), Blok (1969, 1988), and Hess (1973) served to explain its nature as a cultural phenomenon. Similarly, only this time in the United States, two anthropologists offered an inside look into one of the crime families in New York. This inside look did not come in the form of a criminal informant such as Joseph Valachi. Rather, this inside look came from two scientists who employed the participant-observation research method in order to collect their data. In their work entitled *A Family Business* (1972), Francis Ianni and Elizabeth Reuss-Ianni presented data that argued that the criminal enterprises of this family did not consist of a bureaucracy with specific positions of authority, but instead consisted of loosely organized local groups that worked together to achieve their goals. Employing the participant-observer methodological approach, Ianni spent two years living with this family and becoming part of its social milieu. During this time, Reuss-

Ianni was researching the literature on mafia in Sicily. They found no evidence that supported a belief in Mafia as a secret society either in Sicily or the United States.

In 1979, another empirical study, this one taking on particular significance in that it used federal law enforcement data itself to study a family believed to be part of the Cosa Nostra national crime syndicate, found no evidence that allowed for a belief that this group was part of a national organization. Employing economic analysis as her method of research, Analese Anderson (1979) concluded that this family did not constitute a threat to legitimate business enterprises in the city where it operated, and, contrary to the belief generated by the President's Commission 1967 *Task Force Report*, that the Cosa Nostra families were amassing large amounts of profits; this did not appear to be the case in this family.

In a very insightful and useful addition to the literature, Howard Abadinsky (1981) presented a life history as related to him by an informant. In this description, "Vito" portrayed the structure of organized crime not as a national organization but one that was neither complex nor organized in a bureaucratic context in contrast to the narrative presented by Joseph Valachi during the McClellan hearings. This biography served to give a detailed analysis of the decentralized structure and function of organized crime in the United States. It also served to further illustrate how informants differ in their descriptions of organized criminal structure and function.

Using a myriad of archival sources and sound historical and sociological analysis, Alan Block (1979) challenged the conclusions of the McClellan Committee that described a national organization primarily in the hands of Italians. Instead, by studying the nature and structure of criminal groups involved in the illicit cocaine trade in New York during the early part of the twentieth century, Block found that this enterprise was not operated exclusively by one ethnic group and that ethnic ties were not the basis for interaction among these groups. Rather, members of different ethnic groups cooperated with one another. What brought and kept them together was their mutual interest in making money from the lucrative illicit cocaine trade itself. In this study, Block confirmed a finding that seems to be a major characteristic of organized criminals; that is, when there is money to be made, organized criminals seem to be eager and willing to forget their ethnicity.

Two of Block's graduate students, Sean Patrick Griffin and Jeffrey Scott McIllwain, found the same dynamic in their historical studies of "non-traditional" organized crime in the African American and Chinese American communities, respectively. Griffin (2003, 2005) explains the major role of African American organized criminals in the fleecing and victimization of fellow African Americans in and around Philadelphia and their interconnections with numerous corrupt upperworld actors in the larger, multi-ethnic social system of organized crime on the local, state and federal levels. McIllwain focused more broadly on the multi-ethnic turn-of-the-century opium and immigrant smuggling networks in Southern California and Baja California (McIllwain 1998, 2004); the interdependence of Chinese American organized criminals with political machine and police corruption and the manipulation of the Christian reform movement in Progressive Era New York City (McIllwain 2003); and multi-ethnic gambling and loansharking operations in post–World War II Los Angeles County which pitted the Los Angeles Police Department, Los Angeles County Sheriff's Department, and State Attorney General's Office, and the governor against each other (McIllwain 2006). It seems then, that, contrary to popular belief emphasizing ethnic exclusivity, organized crime is, as McIllwain called it, "an equal opportunity employer," comprised of social networks reflecting the racial and ethnic diversity or homogeneity in a given geographic region and marketplace.

Economist Peter Reuter (1983) noted the importance of market forces and how these forces impact the structure, tactics and resulting mutual cooperation between and among organized criminal groups that influence the success or failure of illicit criminal enterprises. The importance of Reuter's work lies in the drawing of attention to the fact that organized criminal entrepreneurs, very much like legitimate business entrepreneurs, find it necessary to understand and abide by market forces and the laws governing supply and demand. So too, in contrast to the popular theme that paints a picture of ruthless loan sharks who continuously threaten and beat up, maim, or kill their victims, Reuter notes that the ties between the lender and borrower in this market are so close that there is minimal need for the use of either intimidation or violence.

We should note here that the effect of these forces have relevance only in those societies with forms of capitalism which allow for market forces to operate in a functioning system based upon the principle and practice of laissez faire. As we shall illustrate in our discussion of organized crime in the former Soviet Union and contemporary Russia in a later chapter, the markets there seem not to be subject to the laws of economics as much as they are subject to the manipulation of a legal system which has been structured to protect and offer immunity from prosecution to those officials of the government and leaders of organized criminal groups who openly engage in a multitude of sophisticated, clever, yet deceitful forms of organized criminal ventures.

These and other revisionist studies served to cast major doubt on the findings of the McClellan Committee, but the controversy continues to this day. It rests with the excitement that continues to surround the Mafia mystique. However, slowly but surely, the essential and glaring contradictions inherent within the McClellan data continue to surface even among those who hope to keep the mythology of the Mafia alive. It has served to create a great deal of entertainment and, for many, this belief in a simple and uncomplicated explanation of organized crime in the United States helps many Americans to define their social reality within a format they can understand. The secrecy that has continuously surrounded this topic allows these individuals to create their own versions of how the system functions. This element of secrecy has made authorities of those who imagine that their own version is the only correct one.

As we move toward our goal of ending this chapter by offering a usable definition of organized crime, we pause to note that the research conducted by academics in the 1970s and 1980s did serve to awaken the awareness of the U.S. government. In its previous investigations, organized crime was made to appear as an enterprise solely in the hands of Italians. There was now just too much evidence to allow this belief to continue. In 1983, then-president Reagan created a Commission mandated to conduct a thorough and region-by-region investigation of organized crime groups in the U.S. This Commission held seven public hearings and examined research and litigation data as well as surveys and data obtained in other investigations. In 1986 it published its report.

The conclusions of this report (President's Commission, 1986) were markedly different from either the Kefauver findings or those of the McClellan Committee. The paramount finding in this report was in regard to the findings of previous investigations; it was felt that too much attention had been given to the Mafia and Cosa Nostra. Several members of the

Committee believed that this had created a barrier for law enforcement by drawing attention away from other organized criminal groups operating in the United States, mainly motorcycle gangs, prison gangs, Colombian gangs, Russian organized crime groups, Chinese Triads, and the Japanese criminal group known as "the Yakuza" (which the report designated as being, in terms of its total number of members, the largest organized criminal group in the world). The report itself was couched in controversy and resulted in the majority of the Commissioners themselves writing and attaching to the final report a statement in which they voiced disagreement over a variety of issues. However, on one point, there seemed to be agreement; that of the misdirection and resulting misconception created by previous governmental findings that employed a narrow view of the history of organized crime in America, thus making it appear that the creation of organized crime itself and Cosa Nostra were synonymous in the United States.

Therefore the government, through the words of this 1986 Commission report, came to agree that the Mafia and Cosa Nostra were given inordinate and unwarranted exclusiveness as constituting the main sources of organized crime in the United States. However, the average American was still beholden to the Mafia mystique, long firmly seconded in numerous films, novels, true crime books, and documentaries. The report did little to diminish the continuing interest and excitement which American audiences displayed in their consumption of books, movies and television portrayals that glamorized the Mafia. Despite the fact that when one considers that the Italians had really not been different from other groups in terms of how they operated their enterprises, it was the Mafia and Cosa Nostra that carried within it the treasure of that magical entity, the Mafia mystique.

Nailing Jell-O to a Wall

Given the information provided in this and preceding chapters, we have occasion to reflect on why agreeing on a definition of organized crime has become so problematic for scholars. Let us now address these issues in hopes of rendering a definition that perhaps will help more clearly distinguish it from other forms of criminality.

The first element is the one that brings about the least amount of argument; that it must consist of two or more individuals. One person, acting alone, simply cannot constitute an organized crime group. Indeed, a network, composed of at least two actors and the relational ties that bind them, is needed (McIllwain 1999). One person can act alone as part of a group, but the nature of his or her crime, in order to fall within the category of organized crime, would have to be related to a group. Thus, if one person commits a murder, this act is not viewed as organized crime. However, if two individuals commit such a murder, then it would constitute a form of organized crime but only if these same two individuals continued to commit murder over an extended period of time as part of a criminal enterprise.

So, we see that the definition now must incorporate the element of time. Two individuals killing once does not warrant their being classified as organized criminals. However, if these two killers create an enterprise in which they kill on a regular basis, we view them as contract killers and now add another element to the definition, profit. But what if these two kill not for profit but, specifically, for their own enjoyment? Are they organized criminals? Many would argue that the answer should be no, in that, traditionally, organized crime has come to be viewed as having a profit motive. But does profit alone have to be a motive to warrant the perpetrators being viewed as organized criminals? Again, the answer would appear to be no in that there are many rebel and revolutionary groups that commit acts of killing and destruction of property not directly for profit, but instead as a means of furthering their cause.

Terrorists, for example, do not seek direct profit but, instead, attack innocent people as an act of demonstrating their anger against certain governments in hopes that these governments will eventually give in to their demands. Yet organized crime scholars do not generally view terrorism as a form of organized crime because it does not represent this type of crime in its traditional form, meaning Mafia and Cosa Nostra. We mention these inconsistencies to emphasize one of the major characteristics of organized crime; mainly, that it can take on many fluid forms. Likewise, its participants engage in many enterprises. Yet, for many of these participants, obtaining a direct profit is not necessarily a major motivating factor. We have already noted terrorist groups as falling into this category. However, other factors like identity and brotherhood are also factors. Outlaw motorcycle gangs allow for an illustrative example.

When these groups first made their appearance after the second World War, they represented individuals who rode in groups in defiance of law enforcement agencies, not because defiance was their goal, though defiance became a byproduct of what came to be called "the biker lifestyle." Unfortunately for both the bikers and the general public, this lifestyle was destined to create social friction in that it was anti-social in its basic orientation. Thus, the bikers who were frequently labeled as "loners," "misfits," and "maladjusted" by those who despised what they stood for returned the compliment by manifesting those types of behaviors that only served to further this image. They chose not to bathe and hence were always purposefully and very visibly, physically dirty. They wore Nazi helmets and swastikas not because they were unpatriotic to the United States, but simply because they knew that wearing these symbols of the Nazi enemy whom, in fact, they had oftentimes helped defeat, would offend mainstream Americans. That was fine by them because the last thing these bikers liked was mainstream American values.

In the same spirit, they added the practice of giving their fellow Americans "the finger" as a further way of making certain that they were not liked. For what was the main goal of these bikers? Making certain that they would not be liked. They were loners. They did not need anyone except each other. Only weaklings needed others. To show any emotion, especially pain when injured, was a sign that one was not worthy of being a biker. Their main joy came from having wild and drunken parties that, of course, often resulted in disturbing "normal" Americans who relished their post-war era of normalcy and conformity. This meant that the police would have to intervene, which often created intense skirmishes between the bikers and the police. All this resulted in the bikers soon becoming defined both by law enforcement and mainstream Americans as being intolerably deviant, after which they were given the label of "outlaw bikers" to distinguish them from law-abiding biker groups.

These outlaws did not engage in any activity for profit during these early days. Fun, in the form of drinking alcohol, doing drugs, and primarily "raising hell" was what life was all about for them. However, fun or no fun, this activity slowly evolved into a form of organized crime. For example, drug use soon became drug dealing and then drug trafficking. Now Interpol and police organizations around the world view some of these outlaw biker gangs as major drug and weapons trafficking syndicates. These groups continue to have their destructive brand of fun, but, today, making a profit seems to be their major goal and their major form of involvement in organized criminal activity. We stress this point to show that organized crime takes on many forms and that organized criminal groups, over time, can and do change the nature of the forms of organized criminal activity in which they become involved.

Another element of organized crime is the use of corruption. However, here again, not all forms of organized criminal ventures require the use of corruption. The early biker groups certainly did not need or use it, although in their new venture of drug dealing, its use became mandatory. When corruption is used, it is often viewed as the criminal doing the corrupting of otherwise honest public servants or businessmen. This overlooks the widespread systemic and cultural reasons for corruption as well as the simple idea that respectable upperworld actors oftentimes need devious underworld actors to help them achieve their personal or organizational goals. Consider, for example, the politicians who need voters to "vote early and often," the banker who needs a capital infusion of drug money to keep his bank solvent, or the government that needs a weapons trafficker to arm rebels in the land of its enemy.

The Organized Crime Continuum

Certainly, it stands to reason that the types of enterprises themselves such as drug trafficking, auto theft, extortion rackets, money laundering, illegal bookmaking, illicit numbers or lottery operations, pickpocketing, confidence game schemes, terrorism, gang criminality, fraud schemes, intellectual property theft, prostitution, and the many other forms of organized crime can largely determine the type of organized crime classification into which each of these can be placed. Still, organized criminal activity, as we have just illustrated with our example of outlaw bikers, does not generally allow for the creation of clear-cut classification boundaries since the same groups may have characteristics that can place their ventures into several different categories at any given time or these categories can change over time as the activity of any given group itself changes.

For this reason, we believe that rather than trying to classify organized crime into a rigid typology, this phenomenon is better understood when viewed as a continuum of types in which each type is described as having certain distinctive characteristics in common, yet some of these character-istics are found in other types as well. We argue that there are four basic types of organized crime that compose this continuum. Each of the four types has at least one basic distinguishing feature that differentiates it from the others. In this endeavor, we build upon Albini's *The American Mafia* (1971) where such a continuum was first constructed. We believe that these types help make important distinctions that can serve as guides that can bring clarity to the very confusing task of analyzing organized crime.

Political-Social Organized Crime

The first type, which we refer to as political-social organized crime, consists of those enterprises and groups which, specifically, do not have financial profit as their major goal. Instead, it would be prudent to empha-size that these groups and their crimes are motivated by attempts to bring about what those engaged in them view as social and/or political change. Included here would be terrorist, rebel, guerrilla and other groups, as well as traditional political machines, which seek to bring about social and political change through the illegal use of violence and force. We need to note, however, a sensitive, but nevertheless important aspect regarding the illegal nature of such groups; that is, those who participate in such activities become criminal by virtue of the laws enacted by the governments that they seek to overthrow or otherwise control. One of the ironies of history can be noted by the fact that the fate that decides whether or not these groups and their leaders are ultimately judged as traitors or heroes depends upon whether or not the group succeeds or fails in its effort. Flipping this dynamic around, it is those governmental leaders who lose power that become the criminals and usually meet with the fate of being imprisoned or executed if the political machine or revolutionary or terrorist groups succeeds in its effort. We must emphasize that this is a fragile type of crime in terms of the judgment of the goals and actions of such groups. It is fragile because the struggles themselves are typically shrouded within the emotional reactions of those who support versus those who oppose the ideologies or central goals being pursued by the reacting group.

Today, for example, many fringe groups like hate groups, such as the skinheads or Neo-Nazis, and extremist militia groups express antigovernment attitudes. These groups continue to bring upon themselves the wrath of patriotic Americans who despise their actions. Yet, other patriotic Americans praise these groups and view their actions as representing a reaction geared toward protecting individual rights under the Constitution. The actions of these groups, they believe, represent the highest form of patriotism. Convicted Oklahoma City bomber Timothy McVeigh called himself a patriot, believing that his act of terrorism represented a righteous form of retaliation against the FBI for its involvement on April 19, 1993, in the killing of Branch Davidians when agents of the FBI attacked the Davidians' settlement at Mount Carmel near Waco, Texas. However, irrespective of the stand taken in these issues, hate groups and hate crimes serve to best illustrate the nature of political-social organized crime in that, here, the perpetrators of such crimes have no financial motives for their acts. Michael Woodiwiss (2001:72–79) aptly illustrates this point in his analysis of the activities of the Ku Klux Klan and his findings remain remarkably consistent with regard to contemporary extremist militias and hate groups.

Mercenary Organized Crime

Of all the types of organized crime, mercenary organized crime is the one most characterized by the outright goal of making direct and immediate profit for the criminals involved. These crimes are predatory in scope in that they cause victims to lose money and/or property through the use of force or the threat of force. Profit is also made through the use of deception such as those involving scams and other forms of fraud. Such crimes as larceny, robbery, burglary, kidnapping, and white slavery, as well as profits made through the perpetuation of various forms of confidence games, are included in this category. This category, however, serves to illustrate the need for a continuum of types when we consider the new forms of cyber-crimes.

Some of these crimes consist of criminal hacker attempts to steal information from the computers of individual users or those of companies. The goal of these intrusions is that of stealing credit card numbers, social security numbers, and other information that the cyber-thief then uses to make a profit by illegally purchasing items via the credit card number. Better yet, they use the stolen social security number, creating new identities for themselves, by which they can initiate illicit loans or use their new identities as a pathway to fraudulently make various other types of purchases. There is no doubt here that these cyber-criminal activities fall under the mercenary category.

However, what if the criminal hacker uses the computer to access secret governmental data vital to the security of the U.S. or other nations? This is theft, but consists of direct profit only if the hacker is paid a given sum for selling the information to the intelligence agencies of a given foreign country. But what if the criminal hacker steals the information for the purpose of helping his country gain access to data that can be employed for committing terrorist acts upon the government agencies and/or citizens of a country which it views as its enemy? If such is the case, then this would fall into the category of political-social organized crime. As a case in point, it was noted (Hosenball 2002:10) that a group known as the Muslim Hackers Club has been using its website to offer instructions to fellow Muslim hackers as to how to create viruses and apply various hacking strategies to create disruptions of government and other computer systems in the form of vandalism, all geared toward the goal of such groups eventually staging an attack which could create a serious disruption of U.S. critical infrastructure. This group, and those like them, would definitely fall into the political-social category. We note these examples as further verification for the need and usefulness of a continuum that allows for these differences to be noted and understood.

In-Group Organized Crime

In contrast to mercenary organized crime, in-group organized crime stands out as being a form in which direct financial profit is definitely not the motive. Typically, this type of crime involves actions that result in the commission of crimes not because committing a criminal act was the original intent of the perpetuators, but rather the acts that result from the group members engaging in activities which they view as daring or adventurous in the context of the group providing a brotherhood or other quasi-familial or tribal dynamic. This behavior is found among street or neighborhood gangs and it also involves gang behavior of the type previously noted in our illustration of the behavior of the early biker or outlaw motorcycle gangs. For this reason, this type of crime can be deceptive given the fact that in many cases the motive for a gang member's theft may not be that of attaining profit from the theft itself, but rather to show bravery as this demonstration of bravery will win for the perpetrator both recognition and acceptance by the other members of the group.

A frequent form of biker gang theft is for a gang member to steal the leather jacket with the patches attached (known in biker language as the biker's "colors") of an opponent. Here, the theft is not for profit, but to humiliate the biker who lost his colors. Typically, the violence perpetrated by gang members is directed toward outsider gangs in the form of fights that are referred to in gang lingo as "rumbles." The basic purpose for such rumbles is to demonstrate and prove superiority of one gang over another as revealed by the bravery and fighting skills of the group that ultimately subdues the other. Sometimes rumbles take place in order for competing gangs to establish and/or protect territorial boundaries. Captured in the same spirit are those cases where members of a particular gang will fight one another. Again, the goal is to establish which member is the bravest and most skilled fighter.

Syndicated Organized Crime

The final type of organized crime is evidenced in the one most commonly referred to as "traditional" organized crime. Yet, as discussed previously, there is nothing traditional about this form of crime since it has existed simultaneously along with the other forms in the United States throughout its history, let alone the history of other nations and cultures. Obviously, different forms of organized crime have made their appearance since technological and other innovations have allowed for new forms to originate. Thus, computer crime could not and did not originate until the computer was invented and put into use on a large scale.

That said, the major reason why syndicated crime came to be called traditional, as we have already explained, was that the government committees investigating organized crime in the United States during the 1950s and 1960s found it useful to establish an über-criminal organization run by Italian Americans that dominated all others. The committees constructed a history of traditional organized crime in the United States that began with a violent transition from the simple, parochial Mustache Petes of the Progressive Era to an urbane, business-like, and modern nationwide organization of the Roaring Twenties run by a secretive and all-powerful Commission of Italian Americans. The Mafia/Cosa Nostra was traditional to those both casting and under the spell of the Mafia mystique. It was the sum-all, end-all of organized crime in the United States. Any other forms were "non-traditional" and they reported directly to the Mafia/Cosa Nostra or suffered the consequences. Hence the commissions created a false dichotomy. This dichotomy emphasized what Jay Albanese called the "ethnicity trap": "when organized crime is defined in terms of the nature of the groups that engage in it, rather than the nature of the organized crime activity itself, and how and why various groups specialize — or fail to specialize in certain activities" (Albanese 1996b:145).

Yet if one pulls out of the ethnicity trap and focuses on the organized crime activity itself, one can begin to pull away from the inherent constraints of the traditional view and recognize what distinguishes syndicated crime, regardless of the ethnicity of the actor, from the other forms. Those who participate in syndicated organized crime have as their major goal and purpose the provision of illicit goods and services to those members of legitimate society who seek these illicit goods and services. Since this activity involves ongoing enterprises that take place on a continuing basis and necessitate that the customer or buyer must interact with the criminal in order to complete such transactions, it becomes necessary for the criminal to provide himself with some form of protection from the legal authorities. This is accomplished through the cooperation of corrupt public officials, police officers, or businessmen.

Another distinguishing feature of this form of crime is that this is the only form of organized crime in which a client seeks out and is willing to pay for the goods and services provided by the criminal. This is a point that is all too often overlooked by those who view the syndicate criminal as one who forces his goods and services on an unwilling and uncooperative buying public. Once again, segments of American society whose members buy these goods and services are only too happy to employ this form of myopia in order to draw attention away from themselves as constituting the real source of the success of organized crime ventures: the continuing demand of customers for the products and services that the organized criminals provide. This is the reality of syndicated crime in the United States. We live in a land where the government understandably enacts legislation that makes certain goods and services illegal or regulates or taxes goods and services to such an extent that there is substantial profit to be made by allowing clients to circumvent government efforts. However, certain individuals need or desire these goods and services and they are willing to pay exorbitant prices in order to meet their demand. Additionally, private and public sector actors are willing to work with professional criminals to ensure the demand is met if the price is right. Consequently, certain individuals will risk their lives and the possibility of incarceration in order to make the exorbitant profits acquired by taking those risks. No matter how many sophisticated treatises are written on this subject, no matter how many distinguished lectures are delivered to explain it, this simple formula that includes the three "Cs"—customer, criminal and corruption—constitute the simple explanation of why syndicated crime is, always has been, and always will be a vital part of life in the United States.

A Definition of Organized Crime

As we end this chapter, we do so by again taking note of the complexity of the phenomenon of organized crime. We have purposefully described it in terms of its history and historiography and have developed a continuum of types. We will continue to draw upon this continuum in the remainder of this work as we now move toward a more detailed analysis of the theories and models that seek to explain the nature of its structure and the causes for its existence. But, despite the fact that we have shown that no one definition has, as yet, served to satisfy the needs of those in various disciplines and governmental and political functionaries who deal with its daily realities, our discussion would not be complete without ending the chapter with our definition. In doing so, we do not in any way mean that this definition will indeed be the definitive one. Instead, we humbly offer it in hopes that it can help bring together in one definition all those elements that make organized crime the complex yet fascinating phenomenon that it is. Our definition then is as follows:

> **Organized crime:** A form of criminal activity occurring within a social system composed of a centralized or decentralized social network (or networks) of at least three actors engaged in an ongoing criminal enterprise in which the size, scope, leadership and structure of the network is generated by the ultimate goal of the enterprise itself (i.e., how the crime is organ-

ized). This goal takes advantage of opportunities generated by laws, regulations, and social customs and mores and can be pursued for financial profit and/or the attainment of some form of power to effect social change and/or social mobility via the leveraging and brokering of the network's social, political and economic capital. Members of the network can be from the underworld or upperworld. In some forms, force and/or fraud are used to exploit and/or extort victims, while in others illicit goods and services are provided by members of the network to customers in a marketplace where such activity is often permitted through the establishment of practices which foster the compliance and/or acquiescence of corrupt public and private sector officials who receive remuneration in the form of political favors or in the form of direct or indirect payoffs.

FIVE

Organizing Crime

How can one begin to make sense of the complexity that is organized crime? We have discussed various theories and models and offered criticisms and suggestions to navigate this milieu. However, another way to appreciate the complexity is to use a case study approach that examines how crime is, in fact, organized. Syndicated criminals engage in a variety of criminal enterprises. Syndicate criminals, sometimes evaluating the current desires and needs of their customers and sometimes seeking to create or stimulate interest in new illicit goods or services, have managed to keep themselves in business for a considerable amount of time from generation to generation. We recognize that syndicate criminals, acting as entrepreneurs, take a financial interest in what they do and are constantly searching for ways to keep their enterprises alive or to adapt and evolve into new ones. They are also particularly adept at understanding the psychology and behavior of their clients.

This discussion provides glimpses into the entrepreneurial genius of these organized criminals and, in so doing, illustrate the limitations of the Mafia mystique. We begin by examining gambling and loansharking, classic staples of organized crime in the United States. Gambling clearly reflects the many faces and complications in a seemingly simple crime. Loansharking provides us with a glimpse of enterprise and power syndicates ("muscle") adapting to the economic realities of the criminal enterprise or else suffering the loss of a client base. Next we will discuss the criminal opportunities related to human trafficking and the practical realization by Chinese syndicates that a monopoly in such a market is impossible to achieve. An analysis of the intrinsic involvement of organized crime within the legitimate economy is demonstrated by its inclusion in the waste and toxic waste industries and how such involvement in something so seemingly benign is comparable to crimes like drug and weapons trafficking in terms of harm and creates numerous, significant problems for the global community as a whole. We then provide an analysis of how crime is organized from a non–American perspective, analyzing the former Soviet Union and its dealings with the challenge of the "Russian Mafia" since the end of the Cold War. These analyses illustrate how syndicated organized crime is not beholden to the Mafia mystique nor just an American phenomenon, but is also one woven into the fabric of all societies.

The Case of Gambling

If there is one constant enterprise in the repertoire of services offered by organized criminals in the United States, it is the service of providing skilled personnel and the equipment for operating various types of gambling ventures. As Jay Albanese (1991a:1–2) emphasizes, gambling, rather than prostitution, merits being called the world's oldest vice. He points out that gambling in its varied forms has been a part of very early recorded history and that the New Testament relates how, following the crucifixion of Jesus Christ, three Roman soldiers, each of whom wanted to keep the robe which Jesus had worn, decided that the only fair method by which to decide who could keep the robe was to throw dice in order to determine who would become its owner. Albanese (1991a:3–4) further notes in the American colonies, horseracing, playing cards and shooting dice, along with lotteries, were common forms of gambling despite the fact that the Puritans of Massachusetts viewed gambling as sinful behavior. Indeed, this puritan attitude, concerning gambling has come to be part of the American psyche in regard to morality as, to this day, there are many in the United States who continue to view gambling as a sinful practice and as a form of vice.

All one has to do to be convinced of its sinful nature, it is argued, is to be closely involved with someone addicted to gambling. These people, known as "compulsive gamblers," live for just one more chance to gamble and win. Unfortunately, the lure for the compulsive gambler and the lure for the recreational gambler are really based upon the same anticipated outcome. It is the belief in this outcome that gives the act of gambling its universal appeal since gambling is a universal practice found in virtually every society in the world; the belief that a player may be able to win a large sum of money by risking a small amount in order to accomplish that win. Compulsive gamblers describe the moment when the outcome of the bet, game, horserace, or card draw is about to occur as representing a high unlike any other form of high they have ever experienced. The recreational gambler seems to feel a sense of exhilaration when that moment arrives but, it appears, this sense does not come anywhere near the form of high described by the compulsive gambler.

Why is there a difference? The compulsive gambler tends to have more at stake in the possibility of losing than does the recreational gambler. The recreational gambler is not obsessed with winning because he or she views the game as fun. The compulsive gambler is enslaved by the fact that he or she has already lost so much that a large win is the only way that he or she will be able to make up for all those previous losses. This certainly becomes a reason for concern when we realize that compulsive gamblers have, in previous bets, often wagered and lost their entire savings, their home, and sometimes, by default, their spouses who simply are no longer willing to tolerate the addiction.

We mention the compulsive gambler because he or she represents an extreme case of the attributes that make gambling so appealing — the desire to win big by investing so small an amount. This is the reality of gambling and is confirmed every time the public is given the occasion to identify with the exhilaration displayed by the person who wins a megabucks jack-pot or another form of lottery that pays millions of dollars to the lucky winner. But there is the rub. Probability wrecks the dreams of idealistic wishful thinking because the process of winning and losing in gambling ventures is based upon chance, and chance is probability that, without any feeling or prejudice, decides who wins and who loses.

There is no question, however, that individuals vary widely in terms of how fascinated they are with the act of gambling and the thrill of win-ning, but it seems that history has shown us that most people, if they do gamble, hope and expect to win regardless of the odds against them. So syndicate criminals know that the demand for gambling opportunities will always provide them with customers. This does not mean that all gambling is under the influence of organized criminals as legitimate forms of gam-bling have, over the past several decades, become increasingly available to the public in the forms of state-sanctioned casinos, lotteries, and on-line gaming. As Albanese (1991a:1) observes, the continuing growth of the legal gambling market, particularly if it becomes better designed, could come to compete so effectively with the illegal market so as to ultimately make illegal gambling an unprofitable activity for organized criminals.

Albini discussed this possibility with several bookies during field research in various cities and each of the bookies claimed that their illicit gambling ventures would never be displaced by legitimate forms of gambling because the bookies have two substantial advantages over their legal competitors. First, they offer better odds. Second, and more importantly, bettors who wagered with them did not have to pay income tax on their winnings. The thrill of engaging in an illicit activity is another element that seems to make illegal betting attractive to certain types of gamblers. Several gamblers whom Albini has interviewed described illegal games possessing an ambiance all its own — the smoke-filled rooms, the eccentric and otherwise interesting types of players whom such games attract, the unpredictability of the composition of the group in terms of level of skills and amount of money that potentially will be wagered, and the thrill itself of doing something illegal. Much more entertaining than celebrity poker tournaments on late night sports television, illegal games with varying components were the games of choice for Albini's gamblers.

Stable and Floating Card and Crap Games

There are generally two types of physical settings where these games take place: "stable," in which a specific location tends to be employed over a relatively prolonged period of time, and "floating," in which the location constantly changes, i.e., "floating card games" or "floating crap games." They "float" from place to place in order to avoid law enforcement or criminals looking to rob the gamblers and/or the house. The organized criminals who operate these games are responsible for expenses incurred, security, and making provisions for operating the games, such as providing the room or rooms where the players will meet, making available any equipment necessary for the playing of the game(s), and providing personnel such as dealers to manage the games. They may also provide other accoutrements such as alcohol and women to serve it and, if necessary, the gambler.

Payoffs to the police are often necessary for stable games to exist.

Depending on the locale, players who attend such games consist of well-known members of the community who need to be discrete in their recreational activities and may include members of city and state governments. Hence, such protection from the police is a very important aspect for some of these operations. Any arrest under these circumstances would quickly dampen any further participation from other clients in future games. That is why the syndicate functionary makes certain that "the fix is in." With floating games, the operation is more protected by its inherent tactic of constantly changing locations. Yet, it stands to reason that, if players can find the location, so can the cops (if they are bothering to look in the first place). Consequently, even floating games will make sure "the fix is in" if possible.

How do the players find the location? Generally, a person known to these types of gamblers is employed. Typically, a bellhop or bartender is given the information with the trust that they "know the ropes" and will give the information only to those whom they know are not affiliated with any form of law enforcement agency. They also know the current code word or phrase that, when used by a stranger, can clear the way for the location to be revealed to the stranger. Even with the use of the code, however, the bellhop or bartender will generally make a call to make certain that the person who he states gave it to him gave the stranger the code. These men really know how to "act dumb" when approached by strangers seeking the information. They know what questions to ask and thus serve as a gatekeeper for those who ultimately are given the location for the game.

The dealers for these games, whether craps or card games, are often "mechanics." "Mechanic" is the term used to designate someone who is skilled at the art and science of cheating at cards or dice games. Albini had the opportunity to interview a mechanic who, in slow motion, showed him how he performed his feats. It is not easy to learn the mechanic's trade and each mechanic has his own methods. Typically, a mechanic will alter playing decks of cards by "shaving" cards. In his garage, with a card placed firmly in a vice locked between two pieces of lumber, Albini watched the mechanic diligently pass a carpenter's plane over the area holding the card. The idea was to "shave" the card so that it would be infinitesimally smaller than the other cards in the deck. Depending upon the card game for which it will be used, the card that is shaved is generally a high one or one that can boost the winning in a particular card game. One would never know that the shaved card was smaller if the card alone were felt in one's hand. However, when it is placed inside the deck and the dealer's fingers are passed gently up and down along the sides of the deck, the card can be felt and found. The dealer can then cut the deck so as to place this card at the top or bottom of the deck in order to make certain it appears when needed.

There are many ways to cheat at cards. John Scarne was an expert on the subject and he has testified as an expert witness in many governmental investigations during the twentieth century. Scarne (1949) also wrote a book that is a classic regarding gambling with cards. He dedicated an entire chapter to describing in detail the various techniques employed for cheating at cards by both amateurs and mechanics. Among the techniques described by Scarne are those of "palming" a card (pp. 13–14), a tactic in which a player secretes a valuable card when the cards have been thrown in for a new deal. He cleverly hides this card in the hollow formed by the palm of his hand and places it under his arm or knee. Later, when he needs the card, he substitutes the palmed card for one of the cards in the hand that he has been dealt, now giving him the winning edge. Another clever technique described by Scarne is the use of "shiners" (p. 170), little mirrors built into cigarette lighters, ball point pens, bottoms of pipes, and any other object that can lie unobtrusively on the card table. The mechanic then passes the cards over these mirrors as he is dealing the cards and the refection from the mirror shows him which player in the game has been dealt which cards.

Lest the role of the mechanic be misunderstood, we need to note that the syndicate functionaries who are offering the illegal gambling opportunity to players want a dealer who can detect cheating on the part of players in the game in order to protect their own interests. Also, the mechanic can cheat in such a way as to help players win as well as lose. These games are played without any cheating on the part of the dealer in most cases. However, in those events where the syndicate game operator wishes for a specific player to win, the mechanic can help make certain that this happens by dealing him the right cards. This usually is the case with players who have political power and, by allowing them to win, can help favorably dispose them to use their power to help further various syndicate interests.

Mechanics also know how to cheat in games involving the use of dice.

They can load a die so as to make certain that the load will cause the heavier side of the cube to allow the desired side to face upright when it comes to rest on the table. Thus, using two dice loaded to given sides will produce the numbers needed to make the desired points necessary to win. Dice are also heated and squeezed in a vice to alter their square or cube shape so that, when thrown, they will be forced to roll in a determined or forced fashion in order to make a given point. Needless to say, the mechanic is skilled in the knowledge of how and when to use these fixed die so as to make it appear that the laws of probability rather than the use of cheating tactics created the conditions for the win. Once again, John Scarne (1961) gives a detailed description of how to detect crooked dice and makes a point of warning honest players in crap games that even a transparent die, although one can see through it, can nonetheless be loaded.

Along with floating games, stable games at fixed locations can be found in towns and cities all across the United States. Once again, police often know these locations, especially in smaller communities. Payoffs are usually made in order to avoid interference from law enforcement. Typically, these illegal gambling places are located in the back rooms of restaurants or private clubs where, after closing, both gambling and alcohol are made available to the players. Since the sale of alcohol in many of these business establishments is restricted by city, county or state ordinance to certain hours of the day or night, the serving of alcoholic beverages in these establishments during certain hours becomes illegal, and, as a result, they have come to be called "after hours" clubs.

Some restaurants, coffee houses and cafes, however, manage to allow for illegal gambling to take place during normal business hours. Cleverly, such establishments devise techniques that are aimed at making the attaining of evidence by the police difficult, thus rendering such evidence ineffective in a court of law. Since money present on a table where an illegal game is taking place constitutes a vital piece of evidence and could be seized by police during a raid, these establishments devise methods to camouflage the financial transactions. One of the cleverest tactics employed is to have no money on the table. Upon viewing such a game, it would look to the average non-gambling patron in the restaurant or café as just a friendly neighborhood game. The waiters in the restaurant, café or coffee house are trained to keep score on the amount of money that is wagered, usually on the check used to take customer orders for food or drink. Needless to say, a very subtle ballet takes place as these waiters make their way to and from various tables after each hand is played in order to record the score regarding who owes whom what. At the end of the game, disguised as the simple act of each customer or player paying his bill for the food and drink consumed, the amount won by each player is paid to him, again disguised as the act of the waiter simply giving the customer his change when disbursing winnings.

The Numbers Game

One of the more prevalent, ongoing and established types of gambling activity in America has been and continues to be that known as the numbers enterprise. This form of gambling has often been erroneously attributed to be, specifically, the favorite gambling pastime in African American communities. Donald Liddick (1999:118) concludes in his study on the subject that numbers gambling is not bound by either ethnicity or race. Liddick's observation is confirmed by the fact that various investigations and studies show that both syndicate functionaries operating the numbers enterprises in various cities and their customers come from a variety of ethnic and racial backgrounds. Although numbers gambling has been a major enterprise for many African American syndicate criminals, this should not lead to the conclusion that this is or has been exclusively the domain of African American organized criminals.

For example, in his study of New York City's Chinatown at the turn of the twentieth century, Jeffrey Scott McIllwain (2003) notes that Chinese immigrants participated in a form of lottery known as "pak kop piu." This lottery had each participant select from eighty characters printed on a five-inch piece of paper, selecting the characters that he wished to play by marking the characters (no two were identical) with black ink. The player would then give his marked ticket with his name inscribed, along with the amount wagered, to a runner or agent who then collected the money and saw that the ticket was delivered to the location where the drawing would take place. Under careful scrutiny by the players throughout the entire process, a measure employed in order to assure against fraudulent practices by those running the lottery, winning tickets were drawn from a bowl and the numbers posted on a bulletin board for all to see. The players then checked the characters that they played to see if they matched those that were drawn. Winners were paid based upon the odds correlated to a client's selecting a certain number of correct characters.

This Chinese lottery is a little more complicated than the numbers lottery as it has come to be played in cities and towns across America. The modern numbers game requires very little skill other than that of selecting a given set of numbers and placing them on a piece of paper. As Liddick (1999:3–6) explains the process, the modern numbers game consists of a player selecting any three-digit number between 000 and 999. The number is written on a slip of paper along with the amount wagered and is given to a collector. A player, however, may place his number directly by going to a "spot" which is either at a front (an outlet disguised as a business place, but, in reality, existing only for the collection of bets) or a legitimate business place that also makes money from taking numbers bets. In his very detailed study of "Morrisburg" (the pseudonym given for a city in a middle–Atlantic state), Gary Potter (1994:74–75) notes that several small lunch counters, restaurants, bars, retail shops, and newsstands in this city served as places where numbers bets were placed. Potter emphasizes that these places of business could not survive financially without the profits made from engaging in these betting services.

Liddick notes that, irrespective of whether the bets are placed through a collector or directly through a spot, the money collected from each bet is passed on to a controller who holds on to the money until the day's tabulations have been completed. The slips themselves are turned over to a controller at the bank, the place where the daily bets are recorded and tabulated to determine the winner and the payoff. Winners receive their payment from their collector who, after taking his cut, passes what is left to his controller who, in turn, takes his percentage before sending the remainder to the person heading the operation — the banker.

Collectors work on commission and keep ten percent of winning bets as a tip. Controllers are responsible for collecting all the slips and making certain that this information ultimately reaches the bank. The banker is responsible for making the necessary payoffs to public officials as well as making certain that clerical workers, maintenance staff, guards and other workers necessary to the maintenance and safety of the building and premises of the bank itself are paid their salaries. Although controllers, collectors, and the banker receive a commission, the clerical workers who record the daily numbers on the betting slips and tabulate the monetary amounts of the wagers as well as all other workers are treated as salaried staff and paid a given salary each week.

The location of the bank itself is often frequently changed and bettors do not generally know its location. The bank itself is generally protected by alarms and equipped with reinforced steel doors at the entrance, all to foil police raids or possible robbery attempts by outsiders. Some banks use special types of paper, called "flash paper" to record the numbers, meaning that, in case of a raid, a lighted match or a flame from a cigarette lighter quickly applied by a staff member to the bin containing the slips will cause the slips to go up in a flash of flames, thus destroying evidence of the bets.

The numbers operation is interesting in terms of the structure of the organized criminal activity that is necessary to its functioning. The banker and those who collect the slips and the money constitute personnel who are directly engaged in the criminal aspect of the enterprise. The clerks who tabulate the data work inside the premises of the bank and, along with the maintenance workers and guards, can be viewed as any other form of corporate personnel. This does not mean that these workers are not violating the laws that make numbers operations illegal, as they are participating in an illegal venture. Yet, they do perform services that would simply be viewed as legitimate in legal business establishments. Hence, tabulating numbers on slips would simply be viewed as clerical work were it not for the fact that these data will be used in a venture that is illegal.

We mention this because, in numbers operations, these clerical workers when combined with the controllers and the street and spot operators serving as collectors constitute a large force of workers. Indeed, those in the numbers racket commonly argue that because of the large number of workers employed in these enterprises, the financial welfare of the communities in which they exist benefits because their employees do not compete for jobs with those in the legitimate labor market. This, the reasoning continues, allows for fuller employment, especially in economically depressed areas. This may not be the most legitimate manner for solving the unemployment problem in such communities, but when one considers that journalist Ray Sprigle (1950:1) found that ten thousand people were employed in the policy enterprises in Pittsburgh alone in 1950, we wonder if these informants may indeed be making an argument that is worthy of consideration.

But numbers gambling also produces an auxiliary industry that emerges from the mysticism accompanying the selection of winning numbers. As Liddick (1999:3–4) explains, the manner in which the winning number is selected has changed over time and some of the methods used by some banks can be very complicated in the mathematical formulas employed to derive the winning number. The more common techniques were those first used in the 1920s that consisted of basing the winning number on those of the New York Clearing House. However, when this became public knowledge in 1931, the Clearing House discontinued reporting the exact numbers. The numbers operators next turned to using the daily quotation of stock prices listed in the New York Stock Exchange. When this was discovered, the stock market exchange also thwarted the numbers operator's method for selecting a winning number by publishing only approximate or rounded numbers. The next method to come into usage was a rather complicated one, but one that computed the winning number by employing the results of parimutuel wagering at designated race tracks.

In Albini's (1971:270–273) study of numbers operations in Detroit, he found that this tended to be the most commonly employed method. However, informants told him that, not only in Detroit, but in other cities where numbers are played, a more devious method of choosing a number had become commonplace. Actually, this method does not involve selecting but, instead, calculating the number. The method guarantees a sure winner for the bank and there are enough sure winners among the players to keep everyone happy. When the slips arrive at the bank, the clerks, using computers instead of calculators, list all the numbers played for the day. The numbers are almost instantaneously calculated, the computer searching for the number that is played by the least number of players. The identified number becomes the winning number. The bank is required to pay only the smallest number of winners in this manner.

Is it fair? Of course not. Playing the numbers is like life — sometimes you win and sometimes you lose. Fairness does not enter the equation. The only thing that numbers players care about is winning. As long as someone wins, who cares how the number was derived? At least this was the attitude of those players whom Albini interviewed. As one put it so aptly, "Hey, it's old Lady Luck — if she is good to you, then it don't matter how she got to the gate because you win. If she doesn't get to the gate, you lose. It's all a matter of Lady Luck getting to the gate. Get it?"

These players know that irrespective of the method for calculating the daily number, the winner is at the mercy of luck. Either way, it's Lady Luck. Get it? So, if you want to win, stop trying to figure out how the number is derived and concentrate instead on getting on the good side of Lady Luck. And it is in the process of getting next to Lady Luck that those auxiliary functionaries make money from the numbers racket. In the game of numbers, mysticism is paramount. Do not rely on probability theory; it just does not work for numbers.

Besides, as David Myers (2002:28) lucidly points out, we always have to accept those occurrences that have no explanation other than being mere coincidences. Myers gives as an example the very odd occurrence on September 11, 2002, when the New York State Lottery's evening numbers game popped up the numbers 9-1-1. It is Lady Luck. It is coincidence. There is no foolproof method for calculating the odds. Instead, the reasoning goes, rely on your dreams. Above all, remember your dreams in detail because they just may contain the winning number. No, Sigmund Freud and his dream interpretations do not apply here. Instead, it is the symbols — the people and objects as well as the theme of the dream — that will give the potential answer and number. So an ancillary cottage industry was born: To help in this process, "dream books" that contain lists of numbers associated with these symbols — people, objects, and themes — are sold to gamblers to help them with their interpretation of a dream and selection of a number.

In terms of the profits made by the criminal syndicates running numbers games, it is safe to argue that making profits from the game is, in itself, a gamble. Peter Reuter and Jonathan Rubinstein (1982), after analyzing numbers gambling in New York City for the period 1966 through 1977, concluded that numbers banks did not always produce the large profits that match the popular and mythological belief about their success. Instead, overhead costs often did not allow for large profits to be made. Furthermore, collectors and their bankers did not have a stable and routine manner of relating based upon the rules allowing for specific commissions to be paid to the collectors. Instead, it appears that these relationships are more of a patron-client nature, the format we have described in reference to other syndicate criminal enterprises. Reuter (1983:59) makes note of the fact that collectors, by virtue of their patron role to their bettors and client role to their bankers, nonetheless become mainstays to the operation and success of the enterprise itself. Yet these controllers are powerful enough to often be able to set their own payout odds, sometimes with and sometimes without the approval of the banker.

One can readily observe that the operation, rules and relationships between the agents and bankers in the numbers game are not written in stone. Instead they vary from place to place. The manner in which the number itself is selected, as we have noted, varies from bank to bank and can vary over time within the same bank. What is important to understand is that those who play the numbers game are motivated by the firm belief that, ultimately, one day, Lady Luck will be there waiting for them at the gate. How she gets there is not as important as her getting there. But, in order to meet her, the bettor has to have a slip with a three-digit number on it that matches the one she is holding. Therefore, the bettor continues to place bets in hopes of one day meeting her. It is a matter of excitement; it is a matter of dreams; it's all about three numbers; it's all about making certain that you have the winning number on the slip when you get to the gate. So you play and hope. One day you may meet the Lady and your dream will have come true. Get it?

Bookmaking

Perhaps the largest source of money made from gambling by syndicate criminals in the U.S. comes from bookmaking. This, like the numbers operation, requires a large organization of functionaries as well as the requisite protection of police and upperworld officials in many communities. McIllwain and Leisz (2006) illustrate just how intertwined bookmaking can become within both the underworld and upperworld, creating a formidable climate of impunity for some operations. Their research focused on post–World War II Los Angeles County and the Guarantee Finance Company, a front for a major bookmaking operation receiving the protection of Sheriff's Department officials and well-connected lawyers and politicians with power reaching from Los Angeles to Sacramento to Washington, D.C.

The bookmaker provides the original funds that form the bank or financial backing necessary to establish the syndicate that runs these operations. Like the numbers game, bets are often placed by bettors at fronts or legitimate businesses where runners or bookies hang out. Some bookies have routes that they travel, daily visiting choice customers at their place of work or in the restaurants, bars or other places where these customers frequent. The bookies then turn over the bets to clerks who record the bets.

The bookmaker sets the odds and can limit the size of bets. Although, in the past, horse racing constituted a major segment of bookmaking activity, today the enterprise consists primarily of betting on sports events such as baseball, football and basketball on the college and professional levels in the U.S., with sports like soccer, cricket, hockey, and rugby receiving significant action in overseas markets. In order to give himself the edge, the bookmaker whose enterprise handles a voluminous number of bets generally hires the services of a "wire man" or "tabber" who carefully and consistently scans the bets and changes the odds or the point spreads on the games in order to better secure the bookmaker's profit margins. Even with this protection, however, a day with several unexpected "upsets" between sport teams can result in a temporary yet serious loss in profits for the bookmaker. The manner in which the odds are established and the use of the wire man and tabber, however, are the vital safeguards that function to keep the banker in business. This service, as Lasswell and McKenna (1971) note, is mandatory to the survival of the smaller types of bookmaking enterprises, as is integrity, because self-interest leads to a high ethical level on the part of bookmakers.

Koleman Strumpf (2003) conducted an economic analysis of illegal sports bookmaking using the records of six bookmakers who operated in the 1990s. He found that the operations were structured like standard business firms and made use of incentive contacts to induce appropriate employee behavior. Prices closely followed the legal market, but individual betting patterns also influenced prices. Risk was still substantial, despite expensive hedging instruments, so maintaining large cash reserves was of vital importance to a successful enterprise. For all the risk the enterprise entailed, Strumpf found that, in the end, "the risk-adjusted profit rate [was] lower than in legal financial markets."

Furthermore, centralized control of bookmakers by a monopolistic organized crime syndicate is not a reality bookmakers face due to the flexible and relatively autonomous nature of their enterprise. This point is illustrated in a criminological study by Phyllis Coontz (2001:239) in which she interviewed forty-seven bookmakers working in the Rust Belt region.

Based on her findings, the author argues that there is no evidence that bookmakers are conduits for centralized organized crime, whether evidenced in their criminal careers or their day-to-day activities. Bookmaking syndicates are decentralized, better able to adapt to market conditions.

Another factor to consider is the element of "the fix" in bookmaking. Sport is a human activity and as such, those who participate in it are vulnerable to human weaknesses. Athletes, coaches, trainers, referees and umpires are all subject to being voluntarily and involuntarily manipulated or extorted to throw games, take a dive, shave points, or inject banned substances into an athlete or animal. They may gamble themselves, owe money, find loved ones vulnerable to threats, suffer from addictions, have something to hide like an affair, or simply respond to a favor asked from a friend from the old neighborhood. Whatever the action or the reason, the fix has been a part of professional and amateur sports and bookmaking for generations, a way for professional gamblers and favored clients to "make a killing" in the face of significant, but covertly surmountable, odds. For instance, two of the greatest hitters of all time, Pete Rose and Joe Jackson, are banned from baseball and the Hall of Fame due to their alleged involvement with gamblers. The NBA was wracked by a scandal in 2007 when it was discovered one of its referees, Tim Donagy, was throwing games in collaboration with a long-time friend and bookmaker, Jimmy Battista (Griffin 2011). Bookmaker-driven point-shaving scandals almost destroyed college basketball in 1951 when a massive criminal conspiracy, including players, coaches, clergymen, politicians, and gangsters, composed a sophisticated network that manipulated the outcomes of many games or protected those who did so (Rosen 1999). Gambling scandals have rocked the spectrum of professional and amateur sports from boxing to horse racing, from college football to soccer, proving time and time again that perhaps there is such thing as a "sure thing" when the "fix is in."

Online Gambling

Decades ago, a revolution in gambling occurred when telegraph lines, then telephone lines, allowed for gamblers in one city to bet on a horse race occurring in another city on the other side of the country or just in the next town over. The last two decades has seen another revolution in gambling occur, riding new technology to a finish worth billions of dollars.

Online gambling is now a very popular outlet, with gambling websites proliferating. Making use of offshore locations that permit various types of gambling, gamblers can easily place bets online. There is still, as is true of many business transactions conducted on the web, the ever-present possibility that the company or, in this case, the onsite gambling enterprise or virtual casino may not be trustworthy. There have been cases where the online bankers went bankrupt and the winning players were never paid. However, online forums exist that allow bettors to first gain information about a given gambling site's reputation for trustworthiness, customer service, and honesty regarding its business practices before using its services. One can understand that overnight types of enterprises, those that come and go quickly, could represent a menace for this new form of gambling. Usually, however, such fly-by-night enterprises go quickly, as dishonest establishments rapidly become known and rapidly go out of business.

As Dan McGraw (1997:54–55) points out, many of these virtual casinos operate as offshore enterprises in countries that permit sports gambling, many being located on Caribbean islands. Customers open an account with either a credit card or a wired bank transfer. Although many of the companies that offer these services maintain that they are legal because they operate outside the jurisdiction of the United States, both state governments and the federal government are attempting to regulate and/or criminalize internet and offshore gambling operations by creating new laws or by using existing laws like consumer fraud statutes and a federal law that prohibits the transferring of gambling information over telephone lines. Other laws have attacked internet gaming from new directions. For example, Section 5363 and Section 5366 of the Unlawful Internet Gambling Enforcement Act (UIGA) of 2006 (enacted in October 2006 as part of the Safe Port Act meant to protect the nation's ports from terrorist attacks criminalized the acceptance of funds from bettors by operators of most online gambling websites. The operators affected are those who are in the business of betting or wagering who knowingly accept proceeds from credit cards, electronic fund transfers and checks in connection with the participation of a bettor in unlawful Internet gambling, which is the sponsorship of online gambling that violates any other federal or state anti-gambling law. Mere participation in online betting or wagering, however, is not banned or criminalized by the Act, welcome news to many online players of Texas Hold 'Em.

The impact of the UIGA on the internet gambling industry has yet to be reliably assessed, though anecdotal evidence suggests at least one major online poker site saw roughly 75 percent of its site traffic disappear after the passage of the Act, leading to the merger of some online betting sites (Hintze 2007). Still, it appears that internet casinos remain quite popular and the UIGA failed to allow the federal government to achieve its goals (Alexander 2008) while at the same time creating a "complex, vague, bewildering set of new federal regulations" for credit card companies as the law "puts onus on credit card banks to stop undefined 'illegal' acts" (Merzer 2009). As one casino industry web site opined, "Ultimately, [UIGA's] real world effect is to increase the risk of operators in the industry, open up doors for small-scale entrepreneurs as the larger ones get out of the spotlight, and make the aspirations and intentions of the United States government known. The one thing it has not done is ban online gambling" (Casino Advisor 2008). Indeed, Congress admitted to such in October 2011 when it held hearings on the topic of "Internet Gambling: Is There a Fair Bet?" "People are playing poker on the Internet in the U.S. for money today," said Rep. Joe Barton (R–TX). "It's not regulated and so these sites are offshore, overseas and, consequently, outside the ability for us to tax the winnings and make sure it's a fair game" (Safe and Secure Internet Gambling Initiative 2011).

As American and non–American gamblers have learned, one of the reasons for their popularity is the convenience they offer; bets can be placed at any time of day or night and they can be placed from the convenience of one's home or place of work. Consequently, regardless of government criminalization efforts and regulation efforts, the customers keep coming. Indeed, *Poker News* provides numerous links to both "Best Choice Rooms" and "U.S. Friendly Rooms." Others, like CasinoAdvisor.com, provide links to online gambling websites next to a declaration, "It is 'NOT' illegal for you to play online if you live in the U.S. Below is a list of the top US online casinos that fully accept U.S. casino players online below which also offer instant deposits though [sic] Visa & Master Card and Amex" (Casino Advisor n.d.).

As McGraw concludes, the investigation and prosecution of online gambling cases present transnational enforcement problems for law enforcement agencies. Hence, it appears that, given the trend toward legalizing various types of gambling, online betting will rapidly become a good candidate for legalization by states seeking to increase their tax revenues. Indeed, when the authors of this book surveyed a number of online gambling sites, all they saw were declarations that real money deposits made by a number of companies providing such a service were "available to all players, except U.S." Since U.S. law applies to the bettor, not the overseas internet gambling company which is out of U.S. jurisdiction, effectively investigating and prosecuting those who choose to ignore the verbal prohibition with all due risk assumed seems very remote, especially given software that makes end users anonymous or otherwise conceals their identity.

Indeed, the UIGA appears, upon closer inspection, to be more indicative of protectionist legislation than legislation aimed at eliminating the online gaming industry. Consider the gaping loopholes in the law discussed by prominent gambling law scholar I. Nelson Rose (2006). He found that American gamblers will have no problem getting their online fix.

First of all, Rose noted, the Act does not expand the reach of the Wire Act, the main federal statute the Department of Justice (DOJ) uses against Internet gambling. Although the DOJ has taken the position that the Wire Act covers all forms of gambling, courts have ruled that it is limited to bets on sports events and races. State anti-gambling statutes have similar weaknesses, including the presumption that they do not apply if part of the activity takes place overseas. This new statute requires that the Internet gambling be unlawful. But it would often be difficult to find a federal, state or tribal law that clearly made a specific Internet bet illegal.

Second, Rose observed, the American gambling capital of "Nevada and other states are expressly permitted to authorize 100% intrastate gambling systems. Congress required that state law and regulations include blocking access to minors and persons outside the state."

Third, Rose found that these same rights, with the same restrictions, were extended to tribal governments: Two tribes can set up an Internet gaming system if the Indian Gaming Regulatory Act authorizes it. This means that tribes can operate bingo games linking bingo halls on reservations. They can also link progressive slot machines if their tribal-state compacts allow. But they cannot operate Internet lotteries and other games open to the general public.

Finally, Rose finds it "interesting that Congress decreed that states can decide for themselves if they want to have at-home betting on horseracing, but not on dog racing. Congress also decreed that tribes can operate games that link reservations, even across state lines, but not the states themselves: state lotteries are not exempt." It appears Congress found ways of taking care of their constituents, be they bettors or Internet casinos, after all.

We conclude this case study of gambling, then, by noting that gambling continues to be an important enterprise for organized crime. However, as more and more state lotteries emerge, and gambling on Indian reservations continues to thrive and expand, the illicit nature of its activity has diminished. Indeed, there is a new surge in poker television programming on major cable and broadcast networks, poker tournaments and parties have mushroomed nationwide in the past year, and gambling games continue to fly off the shelves for game console and computer owners. Gambling, now being a legal activity in so many places, has, for the most part, lost its evil connotation. Organized criminals, however, still know that because of the differences in the odds offered and the fact that winners do not have to share their winnings with the Internal Revenue Service (as well as the thrill some gamblers get from engaging in an illicit activity), bettors will continue to engage in illicit gambling enterprises in large numbers. Professional criminals will continue to adapt to changes in the marketplace and meet their customers' demand.

One of the authors of this book had a favorite lecturer at Pennsylvania State University, Ed Donovan, who observed a change in society's focus on crimes and law enforcement over the years and generations. Donovan recalled being a young officer in the New York Police Department during the 1950s and his sergeants would always end roll call by commanding their officers to "go out and arrest gamblers today!" As the 1960s commenced, those same sergeants would command the officers to "go get a drug dealer today!"

Drugs had become the new emphasis, reflecting a broader cultural shift and the emergence of counterculture norms into the mainstream. The demonized gambler seemingly disappeared as if with the snap of a finger and police officers adjusted accordingly. The societal legitimization of gambling and the emergence of other policing priorities eroded the "arrest gamblers" ethos, with other working-class and lower-class criminals like drug dealers, gang members, hypes, crackheads, drunk drivers, pedophiles, and meth cooks replacing gamblers as police targets. Yet gambling keeps moving along, constantly adapting and necessitating changes in the networks that bind the syndicates operating different forms of gambling, the evolving technologies and strategies they use to carry out their business, and the clientele who can have their whims and preferences for risking their money met by more ways then ever imagined by the likes of Benjamin "Bugsy" Siegel when he pursued his gambling dreams for a desert city named Las Vegas.

The Case of the Loan Shark

Gamblers and others engaged in criminal enterprise need access to capital to start or sustain their enterprise. Since banks and other lending institutions are prohibited from bankrolling criminal enterprise, it is the loan shark who provides the capital in the form of loans made at usurious rates. According to Mark Haller and John Alviti (1977:141), the origins of racketeer loansharking are unclear. They note the enterprise's first appearance in New York City in the 1820s and that, by the 1950s, it had expanded to other major cities across the country. These authors (p. 142) also cite one of the early cases which demonstrate the essence of this racket; mainly, the case of a twenty-year-old clerk working in New York City who was beaten near his place of employment in the Wall Street section of the city by collection agents working for a loansharking enterprise. The reason? He had failed to pay his six-dollar interest rate on a loan he had taken out earlier for ten dollars.

This incident illustrates the basic nature of the loansharking enterprise, an enterprise both Albini and McIllwain learned about through direct, but separate, interviews with loan sharks and their clients. The criminal entrepreneurs operating this enterprise make money available through their various functionaries who in turn extend loans at exorbitant rates of interest to those who apply. In some cases, the person who puts up the money serves both as the entrepreneur as well as the collector, using only a small group of associates to help operate the enterprise. However, it should be noted that for those who apply, the loans are not for the best credit risks the community has to offer. When evaluated in terms of their credit standing, all one need ask is why would these individuals turn to a loan shark for a loan in the first place and choose to pay more interest when they can get far cheaper rates of interest from a legitimate lending agency? The answer is simple: those applying for the loan simply find it difficult to obtain loans from legitimate loan agencies because they typically do not pay their debts and/or do not have collateral. As Duffy (1967:29–30) notes, many of these debtors come from the ranks of gamblers who incur their debts primarily via gambling losses.

Loansharking is a criminal enterprise and the individuals operating such enterprises cannot use the legal court system to right wrongs when contracts are not honored. So, too, considering the financial condition of the person seeking the loan, what can this person present as collateral? In the case of borrowing from a loan shark, a self-enforcing contract is agreed upon in which the loan shark views the debtor's body and the debtor's desire to keep that body in good physical condition as collateral. Hence, the debtor is often subjected to threats that could harm his body if he does not make the necessary payments. Syndicate collectors (either members of power syndicates or freelancers) use violence or threats of violence to extort the necessary payment, in some cases by force. However, typically, they do not have to use violence because the mere fear of its potential use is enough to persuade the borrower/victim to make the payments.

The problem is that the victim is such a poor money manager that he simply keeps going deeper into debt as he cannot meet the added interest that is applied to his original loan each time he misses a payment. As a result, victims just go deeper and deeper into debt. When violence is employed, often it is meant to send a message to other victims who owe payments, indicating to them that they will receive similar treatment if they do not pay their debts on time. But, here the loan shark must be careful because if the method used to inflict the pain meant to persuade a debtor to pay the debt is such that it becomes public knowledge outside the loansharking pipeline, this can serve to increase the likelihood of police action being taken against the loan shark. Normally, this knowledge travels through the grapevine of debtors who often know one another from having dealt with the same collector. However, there are those rare cases where the method employed was so brutal and carried out in a public place that the incident is reported on the evening news and in newspaper stories, bringing about a reaction both from citizens and the police. Such cases are rare but, when they do occur, they only serve to convince loan sharks that this is not an appropriate method to use if they want to keep the police from being forced to take action against them and temporarily disrupt the functioning of their enterprise.

Even in those cases where violence is used, care is taken to give the victim pain without incapacitating him. After all, it is difficult for a corpse or a cripple to adequately seek and find the money to pay the debt. Indeed, it is in the use of violence in this enterprise that we come to note the required skill of the enforcers used to inflict this violence. Normally, their appearance is very intimidating and they have a reputation for violence. This, in itself, often is enough to produce fear in potential victims. However, their major skill lies in their ability to know the art and science of inflicting pain in such a manner that it produces visible bruises and cuts, but does not do permanent damage. Hence, the common belief that these musclemen break the legs and arms of victims is part of the folklore that surrounds loan shark and their operations. The pain resulting from the inflicting of the bruises is usually sufficient to convince the victim to pay up.

The enforcer must also know how to persuade the victim to find money that the victim maintains he or she does not have. Thus, when in severe pain or facing the prospect of severe pain, some victims suddenly remember that they can borrow the money from a relative or a friend; thus, the amount owed is paid, a profit is made, and the debt is somebody else's problem. Enforcers usually have knowledge about the current financial condition of their debtors and thus know how to use intimidation and the application of pain in order to cause the victim to make an arrangement that will result in his ultimately being able to pay the debt, if not in cash then in goods or services. In other cases, a debtor is permitted to pay back a loan through an arrangement with the collector for the debtor to work in a criminal enterprise operated by the collector, an arrangement where the debtor pays off his loan by means of the salary he makes on the job or settles the debt by exchanging the money owed for a service he may perform for the collector. Thus, a truck driver who owes money may tip off the loan shark as to the times and routes of loads of valuable goods that can be hijacked or the driver may be asked to use his truck to make a delivery of illicit drugs for a drug distributor who is an associate of the loan shark. Making such a trip will then be viewed as a settlement of the debt.

Working off a debt is referred to as a "boiler room" technique. In a variation of the "boiler room" tactic, the owner of a business agrees to pay off his loan by giving the loan shark a percentage of his business profits. In some cases, the profits cannot meet with the increasing amount of the loan and so the business owner agrees to pay the loan by giving the loan shark a percentage of the ownership of the business itself. Eventually, this may result in the loan shark owning the entire business, a method commonly used by organized criminals to gain control of legitimate businesses. Once in control the loan shark and/or his syndicate can launder illicit profits through the business or run up debts against the business until bankruptcy is declared. Better yet, as memorably shown in the film *Goodfellas*, an arsonist can torch the business at the point of bankruptcy so fire insurance monies can be collected as well.

We should also note, along with the findings of Peter Reuter (1983:98–99), that not all loan sharks employ the use of violence. Indeed, many do not use it at all. Whether or not a loan shark will use violence seems to depend upon the individual personality of the loan shark himself. Some have personalities that foster trust and understanding among their debtors to the point that the debtors come to feel a personal sense of obligation to pay back the loan while others, often because of personal insecurities, resort to violence as a means of further insuring themselves of the respect which they feel they may otherwise not get. Above all, we should note that loansharking operations vary widely from one city to another. Operations are unique to each set of operators in terms of the varying characteristics of their clients at any given time, the personalities, and other characteristics of the personnel they use to collect the debts and the methods they employ.

The Case of Human Cargo and Ethnic Chinese Human Smuggling Networks

In a heart-rending description of a common occurrence in a country where poverty is a constant in life, Gordon Thomas (1991:13–14) describes the night when the slave traders came for little Shambu who lived in a village in India. Shambu had witnessed on numerous occasions the sight of many children being placed into the trucks used by the traders and knew these children were never seen again. Could he run away? Yes, into the jungle, but only to face the fate of being torn apart by animals. Was he being kidnapped? Not really. What makes the story even more emotionally gripping was the fact that he was being sold by his father in order to have funds to feed and clothe his other children. Unfortunately, this was not a unique occurrence, for as Thomas notes, human rights organizations report that in 1990, each day, an average of one thousand small boys drawn from the Indian subcontinent were sold into slavery. This translates into 7,000 cases a week, amounting to a total of 365,000 a year, enough to equal the population of a midsize city.

These are the children for whom treaties are signed to protect but do little to stop the trade. These children enter an unregulated and officially non-existent workforce used to supply workers for industrial corporations, clandestine workshops and brothels in India and other countries like Peru, Morocco, China, Thailand and the Philippines (Thomas 1991:18), working in the sweatshops of these countries and other parts of the world under abominable conditions, held in slavery by fear and the thought that they, despite these abominable conditions, are much better off in the sweatshops than if had they remained with their families in their village. In many instances, as Thomas notes throughout his work, children, both male and female, are sold or are purposefully abducted in order to be transported to various parts of the world where they will become sex slaves, used for the sexual desires of those whose deviant tastes require small children for their satisfaction.

Children are sold to merchants who will place them into enterprises involving child pornography and child prostitution or, in other cases, to militias who will use young boys to fill the ranks of child soldiers (Heppner 2002, Singer 2006, Eichstaedt 2009, Wessells 2009, Dallaire and Beah 2011). The number of children involved in such exploitation and trafficking is staggering. The International Labor Organization estimates "worldwide that there are 246 million exploited children aged between 5 and 17 involved in debt bondage, forced recruitment for armed conflict, prostitution, pornography, the illegal drug trade, the illegal arms trade and other illicit activities around the world" (Department of Health and Human Services n.d.:2). Syndicate criminals in all parts of the world make a business of procuring, transporting, smuggling and exploiting children from country to country as the supply and demand of these markets continuously change.

In human trafficking there is another side to the drama; that is, in many cases, the victim himself or herself seeks to be smuggled and transported into another country. In countries like China, which has a serious problem with overpopulation, the dream of many workers who live in poverty is to go to such countries as England, Australia, Italy, Germany and, above all, the U.S., where they believe that they can make a better life for themselves. By doing so, they can also help support their families who are forced to remain in their country of origin.

We have previously discussed the role of and composition of various types of Chinese criminal organizations and emphasized the point that the smuggling of Chinese nationals into the U.S. began during the late 1800s (McIllwain 2004). However, as Zhang and Chin (2002) argue, the current organized enterprise of smuggling Chinese aliens into the U.S. is a new phenomenon and now involves an entirely different breed of criminal, differing from the traditional "Triad" societies and developing unique organizational and operational attributes, achieving optimal efficiency in the face of uncertain market conditions.

The aliens enter the U.S. by a variety of routes, the wealthy arriving by air with those of lesser means arriving as smuggled cargo in fishing trawlers or freighters. The smugglers themselves, as Zhang and Chin note, are called "snakeheads" and have remained elusive to researchers and the media. In their study, Zhang and Chin used informants drawn from Chinese communities in New York City and Los Angeles, two areas commonly used as entry ports, and Fuzhou, China, the city from which a majority of their illicit human cargo are dispatched.

The organizational structure of this enterprise is indeed different from that of traditional Chinese organized crime groups and the backgrounds of those involved reveal a new enterprise structure necessitated by modern-day markets. This structure includes a variety of functionaries drawn from a variety of occupations such as government officials, housewives, police officers, handymen, masons, taxi drivers, massage parlor owners, fruit stand owners and gang members, in essence what we previously referred to as a network of underworld and upperworld actors comprising a social system of organized crime in our definition of organized crime. Unlike previous structures, they assert, this structure was found not to include members of the Triads or other traditional Chinese organized crime groups. In other words, the enterprise was not in the hands of criminals who were members of established criminal organizations or gangs whose relationships had been established over a long period of time.

Instead, as Zhang and Chin (pp. 745–747) describe its structure, the complexity of the enterprise drives its structure. The enterprise lends itself to networking or patron-client types of relationships in a form of frontier enterprise in which anyone with the right connections and fortitude can participate. In other words, monopolistic control is not a goal of the actors involved in the enterprise since there is too much opportunity and demand to go around.

Consequently, Zhang and Chin found a distinction between "big" and "little" snakeheads (p. 748) referring to the task the individual snake-heads performed, rather than representing a distinction in status or rank position within the organization. Thus, it seems that big snakeheads invested more capital in the enterprise and thus made the larger profits. The task, roles and duties of those functionaries involved in a typical oper-ation ranged from "recruiters," who made referrals for clients to the smug-glers, a task for which they received a specified fee; "coordinators," who served the very important function of making the necessary connections and arrangements for the transportation process itself; "transporters," who in China personally took the client to the port or airport from which they would depart while those in the U.S. would transport new arrivals from ports or airports to safe houses; "document vendors," who provided the necessary documents (legal or forged) such as passports or other papers needed to gain entry into the destined country; "corrupt public officials" in the form of law enforcement authorities both in China and the countries of destination whose task was to aid the smuggled victim in entering or exiting a country; "guides and crew members," who moved immigrants from one transit point to another; "enforcers," mostly illegal immigrants themselves, who were hired by snakeheads to work on the smuggling ships, distributing food and water and maintaining order; and "debt collectors," who were responsible for locking up the newly arrived immigrants in safe houses until their smuggling fees were paid (pp. 751–754).

Interestingly enough, Chin and Zhang's argument about the newness of such complexity may be a reflection on the paucity of historical crim-inology on the subject of human trafficking, not on the inherent nature of the enterprise or the syndicates and networks engaged in it. The com-plexity Chin and Zhang illustrate, in the forms of the disparate tasks, roles, and duties of those involved in the enterprise, the decentralized nature of this enterprise, and the diversity of networks engaged in it, are apparent in the limited historical research available. For example, George

Paulsen (1971) implicitly made similar findings in a study of corruption and Chinese immigrant smuggling from Sonora, Mexico, into Nogales, Arizona, during the beginning of the 20th century. Similarly, Jeffrey McIll-wain (2004) detailed how Chinese human traffickers engaged the services of corrupt officials in multiple countries, various multinational and domestic companies, and a substantial number of non-professional criminals around the globe to ensure their clients arrived in San Diego between 1897 and 1902.

A specific example of this complexity as manifested in the past is found in a letter between smugglers submitted as evidence to the U.S. Senate's Committee on Immigration in 1902. Written on or about May 1, 1898, the letter from the head of a smuggling syndicate in Canton (modern Guangzhou) to one of his business partners in San Francisco is worth quoting at length:

> You say how that when you had already bought up the Counsel's inter-preter at Canton so as to have a way of getting certificates, afterwards had to know that others secretly obtained certificates and went ahead. Going on, you tell us at San Francisco to conduct some scheme by which others could be sent back, hoping thus to cut off other people's road, so that our concern can do all of the business and our concern get all the profit. Your idea is excellent and the way good, if only practicable.
>
> Not only these five, but others, also, I have seen come with certificates from Canton. You have schemes, others have schemes. You have influence so as to open up a way, others have greater influence still, and they do the work even more easily. So that others having the money to place will get the certificates. If they can issue them to you they can issue them to others. This is true everywhere. Take San Francisco, for instance; you can nei-ther stop other people's fraudulent comers here. Even though you go to the customhouse and point out those newcomers, prove they are really not merchants, all you can accomplish is to detain them a little and cause them to expend more money. Should the customs people not allow them to land after certain firms had endorsed them, other people then get lawyers and have papers made. Those firms who are engaged in bribing the men over then sign their names and come forward positively identifying the new-comers as relatives or partners. The collector is a most upright man and full of intelligence — never receiving one cent. He is an experienced lawyer, determining cases according to law.
>
> There is no way to hinder these people. The only thing we can do is cause them to go to greater expense. Then, again, there are other things to be considered. There is no certainty in connection with the different posi-tions of the customs officials, whether inspectors or chiefs — some pro-

moted, some degraded. This makes it difficult to hinder others. To have a monopoly or worldly profit is an impossibility. If you have the schemes and the means, you import more; if not, you get through less. Each concern does its own work with the means that each has. If you are hoping to contrive a way by which we could have a monopoly of this business — Canton end as well as San Francisco end —[and] send back those that others may send, I am afraid that your hope will soon see night. Things are very good as they are and as they have been some time back. Should Congress change the laws and there be other changes, the opportunity may go and with it the profit hoped for. Never look for the time when we can get it all. That time will never come. There is nothing like making the most of the present opportunities, few or many, but the more the better. Sooner done, sooner won....

Don't let the present opportunity go by.... There is business in Hong Kong and there is business in San Francisco, both well-connected, with big profits as the result. Don't let our concern be the only one hoping for a monopoly. While working for a monopoly, time will be lost. One half a year goes. There is no good doing this. The thing to do is hurry all you can, for fear later on there may be some changes in the law, and so forth. Once a law is passed against these newcomers our profits will come to an end [U.S. Senate, 1902].

This candid, first-person appraisal of the market forces shaping Chinese human trafficking enterprise from over a century ago, the complexity of the networks engaged in it, and the massive social system these syndicates and their networks created illustrate that transnational criminal enterprise is inherently modern (save for changes in technology and communications and the opportunities they generate). Indeed, the same holds true for other transnational criminal enterprises like arms trafficking (Chan 2010), drug trafficking (Block 1989, McIllwain 1998, Meyers and Parssinen 2002), and sex trafficking (Hirata 1979). As more scholarship is developed in this area, it appears Chin and Zhang will find generations' worth of historical case studies that support their central arguments.

The tenacious nature of the human trafficking enterprise speaks to its structure and function. Thus, Zhang and Chin conclude, human smuggling is an enterprise that is haphazard in its business formation, irregular in its planning and execution and uncertain in its outcome. We occasionally encounter horrible stories in the media about smuggling victims found suffocated in containers without adequate ventilation systems, lost in disasters at sea and lost in other tragedies. In reality, however, as Zhang and Chin (pp. 754–756) note, most operations are successful, violence against snakeheads or their clients are rare, transactions involve cash payments and, above all, the desire to build and maintain an image of trust has become a major feature which seems to assure the future continued success of this business. The snakeheads also have learned from experience to trust only relationships based upon a shared ancestry of family and ethnic ties, to use underground banking methods and encrypted mobile telecommunication systems and spontaneously selecting meeting places.

In his description of the smuggling of Chinese aliens, Peter Huston (1995) presents a portrait that has much in common with the findings reported by Zhang and Chin. However, Huston describes the various steps in the process such as recruiting, transporting and placing the aliens into jobs as being in the hands of different gangs, with each gang specializing in its relegated activity but all working together to complete the process. Huston found that a major tactic employed by these gangs is to send the aliens to their destination via roundabout routes, often in response to U.S. embassies' discovering information about a shipment of aliens taking a specific route to the U.S. Immigration officials then plan to intercept the aliens and send them home. Once the gangs discover that a route is being monitored, however, they simply alter the route and use a new one. These routes, Huston (pp. 183–186) notes, can take aliens originating in Fuzhou, China, first to Hong Kong, then to Kuala Lumpur, to Frankfurt, to Amsterdam, to Belize, then to New Orleans. Or another route originating in Fuzhou would first go to Hong Kong, then to Bangkok, to Moscow, to Havana, to Managua, then to Tucson.

In some cases, aliens, as part of their agreement to pay their smuggling debts, will agree to work in businesses selected for them by the smugglers. This, he argues, can sometimes turn out to be an exploitive venture with the worker being placed in a job in which he encounters low pay and abominable working conditions. Huston argues that some of these gangs have turned this enterprise into an exploitive one in which business owners overwork the alien employee while paying him or her a low wage, while the gang can wield power over both the employer and alien worker and thus come to serve as a "labor broker" to employees, continuously offering them a steady stream of hardworking, docile workers at a low cost.

A major route employed for smuggling ethnic Chinese from Hong Kong into the U.S. goes through Panama, with the final destination being New York City (Huston 1995:183–184). The Panama Canal has begun to receive a great deal of attention due to use by Chinese criminal groups who manage to skillfully deceive port authorities by using a variety of deceptive techniques to camouflage contraband on the ships that pass through the canal. The Panama Canal generates massive revenue from the passage of thousands of ships through its waters each year, in a country perceived as suffering from serious corruption (Transparency International 2010). It follows then that the most frequently used technique by smugglers is that of simply bribing port inspectors to look the other way, thereby making the discovery of the camouflaged cargo highly unlikely. With the war on terrorism and the fear of the cargo on ships possibly including terrorists or radiological or "dirty" bombs, this issue is of serious concern to U.S. officials and agencies responsible for homeland security and has increased the likelihood of detection of all smuggled cargo as the U.S. works with Panamanian officials to insure the safety of the canal and destination ports. Still, the sheer volume of cargo needing to transit swiftly between the Pacific, the Caribbean and the Atlantic has recently led to a Chinese initiative to build railways across Colombia to move more goods and natural resources swiftly to market (*Homeland Security News Wire* 2011), an initiative that will result in even more regional security and criminal justice concerns.

Although organized criminals from a variety of ethnic groups and countries have begun specializing in these various human smuggling enterprises, the organized ethnic Chinese criminals have arguably become the most specialized and major players in this arena. As Zhang and Chin note, most human smuggling projects reach their destination as planned, but there are those unfortunate situations where the alien cargo is discovered at sea, forcing the return of the aliens to their port of origin. In other cases, due to the lack of sound judgment on the part of the smugglers, they are placed into situations where their identity is exposed, as was the case with a group of sixty Chinese males who landed in Macksville, a seaside town near Sydney, Australia. After paying $20,000 for the service, they were naively put ashore dressed in dark business suits in hopes that they would blend into the local scene. Instead, they stood out, as the standard dress for most of the inhabitants of this town is that of a comfortable T-shirt and shorts. Needless to say, all sixty of the men were discovered and deported immediately (*The Economist* 1999:40). Despite this occurrence, it appears that the smugglers continue to deposit their human cargo close to those urban centers located on the east coast of Australia where they hope that the aliens can and will quickly merge into the local populations (Adams, 1999: 31).

Along with the smuggling of humans, cargo theft, the smuggling of weapons and other goods by organized criminals is an expanding criminal enterprise. The extent and daring nature of the tactics used in this enterprise is evidenced in the recent appearance of "phantom ships," ships that have a phantom identity created by false information provided to registration authorities regarding the vessel's previous name, tonnage, and dimensions and the owner's identity (Abhyanker 1997). The cargo on these freighters, trawlers and other vessels could contain anything from people to weapons. As such it presents an ever-increasing menace to virtually every country in the world as the criminals continue to develop clandestine routes for the trafficking of illicit goods.

The Case of Garbage and Hazardous Waste Disposal

If there is one thing that is as sure as death and taxes, it is garbage. Garbage, if not hauled away, can produce all types of problems. It can clutter valuable space; it can serve as a breeding ground for vermin and others pests; it can form mold that threatens the health and welfare of those working and living nearby. Garbage must be removed from populated areas or else all manner of pestilence will rise from its rotting heaps. Given the importance of this fundamental truth of human existence, it is no wonder then that garbage equals money for those in the waste business.

As every major city awakes each morning, an army of trucks and garbage collectors are maintaining the very continued functioning of both major industries and the average household by moving, *en masse*, tons of garbage to make way for even more garbage on the following morning. Garbage has, as one of its unintended features, the power to oppress the masses, evidenced by the virtual paralysis of cities in cases where garbage collectors have gone on strike or where overwhelming snowstorms present obstructions to the normal garbage collection process.

This is a perfect setting for organized crime to help out city managers, businesses and residents by efficiently collecting this garbage every day. There is only one problem; these organized criminals are not satisfied to remove some of the garbage. They want to be in charge of removing all of it. They want no competition, because competition in the free market system of doing business means that they will not be able to form a monopoly and they will operate the system only if they constitute the monopoly. Once again, this is a form of business enterprise in which control over a vital industry is secured by eliminating competition through the use of bribery, violence and the threat of such.

Indeed, for the past sixty years, organized crime groups in the City of New York have done just that. It took the efforts of an undercover New York City detective who stumbled into the murky world of syndicate involvement in the waste industry after investigating a "routine firebombing" at a Brooklyn warehouse. He spent the next five years in a jungle of syndicate criminal enterprises where garbage was literally a matter of life and death, especially for him, as the investigation almost cost him his life. The story is told in detail and with all of the drama it entailed by Cowan and Century (2002) in their book whose title designates the outcome of the investigative effort itself, *Takedown*. This book takes us into the world of syndicated garbage disposal, where these gangsters do not get dirty from collecting the garbage itself, but from using the tactics long associated with labor and industrial racketeering to control the industry, from the stops where garbage is picked up, to the carters selected to haul the garbage, to the dump sites and incinerators used to dispose of the garbage.

The garbage gangsters, dressed in the latest fashions and wearing the latest in expensive jewelry, succeeded in operating, until their takedown, an illegal enterprise in which they had the power to literally shut down the City of New York. This reality was made clear in a chilling appraisal of their power by Cowan and Century (2002:18–19) when they describe the scenario of what would happen if they called a strike involving the garbage workers. Within a few days, New York, with mountains of garbage overflowing in front of the New York Stock Exchange, Madison Square Gardens, Bloomingdale's and the United Nations, would become host to an army of millions of rats, cockroaches and flies and the city would risk becoming a site for the spread of diseases such as cholera, yellow fever and bubonic plague. The mayor had the choice of either settling the strike on the mob's terms or declaring a citywide health emergency.

The garbage empire came to a crashing halt in 1998 due to the efforts of law enforcement and the agile, effective and courageous stamina of the undercover detective involved in this case. It was a takedown to be remembered, yet it left in its trail the tale of New York syndicates whose members had used beatings, murders and firebombings to keep their garbage empires intact. This stands to reason, given the high stakes involved in protecting their interest in the *status quo*. In the case of the New York City syndicates, their control of the carting industry netted them a profit of 1.5 billion dollars a year. The disruption of the monopolistic control of these syndicates has created, bona fide competition within the carting industry as evidenced by the fact that the waste-hauling costs for large office buildings have dropped between thirty and forty percent and, for smaller businesses, by as much as twenty-five percent (Jacobs, et al. 1999:204–205).

With the appearance, however, of toxic waste and the hazards it presented to the health of most of the earth's population, and with the high costs involved in the removal of such waste, one can understand how this was destined to and has become a profit-making venture for organized criminals in various countries. Alan Block and Frank Scarpitti called national attention to this menace during the mid–1980s in their book, appropriately titled *Poisoning for Profit: The Mafia and Toxic Waste* (1985). In this and another work that followed shortly thereafter (Scarpitti and Block 1987), these authors emphasized that industrial poisons were seeping their way into the food chains and the drinking water supply of the United States and that this process was not likely to stop as the disposal of the toxic waste materials was in the hands of organized crime.

Some of the most prestigious companies in the petro-chemical industry themselves employed "midnight dumpers" or organized crime disposal firms because they provided a cheap method for getting rid of this harmful waste. So, too, the government failed in protecting the public welfare regarding the danger of this enterprise by passing laws that were basically ineffective, not based on market realities and by the lax enforcement of applicable laws and regulations due to rampant corruption or a lack of political will (Scarpitti and Block 1987:116). Once again we find that, as Scarpitti and Block (1987:117) explain, there is a repeat of the use of labor racketeering methods in which a monopoly over a territory is established by one hauler, thus eliminating competition, and one in which workers are controlled by union officials with the threat and perpetuation of violence employed in order to assure compliance on the part of all parties involved.

Yet labor racketeering methods alone were not the only methods available to these syndicates to exert control and keep profits rolling into the bank. As Scarpitti and Block show throughout their work, government officials, regulators, law enforcement and politicians on the local, state and federal levels provided a form of upperwold muscle to ensure protection of their interests, whether in the form of thwarted investigations, manipulation of zoning ordinances or the classification of waste sites. It did not matter if liquid hazardous waste was dumped on turnpikes and expressways or into abandoned mining shafts or if barrels of PCBs or toxic sludge were dropped into rivers, ponds, and lakes. It did not matter how many children got sick with cancer or how many homes lost their value due to being near what would become a Super Fund clean-up site. The social system of organized crime protected its members and their interests with the full power of the government and the mob, just like it was designed to do.

Not in My Backyard

The dread of this enterprise is made more alarming by the risk presented to the health and well-being of individuals everywhere. As Frederick Martens (1991:3) observes, the disposal of such waste in oceans and on land has affected ecological balance and represents a potential threat to the economies of many countries whose water supplies and beaches, should they become polluted, could present health hazards to the populations of such countries. Yet, as Martens points out, the search for lower costs in the disposal of such waste has resulted in the practice of sending such material into underdeveloped countries whose economies welcome the infusion of the money from such an enterprise, but whose populations are not prepared to meet the potential health hazards and environmental implications presented by importing such waste material. One can be certain, argues Martens, that those who operate such enterprises will, whenever necessary, skirt or avoid laws that deal with the proper disposal of the waste. For example, as reported by Cahal Milmo in *The Independent* (2009), the illegal, transnational shipment of hazardous waste leads to child laborers being compelled to work in the toxic dumps the waste creates:

> Tonnes of toxic waste collected from British municipal dumps is being sent illegally to Africa in flagrant breach of this country's obligation to ensure its rapidly growing mountain of defunct televisions, computers and gadg-

ets are disposed of safely. Hundreds of thousands of discarded items, which under British law must be dismantled or recycled by specialist contractors, are being packaged into cargo containers and shipped to countries such as Nigeria and Ghana, where they are stripped of their raw metals by young men and children working on poisoned waste dumps.

Conditions are no better in China, even though the Chinese government has halted the legal importation of "e-waste" derived from consumer electronics. Corrupt officials allegedly allow smugglers to import such waste *en masse* and the government allegedly covers up the seriousness of the toxic pollutants in numerous Chinese communities (Lorenz 2005). As Greenpeace (2007) reports, towns like Guyiu find their groundwater undrinkable and their landscape "filthy to apocalyptic" due to massive piles of e-waste from the European Union, the United States and China itself.

Such conditions have inspired the global community to respond. According to United Nations Under-Secretary-General Achim Steiner, Executive Director of the United Nations Environment Programme (UNEP), a recent UNEP report "gives new urgency to establishing ambitious, formal and regulated processes for collecting and managing e-waste via the setting up of large, efficient facilities in China" (*Science Daily*, 2010). He further observes,

> China is not alone in facing a serious challenge. India, Brazil, Mexico and others may also face rising environmental damage and health problems if e-waste recycling is left to the vagaries of the informal sector. In addition to curbing health problems, boosting developing country e-waste recycling rates can have the potential to generate decent employment, cut greenhouse gas emissions and recover a wide range of valuable metals including silver, gold, palladium, copper and indium — by acting now and planning forward many countries can turn an e-challenge into an e-opportunity.

Though well-intended, Steiner's remarks strike one as a bit optimistic. This "e-opportunity" will continue to beckon organized criminals who, by not following costly and cumbersome laws, codes, and regulations, will provide this service with lower overhead and labor costs across the board and thereby provide a cheaper alternative to those looking to dispose of their e-waste. It should be noted that those contracting organized crime for this service might not know that they are dealing with a criminal organization (CBS News 2009). Just as Block and Scarpitti (1985, 1987) noted over twenty years ago, many companies and governments require contracts go to the lowest bidder. By daisy-chaining company ownership through countries with corporate and bank secrecy laws, a seemingly legitimate company can take the money and illegally dump the waste of governments, schools, and companies in a foreign land thousands of miles away without the producer of the waste knowing the result. Indeed, through corruption and fraud, a paper trail showing its legal disposal can be created to assure the producer. Still, if that does not work, the waste company can go out of business if the producer and/or the authorities wise up to the scam (indeed, the employees of the company may not even know they are part of the scam given they are distanced from the end result themselves; they just know they are out of a job and facing fines, liability claims, and criminal prosecution). As the end link in a global daisy chain of corporate subsidiaries and shell corporations, the chances of finding the organized criminals behind the crime, bringing them to justice, and forcing them to pay damages is the legal equivalent of a snipe hunt.

The political and economic realities of this issue were dramatically illustrated in 2001 by the actions of Russian government officials and Russian legislators, which defied the overwhelming reaction of public opinion as expressed by Russian citizens and voted into law an enterprise that would allow Russia, in the future, to import 22,000 tons of spent nuclear fuel from nations that wish to ship such fuel out of their countries. As Colin McMahon (2001:1A) reported, the Russian government, in defense of its actions, maintained that it intended to reprocess the fuel and then return it to the nations from which it was obtained. However, as McMahon makes clear, nine out of the ten Russians who opposed the plan did so because they believe that the Russian officials, in passing the laws, intend to merely reap the profits from the enterprise, that they would never reprocess the fuel and return it to the countries from which it was obtained, and they would leave the problems involved in dealing with the environmentally hazardous waste to the coming generations of Russians. We note, along with McMahon (p. 17A), the observations of a Duma member, Grigory Yavlinsky, who, in opposing the measure, pointed out the glaring defiance of the legislators toward the Russian public by noting that one hundred million Russian citizens were against the measure while only five hundred people were for it — that is, the three hundred members of the lower house of the Duma and the two hundred bureaucrats who stood to make money from the enterprise when the payoffs and bribes that have become synonymous with Russian politics and governance were delivered. The will of one hundred million subverted to the greed of five hundred. This fact illustrates how power is distributed in the nominally democratic system of government in Russia.

By focusing on a global manifestation of organized crime, this case study and the case studies on gambling, loansharking, human trafficking and waste disposal before it, shed valuable light on the deficiencies of the Mafia mystique that has historically held such sway in textbooks, the media and policy. Indeed, a detailed examination of the impact of globalization on organized crime would go even further to illustrate its numerous parochial presumptions, an examination we will conduct in a coming chapter. Before moving forward, however, we believe it is important to observe how organized crime can affect the evolution of a particular place and have its evolution affected by a particular place in return.

SIX

Survival of the Fittest: From Russia to the Original Sin City

Now that we have explored the complexities of how crime is organized, let us focus on two case studies of how organized crime evolves in a specific place. We will begin where we left off, examining the interplay between politics and organized crime in Russia before and after the breakup of the Soviet Empire. We will then turn to a city that has long been synonymous with organized crime. Indeed, some would argue it was built by organized crime. That city is Las Vegas.

The Case of Organizing Crime in the Former Soviet Union

One of the most intriguing case studies one can examine in this regard is the phenomenon of organized crime that evolved as a result of the fall of Soviet Communism and the collapse of the Soviet Union in 1991. This phenomenon is unique and, because it occurred under the watchful eyes of researchers and journalists (i.e., Albini et al. 1995; Handelman 1997; Williams 1997; Klebnikov 2000; Varese 2001, 2011; Satter 2004), it thereby serves as a living laboratory for helping identify the multiple types of factors and social conditions that serve to produce organized crime in various settings and at various times in history.

The major point that is stressed in our analysis is that although syndicated crime experienced a rapid growth after the fall of Communism in 1991, in no way does this render truthful the mythical belief perpetrated by the Russian Communist Party officials during the reign of Joseph Stalin (1928–1953) that virtually no form of criminality existed in the workers' paradise that was the Soviet Union. This mythology was the result of the communist ideological belief that crime was a product of the capitalistic system and hence would not occur in a socialist society. Without question, however, it became publicly apparent that both mercenary and syndicated forms of organized crime were emerging after Stalin's death in 1953 (Albini and Rogers 1998).

Interestingly, in noting the various types of social conditions that give rise to organized criminality, these forms grew out of a political decision and form of strategy by Russian military strategists who believed, in the early 1950s, that the U.S. was gaining military superiority over the Soviet Union. Historically, this was a period of apprehension, a period when the U.S. and the Soviet Union viewed one another as potential enemies on the battlefield. Soon, the threat of a potential nuclear holocaust hovered over the entire world as the Soviets and Americans developed their missile technologies and nuclear weapons. This apprehension was to have its effect upon organized criminality not as a direct intended effect but as a byproduct of a program that sought to bring about the superiority of the Soviet Union in the coming quest for missile readiness.

The Brezhnev Era

The program that we are referring to was instigated and put into effect by Communist Party leader Leonid Brezhnev, whose reign lasted from 1964 to 1982. This period provided the breeding grounds for the emergence of syndicated forms of organized crime. The Brezhnev era provided a stimulus for the creation of these forms of criminality while not advancing the welfare of the average Soviet citizen. Instead, it thwarted progress as evidenced by the fact that the period has come to be known as "the period of stagnation."

The basic ingredient that created the breeding grounds for the emergence of this form of syndicated crime was found in Brezhnev's program which stipulated that, beginning with his reign in 1964, Soviet capital investment was to be allocated to the Soviet military in an effort to gain missile parity with the United States. This would be achieved at the expense and sacrifice of the standard of living of the Soviet people. As a consequence of this economic upheaval, stagnation indeed did take place in Soviet society, but not for those who now saw the opportunity to spawn careers as organized criminals brokering and meeting the unmet demands of Soviets tired of waiting in breadlines and desiring to listen to a Michael Jackson cassette tape.

To set the background for what took place, we must note that there are many similarities between Sicily and the former Soviet Union, similarities that helped develop the breeding grounds for the emergence of syndicated crime. Neither the Sicilians nor the people of the Soviet Union trusted their governments. The Sicilians developed this distrust from the actions of the multitude of foreign powers that invaded their country. By contrast, the tyranny of oppression of the Russian citizen came from Russia's own rulers. For centuries, beginning in 1565, these rulers (or tsars) employed secret police as one of their unique mechanisms of political and social control. This produced a social climate of fear, terror and distrust wherein the average Russian was made to harbor distrust toward government officials. This resulted in their coming together with relatives whom they knew and could trust. Empowered clans emerged and became the key node for trust in broader social networks.

The power emerging from this trust has continued to the present day as we find that the clan remains one of the major powerful forms of social organization among the contemporary Russian populace. Like the Sicilians, the Russians also came to rely on the development and use of a patron-client system for developing relationships with the ultimate goal of using this system to exchange favors that would lead them to avenues for gaining influence and power. However, whereas in Sicily the catalyst for the development of mafia as a method emerged from the ownership of land in the gabellotto or landlord system, in Russia no such system ever emerged. Instead, the catalyst for the emergence of syndicated crime came not from land, but from possession and control of state-owned goods and services and the explicit power to use discretion as part of one's official service to Party and the Motherland over the matters of every day life. Therefore, what land was to the spawning of syndicated crime in Sicily in the 1860s, state-owned goods and services and the power to allocate them became for the 1960s-era Soviet Union the bargaining ingredient which generated the development of Soviet syndicated crime.

We must understand that under the Soviet system, all goods and services in the Soviet Union were owned by the state. As such, there could be no private enterprise (or at least the theory held in Soviet classrooms).

During the Brezhnev era there emerged the practice whereby goods and services were indeed stolen from the state by those who had the power and opportunity to do so. Yes, this constituted a crime, but it seems that, in order to survive, the people needed goods and services for life's daily necessities. Also, we must remember that during the Brezhnev era, the state faced a fundamental dialectic; it wanted to equal its military might to that of the United States, but it also had to provide goods and services to its populace. When it did not provide the latter, the people at all levels of society began using patron-client networks in order to provide for themselves these necessities of life. Hence, a state employee would offer private repair work to someone who could reciprocate by giving him and his family shoes for the winter. Another state worker whose job entailed driving state officials around in a state-operated vehicle would siphon gas from the tank and use this to bargain with someone who could provide warm coats to protect his children against the harsh Russian winters. The system was one in which bartering for goods and services became the means by which the average Russian survived. It is ironic, then, that the state built on the communist ideology of Karl Marx, Vladimir Lenin, and others owed its artificially long tenure to the "invisible hand" of Adam Smith's market-based economics of self, not Party, interest.

At this stage, however, syndicated crime as such did not yet exist because virtually everyone was engaging in this practice of theft and bargaining of state goods and services. There was no need for violence and, since government officials as well as the common citizen were all involved, there was no need for the employment of political protection. However, this period became the training ground for the emergence of syndicated crime. The practice of theft of state goods and services became a way of life. Indeed, the practice itself became the social norm.

Opportunity in the Fall of Communism

It remained for the fall of Communism, however, to provide the conditions under which syndicated crime emerged. This took place in the late 1980s and early 1990s as Russia experienced what can best be described as a state of social, economic and political convulsion, one of the most rapid periods of social change in the history of social change. The government of a country that had for decades been bonded to a belief in communism, where the state owned everything including responsibility for the life and welfare of its citizens, suddenly collapsed. With this collapse, the life, thought, and incentive of every Russian individual was suddenly catapulted from a belief where the individual belonged to the state to one, suddenly, where the individual was now asked to participate in an official market economy where privatization became the new mode, in theory at least, of both business and industry.

When the collapse finally occurred, the now former Soviets were in a state of shock. Indeed, Daniel Yergin and Thane Gustafson (1995:7) are correct in calling the fall of the Soviet Union one of the classic examples of a "surprise" in history. Mikhail Gorbachev, the president of the Soviet Union, went on television on Christmas Day 1991 to announce that the Soviet Union would soon disappear from the political stage of the world. Six days later, on December 31, 1991, it did, falling quickly and quietly into the dustbin of history. Yergin and Gustafson (p. 21) describe its quiet farewell when they write, "There was no great celebration, no honking of horns, or ringing of bells, just a great silence in the dark, and the uncertainty as to what the dawn would bring."

What the dawn brought was more convulsion as the shock of the old and the new began to battle one another for survival. Although Russia sought to develop a new form of capitalism based upon a system of laissez faire and free enterprise, the Communist bosses, known as the "nomenklatura," who had held power for decades, were not about to relinquish that power without a fight. Consequently, the old and the new struggled for prominence as a new government sought to establish democracy and capitalism in Russia.

During September 1993, there was fighting in the streets of Moscow as the forces of the old totalitarian bosses tried to recapture the reigns of government, which they had lost. As noted in the very accurate and compelling account of this period by Strobe Talbot (2002:86–91), the former Deputy Secretary of State (1994–2001) and Ambassador-at-Large and Special Adviser to the Secretary of State on the New Independent States (1993–94) during the Clinton Administration, the U.S. offered both moral and financial support to then Russian president Boris Yeltsin. Meanwhile, as the conflict between these forces was going on, other conflicts were taking place within the former Soviet Empire, conflicts between the former republics that had been, until its collapse, part of the Soviet Union, and

Mother Russia. In 1989, many of these republics, including Ukraine, Uzbekistan, Georgia, Dagestan, and others, began demanding their independence from Russia. These demands often took the form of the creation of insurgent and terrorist groups within these republics that demanded action from the Russian military forces to keep these countries from gaining their independence. Russia was now faced with the emergence of social-political organized crime within the borders of its former republics.

The need to quell these uprisings only added to the already-existing forms of convulsion and chaos that the Russian government was dealing with within Russia itself. Russia had difficulty keeping the political control that it previously had over these former republics prior to its collapse. So, instead, after the Soviet Union was dissolved in 1991, these former republics joined a voluntary agreement with Russia to form a union called the Commonwealth of Independent States (C.I.S.). Stephen Cohen (2000:78–79) notes the inherent instability of the motives and factors that gave birth to this union, an idea that basically came into existence on paper, and one in which the republic leaders who signed the agreement did so for conflicting reasons, with some viewing the signing as a gesture aimed toward ultimately gaining total independence. Hence, he does not view this union as one that can or will survive the complexities resulting from the political turmoil that has, since the collapse, been taking place between the former republics themselves and those between each individual former republic with Russia itself.

We highlight these forms of turbulence in order to note the turbulence itself that was taking place within Russia. Since the old power system and the new were not clearly defined as Russia struggled to blend the two into a workable government, one group knew where to find a specific type of power. This group consisted of those government officials who saw the money ready to be made under the cloud of the ongoing chaos, the organized criminals. Recognizing the fact that the new form of capitalism was not, either legally or socially, specifically bound by the new or the old rules, they took to making the rules for themselves. Yes, privatization was definitely established as a governmental policy in 1992, but no one anticipated or expected the novel ways which the organized criminals — mainly the former communist bosses, the world-renowned and feared Russian intelligence agency known as the KGB, and some clever and eager new young entrepreneurs — would manipulate the system in order to control former state assets (like land, energy, natural resources, weapons, and modes of production) and net themselves substantial profits.

We must remember that all goods during the Soviet era belonged to the state as controlled by the Party. Hence, a system of bartering which consisted of stealing goods from the state was already in existence before the collapse. This system, because it involved the shady practices of stealing goods from the state, came to be called, "the shadow economy." When the Soviet Union collapsed, the public needed and demanded the same types of goods from the shadow economy. But now, it was those in power, primarily former Communist officials and bureaucrats who had access to these goods, who were in a position to sell them at exorbitant prices. So, too, as the movement toward privatization began to emerge during 1989 and 1990, the various forms of power groups — business, political and criminal — began to clash. We must remember that although the government of Russia at this time appeared to be undergoing a legitimate form of reconstruction, in reality, it was in a state of disturbing confusion. This is evidenced by cases where young entrepreneurs who actually took to heart and believed in the new spirit and program of privatization did create new businesses. However, at the point when it was evident that these business ventures were going to be successful, it was not uncommon for bureaucrats to step in, have these young entrepreneurs arrested as "mafiya profiteers" and seize their businesses. This aptly illustrates the reality that one does not need a gun to steal. One simply needs power and, preferably, impunity to exercise it.

Along with seizing these new businesses came the practice of these bureaucrats, now clearly manifesting criminal practices and intent, to demand extortion fees as payment for the service of protecting the lives and property of these new business entrepreneurs. As is typically true of the nature of extortion, it indeed became necessary for these new business owners to provide themselves with protection since criminal groups were now violently competing with one another. So privatization was an ideal whose reality could be brought to an end by the powerful forces of the former communist officials. Yet it was an ideal that the young Russians took to heart and it helped clutter the reality of life for them during the middle 1990s. There was one reality, however, that was not cluttered: the rapid growth of organized criminality in its many forms.

The primary forms of organized crime that immediately manifested themselves in the post–Soviet Union were those of mercenary and syndicated organized crime. Suffice it to say that mercenary types of crime took, among other forms, the form of various types of frauds in banking, counterfeiting of money, and theft carried out by mugger gangs and auto-theft rings. Most evident and profitable, however, were the enterprises of syndicated crime. With political protection now being provided by bureaucratic officials who themselves had turned criminal, the patron-client system allowed for various criminal groups to join together to provide illicit goods and services to segments of the Russian public that demanded these goods and services, with prostitution, intellectual property theft, fencing of stolen vehicles from Western Europe, and illicit drugs becoming major enterprises as the emerging middle and upper classes, coupled with their disposable income and newfound freedoms, began to make their presence felt. Smuggling of illegal goods into and out of the country became commonplace. By this time three major ingredients for the creation and operation of syndicated crime had come into existence: the use of violence, the making of illicit goods and services available to the public, and the political and police protection provided to the criminal.

Ironically, the former KGB came to serve as a major facilitator for many of these criminal entrepreneurs. Reorganized in 1991, it became known as the Ministry of Security of the Russian Federation (FSK). However, it continued in its traditional roles. Because its agents, during the reign of the Soviet Union, had, as part of their role, the obtaining of intelligence and security information both in the Soviet Union and abroad, this information now allowed for these agents to serve as valuable resources, contacts, and brokers between criminal elements both in Russia and in foreign countries (Albini and Anderson 1998). Not surprisingly, many of these agents were called upon to make contacts in enterprises involving banking and other types of business fraud. Since these criminals were engaging in all manner of bank frauds and, since they were aware that other Russian criminals were doing the same, they knew better than to trust their new stolen funds to Russian banks. Hence, they made certain to deposit their newly acquired funds in offshore banks located in foreign countries. The money-laundering skills of the former KGB agents were extremely effective in this process. Additionally, since KGB agents were skilled in the use of violence, it is logical that they would be called upon as they were by the new syndicate criminals to serve, when and where required, as muscle.

By the middle 1990s, the former Soviet Union as a state had been stolen.

Russian society was now, for the most part, in the hands of organized criminals and their upperworld patrons. As Paul Klebnikov (2000:2) so aptly describes the new Russia, it had now become a gangster state and its political system consisted of nothing more than a government consisting of organized crime. Thus, the state itself had become a form of organized crime. Among other features of the new Russian government was a provision in its new constitution that stipulated that no political official could be tried or convicted of a crime during their term in office. Hence, in Russia today, those influential people who are about to be indicted for a crime immediately run for some political office in hopes of being elected before the indictment can take effect. That is power and impunity unlike most organized criminals have ever possessed. This has spawned a new era for organized criminals, for when a government itself tolerates and protects the organized criminal, what avenues are left for combating his crimes? This calls to mind an observation made by that great American statesman, Alexander Hamilton, who many years ago asked the question, "Why has government been instituted at all?" His answer, "Because the passions of men will not conform to the dictates of reason and justice without constraint" (Brin 1998:108).

The historical and other variables that have been offered as explanations for the existence of organized crime in previous chapters do not help explain the origins and nature of organized crime as it developed in Russia. If anything, the Russian case only serves to raise new questions. For in the case of Russia, the slums did not give rise to organized crime as has been argued to be the case in the United States. Instead, in Russia, it was the influential classes of powerful bureaucrats that gave it birth. So, too, there exists no evidence for ethnic succession as, by all indicators, Russian criminals, like their American counterparts, often join groups whose ethnic origins are similar to theirs, but more commonly, will forego ethnic allegiance to join with groups that offer the promise for bringing them rapid and substantial wealth. As we shall see in our study of Las Vegas, this is not a unique trait when it comes to organizing crime.

The Case of Organizing Crime in Las Vegas

For all the effort on the part of various sensationalist writers to portray organized crime in Las Vegas by depicting its most debased form of origin and existence, such a portrayal is in denial of the uniqueness that Las Vegas represents in the development of the history of organized crime in the United States. To selectively give credit to Benjamin "Bugsy" Siegel as the creator of Las Vegas, as many are wont to do, is to miss recognizing the many factors that joined together to make it the city it has become. This is not to say that Siegel and the enterprises of other syndicated organized criminals did not play a significant role in its development. Rather, if one carefully examines its history, one finds that organized criminals constantly adapted to an ever-changing community to which they were symbiotically tied, a community that eventually made such adaptation an ever more difficult thing to do.

The first point to emphasize is the fact that Las Vegas was first and foremost a daring experiment, particularly at the time of its early development. While the rest of the nation was obsessed with sparking religious efforts and laws to stop individuals from participating in activities judged illegal and immoral, Las Vegas and the State of Nevada were willing to recognize "human nature" for what it is; many people have a curiosity or need to delve in those pleasurable areas of life that they are told are immoral and off limits.

Those who developed Las Vegas did not bother themselves with the question of what was moral and what was not. Las Vegas was, after all, an experiment, and who can predict how an experiment will turn out? Yet, the best argument that can be made to counter the belief that organized crime in itself was the major spawning force for the creation and development of Las Vegas lies in the fact that Las Vegas had a characteristic that violated a very basic tenant of the successful functioning of syndicate criminal activity. Specifically, most goods and services that were illegal in cities where criminal syndicates were entrenched were legal in Las Vegas. This is not to say that every activity or vice was legal in Las Vegas, but one of syndicated organized crime's major enterprises, one highlighted by the Kefauver Committee itself, was that of illegal gambling and that definitely was legal in Las Vegas.

The system of syndicated crime, when functioning in locales where such activity is illegal, has as a very vital component of that functioning, the need to have to camouflage or hide their activity from public view and use political protection and payoffs in order to keep such services functioning. Syndicate criminals can justify the high cost of operations because their customers are willing to pay the expensive prices charged in order to continue to have access to those services. The last thing that syndicate criminals want is to have their illegal goods and services become legal. Imagine what would happen if, suddenly, illicit drugs were legalized. There is little chance that this will happen any time in the near future. However, one can appreciate that if a very lucrative illegal enterprise were to be legalized, financial rewards and other incentives would diminish significantly.

Since it did not consist of making available illicit goods or services to the public, organized crime in Las Vegas did not take on the usual format of syndicated crime but, instead, consisted primarily of mercenary forms of crime. Organized criminals committed some crimes in order to make direct profit for themselves while others provided services for other organized criminals, some of whom were operating in Las Vegas itself and others operating outside Las Vegas. These services consisted primarily of casino skimming and money laundering.

This is not to say that these are minor enterprises, as skimming tactics have netted organized criminals millions of dollars. Indeed, Carl Sifakis (1999:343) makes the argument that gambling is the one enterprise from which syndicate criminals can make large profits irrespective of the fact that the enterprise is operated legally. The reason for this, he argues, is the use of skimming, which he defines as the stripping away of money made in the gambling ventures before the actual figures of profits are made available to the tax authorities. Sifakis explains that this can be accomplished by having casino personnel themselves enact the skim before the money reaches the iron-barred casino counting rooms or through big payoffs made to customers at the tables themselves. In the latter scenario, the customer who has scored a big win simply is allowed to walk away with the money before an IRS agent can obtain his or her identity. Estimates of the profits made from skimming range from about triple the amount of reported profits to approximately 20 percent of the total amount of money that is bet.

Nicholas Pileggi (1995:15–17) offers a visual picture of the magnitude of skimming as an enterprise in itself by taking us into the inter sanctum of one of America's most heavily guarded temples, the casino count cage. Tons of coins, paper money stacked into inch-thick $10,000 bricks, double-locked metal boxes of money emptied from under the table games on every floor of the casino arrives to the count rooms of every casino every day. Bulks of money arrive at these rooms, bulks so large that the money is assembled into various denominations and weighed. For example, a million dollars in $100 dollar bills weighs in at 20½ pounds while a million in five-dollar bills weighs 408 pounds. This massive assault of hard currency requires the use of hydraulic lifts to move it from place to place within the count rooms themselves. Guards check the clothing and other personal items of those who enter and exit after each visit. Cameras are oftentimes in use. Two independent clerks and supervisors must check and sign off on the final count for every drop box on each shift. Even the casino owners themselves are barred from entry by law.

Despite all of these measures, money still vanishes from these rooms. It is stolen, sometimes brazenly by workers who simply grab a fistful of cash before the boxes are even counted and other times by owners who themselves manage to obtain keys to the iron boxes before the count takes place or by scams which include misdirecting fill slips and rigging the scales that weigh the money in such a manner that they ultimately come to weigh only one-third of the money that passes through the count room doors.

Is skimming then a worthwhile venture for organized criminals? You bet it is. It is no surprise then that skimming became the major enterprise for the organized criminals involved in various casinos in Las Vegas despite licensed gambling's legal status. It also became an enterprise for many syndicate criminals operating outside Las Vegas as this allowed them to launder money (make profits and divert and hide money made through their criminal ventures) via the casinos themselves. Hence, as Denton and Morris (2001:103) so keenly observed, in the 1950s, Meyer Lansky was using funds skimmed from the Nevada casinos to fund his newly formed enterprise of providing Americans with illegal drugs by developing routes for trafficking Turkish heroin through laboratories located in Marseille, France, and by effectively bribing officials in the Middle East and Europe. Yet Denton and Morris note that earlier, in the 1940s, Lansky's profits obtained from his Mexican opium smuggling enterprise had helped finance several casinos in Las Vegas.

Some forms of syndicated crime did make their way into Las Vegas. For example, former FBI agent William Roemer (1994:163) notes the involvement of Tony "The Ant" Spilotro (played by Joe Pesci in the Martin

Scorsese film *Casino*), who, working in conjunction with syndicate criminals in Chicago, and serving in Las Vegas as an enforcer for these individuals, operated his own loansharking business which, according to Roemer, made loans to debtors both in Las Vegas and in other cities. This enterprise, Roemer notes, was tied to another of Spilotro's ventures that involved illegal bookmaking where bets were placed with bookies operating outside the casino and outside the law. Since some of these bettors were often poor credit risks, they frequently found it necessary to borrow money from loan sharks, organized criminals who charged exorbitant interest on their loans and made use of threats and violence in order to collect on late payments. Spilotro was head of this operation as well (Roemer 1994:159–163). Spilotro also was the organizer and leader of a burglary ring that operated out of his jewelry store located one block from the strip. He used this store to fence jewelry that had been stolen by professional burglars (Roemer 1994:121–131).

Pileggi (1995:18) notes Spilotro's indictment on charges of running a loansharking, extortion, and burglary ring out of his jewelry shop and records a violent era in the history of organized crime in Las Vegas in which the two major players were Tony Spilotro and his associate, Frank "Lefty" Rosenthal. However, it must be noted that loansharking is an enterprise that does not necessitate a large group of individuals to carry out its functions. It primarily involves the occasional intimidation of those who do not pay the exorbitant rates of interest on the original loan made by the loan shark. In some cases, the operator of a loansharking enterprise may provide himself with police or political protection (McIllwain and Leisz 2006). However, since this enterprise can usually be operated in a stealth manner (the victim, who generally has a very poor credit rating, most likely is not going to make a complaint to the police), there is little need on the part of the loan shark to provide himself such protection. Extortion can involve enterprises where police protection is employed, but often those being extorted themselves originally sought out the protection of the criminals. As to the extent of Spilotro's illegal bookmaking enterprise, we are reminded by Richard Sasuly (1982:204) that caution is in order regarding any data involving estimates of the number of participants involved in such enterprises. Sasuly argues that the number of bookies and other functionaries involved in such enterprises is not known with accuracy, if in fact it is known at all or ever could be known. Burglary rings, on the other hand, since they involve outright theft, do not constitute forms of syndicated crime but are, instead, forms of mercenary crime.

Pileggi (1995:241) brings perspective to Spilotro's sideline enterprises by showing them for what they really were: Spilotro and a crew of bookmakers, shakedown artists, loan sharks and burglars who never managed to operate at the top of the casino business arena. It appears that Spilotro served primarily as the enforcer for the Chicago syndicate. In this arena, Spilotro was efficient since, as Pileggi (1995:141, 163) also makes clear, when Spilotro arrived in 1971, Las Vegas was a relatively quiet place, but, during Spilotro's first five years of residency, the city experienced more murders committed than it had seen in the previous twenty-five years. Although these crimes indicate that a few syndicate criminal enterprises did make their appearance in Las Vegas, it seems reasonable to argue that the profits earned in such enterprises did not come anywhere near those earned by the organized criminals who made skimming their major endeavor.

The Benjamin "Bugsy" Siegel Era

Although Benjamin "Bugsy" Siegel is generally given credit for giving Las Vegas its jump-start both as a prosperous city and as a full-blown new haven for organized crime, Denton and Morris (2001:97–98), in their very comprehensive work regarding the development of organized crime in Las Vegas, make clear that Prohibition-era organized criminals had already made their way to Nevada and organized crime was in control of most of the lucrative gambling in the state during the 1930s. It is true, however, that Las Vegas itself did not seem to receive the attention that it has since come to acquire until Benjamin "Bugsy" Siegel arrived in Las Vegas. Denton and Morris (2001:51) attribute Siegel's reason for coming to Las Vegas in the early forties as being that of taking over the wire service since the Nevada legislature had just legalized betting on horses by wire. Siegel succeeded in establishing a monopoly over the bookmaking enterprises of the existing casinos by establishing his new wire service known as Trans America Wire Service. Evidently, he began to see the possibility of growth and profit that the then-small and undeveloped strip had to offer. He began investing his money along with that given him by Meyer Lansky and Lansky's partners in various casinos. According to Denton and Morris

(2001:52), when Siegel arrived in Las Vegas he had already become known to federal authorities as one of world's biggest dope ring operators. The money made from this enterprise, although it was not common knowledge to state officials or the people of Nevada, was being invested in Siegel's new casino ventures. He now began investing in building casinos and, in doing so, as Denton and Morris (2001:54) note, he paid and otherwise corrupted public officials in order to persuade them to lift a building freeze. This they did by falsifying records, affidavits and permits.

Siegel's downfall and death came with his dream project, that of building the biggest casino in Las Vegas, the Flamingo. There are many theories as to what happened and why. Some say he squandered the funds of organized crime partners who had invested in the project and later angered them when he refused to pay back these funds. One thing was certain, for a variety of reasons, Siegel's Flamingo dream turned into his nightmare. It may, indeed, have cost him his life, as it is believed that his murder was planned and executed by his former organized-crime associates. The reason for his death itself will forever be shrouded in mystery. The mystery itself was generated by the style of killing employed. It has become a generally widely accepted belief in the underworld that the modus operandi employed in Siegel's murder, one in which he was shot from a ten-foot distance through a window while sitting in the living room of his girlfriend's mansion in Beverly Hills, California, simply was not in keeping with the usual style employed in mob killings. Normally such homicides have a format where Siegel would have known the killer, and thus, trusting the killer, Siegel would have allowed him into the mansion and Siegel would have been shot at close range. Because of this diversion from the typical style of mob killings, many have come to believe Siegel's death was most likely the result of a personal vendetta rather than a mob execution.

In death as in life, Siegel imprinted his legacy on Las Vegas. There is general belief that what Siegel saw on that barren and sandy strip in the desert, others also saw in Las Vegas and that his dream and efforts would, as they did, rise out of the sand with or without him. There are many reasons as to why they did, although, as we said before, there were always those intangibles that could have kept it from happening. On the other hand, there was that underlying force that seemed to mitigate its triumph as though Las Vegas had its own die cast on the table of history.

The Howard Hughes Era

There was another person of great importance who came to Las Vegas, but he did not seem to arrive guided by a planned mission of turning the city into an emerald of his dreams. Unlike Siegel, he was not an organized criminal. He was, instead, one of the world's wealthiest business entrepreneurs. Howard Hughes was an enigma to those who knew him well and to those who have been burdened with trying to explain Hughes' actions, which resulted in a transformation of Las Vegas. The story was never told by Hughes himself as he was a recluse while living in Las Vegas, living in his hotel penthouse on the ninth floor, the windows having been darkened soon after his arrival by the placement of thick curtains over them to make certain that no one could see him from the outside. His story is told instead by a man who came to know Hughes as much as he would allow himself to be known by another, Robert Maheu, his closest advisor. We employ information gained from Maheu regarding his work and interaction with Hughes as Maheu was himself instrumental in negotiating and completing the plans for many of these transactions. However, our discussion of the Hughes' phenomenon draws more heavily upon the more current research presented by Richard Hack (2001) who, based upon interviews with many of those individuals who had varying types of knowledge concerning the various aspects of Hughes' life and career as well as using memos, corporate records, inventories, letters, court transcripts, and information gained from recently declassified FBI and CIA surveillance reports, has written what is considered the definitive biography of Hughes.

To set the stage for this discussion, we note the observation made by Maheu (Maheu and Hack 1992:166) regarding the impact that Hughes had on Las Vegas and the impact that Las Vegas had on the life of Hughes himself. On April 1, 1967, Las Vegas entered a new chapter in its history when the Desert Inn, which had been for so long viewed and described as a "citadel of organized crime," went legit. The person responsible for this drastic change arrived in the dark of night at the Desert Inn on November 27, 1968, and was transported quickly and quietly on its service elevator to its ninth floor penthouse. He would soon own the property. The purchase, as Hack (2001:284–290) relates, was not without drama in that Hughes' stay when he arrived on November 27th was only supposed to last until shortly after the Christmas holiday as the then owner of the

Desert Inn, Morris "Moe" Dalitz, was already preparing for the large crowd coming into town for the New Year's Eve celebration. The hotel room reservation list was full. After Christmas, Dalitz insisted that Hughes move to another hotel. Hughes did not want to move. He had come to like his new, dark penthouse. As the New Year was rapidly approaching and he needed the rooms for his guests who would soon be arriving, Dalitz finally told Maheu to tell Hughes that he absolutely had to vacate his rooms at the hotel. Instead of his being moved by this demand, Hughes told Maheu to just go ahead and buy the entire hotel for cash.

This is how one of the largest and most powerful real-life games of monopoly ever played in the U.S. began, with Las Vegas properties serving as the playing board. Hughes played the game with zeal. As Hack (2001:292–293) so vividly describes what was happening at the time, he notes that, despite the fact that his physical condition made it difficult for him to shift from his chair to his bed in his penthouse, Hughes' mind and body were now energized to the point that he would stay up for two to three days at a stretch without sleep. Howard Hughes felt the power of control. His wealth was his weapon and his war cry became "Buy!" as in "buy every property that becomes available in the city." He ordered overlay maps and, acting like a conqueror, notes Hack, he marked out his territory with a green marking pen. The Sands Hotel, KLAS-TV (a CBS affiliate), the Frontier Hotel, the Castaways Hotel and the North Las Vegas airport soon belonged to him. He felt his power and so did Las Vegas. It appears that the forces that had spawned Las Vegas now had a new force that, in the sole effort to make his force felt for the sake of confirming his power to himself and to the world, was changing the face of Las Vegas. Yet, throughout this drama, as Hack observes, no one in the city laid eyes on Hughes. He did not see, nor was he interested in seeing, the properties he bought by looking through the covered windows of his penthouse; he knew they were out there in the desert and all he cared about was making them his property.

What about organized crime? Hughes, as Hack (2001:332) notes, went along with Maheu's management plans and left many of the previous casino bosses in place and was aware that money was being skimmed from the casino banks. This did not bother Hughes as he was not interested in the profits themselves. Instead he wanted control and he felt that allowing the bosses to remain but to answer to him was the best way, at least for the moment, to assure that control. As a reward for his efforts, Hughes soon became the subject and target of the federal government's anti-trust laws. But, in the end, it was not the threat presented to Hughes by these anti-trust laws that ended his quest for continuing his monopoly game; instead, it was a scientific development that changed his mind — the nuclear bomb and the fact that new tests were to be conducted in the vicinity of 120 miles from the city of Las Vegas. As Hack (2001:298–302) notes, Hughes became obsessed with the fear of nuclear poisoning and began dedicating his attention to stopping such tests in the state of Nevada. Eventually, this fear, the fact that his casinos were losing money, and his rapidly deteriorating physical condition caused him to leave Las Vegas. He died, frail and tired, at the age of seventy while being transported by plane from a hotel in Acapulco, Mexico, to a hospital in Houston, Texas.

A debate continues as to the nature and extent of Hughes' contributions to Las Vegas. One thing, however, seems obvious. Howard Hughes helped turn the casino enterprises into corporate structures. As Kilby and Fox (1998:8–9) explain, following Hughes' entry into gaming in 1969, a Corporate Gaming Act was passed by Nevada's gaming regulators. Before the passage of this act, every owner of a casino was required to be individually licensed. However, with the emergence of public corporations, the task of licensing thousands of stockholders would have been highly impractical. Hence, the passage of the Gaming Act allowed publicly traded corporations to own casinos without requiring that each stockholder be licensed. Today, as Kilby and Fox go on to note, the general requirement is for a stockholder to own ten percent of the voting stock of a public corporation before being required to obtain a gaming license. Here again, however, the debate continues as to whether or not the change from mob control to corporate control of the casinos ultimately resulted in the improvement of the function and efficiency of the casinos themselves.

Albini conducted field research on gambling beliefs in Las Vegas between 1989 and 1991. As part of this study, Albini asked a sample of forty-three dealers working in the various major casinos in Las Vegas to evaluate the role of corporate control in improving the casinos. The question was phrased so as to elicit each of the dealer's personal viewpoints. With outright and unwavering agreement, each of the dealers noted that they felt that the casinos were operated more efficiently when they had been in the hands of the organized criminals. They cited primarily the fact that the management during that time period had created a much warmer atmosphere and a friendlier working environment for the workers as compared to the management of their newer corporate counterparts. No doubt, since organized criminals often select personnel known to them through friendship and acquaintances, the probable result very well may have been that they would have behaved more congenially toward their fellow workers. But the dealers noted also that the customers visiting casinos during the previous era were showered with more complimentary gifts, including free dinners and passes to the nightly shows at the casinos. The former and pre-corporate owners seemed, according to the observations of these dealers, more interested in treating customers on an informal and much more friendly level of interaction. The corporate structure, they felt, because it was based upon a more informal and bureaucratic format, simply did not seem to create that style of interaction as effectively. We should add, however, that part of what these dealers may have been reflecting was a form of nostalgia generated by memories of a former Las Vegas and that their reaction was one that reflected their feelings toward the process of the growth and expansion of Las Vegas itself from a small and intimate type of small-town atmosphere to one that manifested the distance and informality typically found in social relationships among the inhabitants of larger cities.

In any respect, it appears that Howard Hughes did have a significant effect on the casinos of Las Vegas by helping create their corporate structure. Syndicated organized crime had power and money. Hughes had an exponential amount more of both. This transition happened and it did certainly have its effect on the ownership and management of the casinos. Most writers argue that, as a result of the Hughes effect, the reign of organized crime came to an end. They see the casinos and other businesses in Las Vegas as now being free of its influence. That is true. Yet it remains for us, before bringing this discussion to a close, to note some of the other important factors that came to play a major role in that outcome.

The Unique Experiment of Las Vegas

There is no question that gambling as a legal enterprise in Nevada set an important precedent for the unique format that organized crime was forced to take in Las Vegas. Mainly, the organized criminals did not have to hide their services. Some of them did through their practice of making money from skimming, but, as we have already noted, this was theft and represented a form of mercenary, not syndicated organized crime. Las Vegas certainly did not, even with the violence perpetrated during the Spilotro and Rosenthal era, match the number of deaths resulting from the violent conflicts fought during the reign of syndicated crime in Chicago and New York. But there were still other factors that need to be addressed in order to understand what the experiment of Las Vegas has come to reveal for those who study organized crime.

Mark Haller (1985:152) notes that it was the ex-bootleggers that provided the personnel and the capital for the development of the original Las Vegas casinos. In fact, he presents a thesis that argues that without the ex-bootleggers to found and staff the first generation of casinos, Las Vegas may not have become possible. Certainly, one has to agree with Haller's premise, that the early casinos would have had to draw from a sector of society — the organized criminals — for personnel skilled in the operation of gambling games and devices. Although there are now schools that teach dealers the art and science of gambling techniques, such were not available to the owners of the legal gambling enterprises of the casinos in the early era of the Las Vegas casinos. Hence, here was an instance where entrepreneurs of legal gambling establishments had to turn to that formerly criminal segment of illegal practitioners of the art from which to draw their dealers.

So, too, Haller (1985:153) concludes, and we agree, that the remarkable expansion of Las Vegas during the 1970s was due primarily to the enactment of gaming laws by the Nevada legislature in 1967 and 1969, which allowed for publicly held corporations to obtain casino licenses (although he also recognizes that Hughes was a powerful influence). This, argues Haller, had resulted in the top twenty largest corporate-owned casinos generating half the gross gambling revenue and providing half the gaming employment in the state of Nevada by 1980. This was definitely an indicator that the casino industry had been reorganized.

However, there is another factor that played a major role in the growth and direction of the flow of influence that resulted in the formation of what is now modern Las Vegas. That is a force that has always been present but is difficult to attribute to any one group. It is the force that has always concerned itself with the image of the city. There is no question that the influential leaders, both those in the business sector and those in the political arena, particularly after Hughes' transformation of the casinos into corporate enterprises, were averse to an image that reflected Las Vegas as being a city whose inhabitants and enterprises were tinged in any way by an association with organized crime. The Kefauver Committee in 1950 had cast a shadow of suspicion over Las Vegas as being a city that reflected both a presence of organized crime and the corruption that generally follows from its presence. It was a shadow that lingered and produced a suspicious image that only served to further cloak the image of the city for years to come. It was a vague shadow but nonetheless one that hovered over the city well into the early 1980s. As historian Eugene Moehring (1989:89) so aptly observes, Kefauver and his associates were in Las Vegas conducting their investigation for less than two days, yet they were convinced, after leaving for California to continue their crusade, that they had uncovered a major connection between organized criminal forces in Las Vegas and the local casinos. When they left, as Moehring notes, the damage had already been done; "Kefauver had linked southern Nevada inextricably with the syndicate."

The city fathers, the new corporate owners of the casinos, business entrepreneurs and the masses of new inhabitants who had now come to view Las Vegas as their home were particularly sensitive to this reputation. They wanted it removed and the only way that this could be done was to make certain that any activity that was likely to be viewed as immoral by those who themselves did not wish to engage in such activity should be made available in such a manner as not be visible to the average tourist. Las Vegas had become known as "Sin City," and it drew its tourists from a population around the country that was interested in certain types of sinful activities. Las Vegas has never tried to hide the fact that many types of pleasure, sinful and otherwise, are available to those who visit. But, although its leaders and inhabitants did not mind it being called "Sin City," they did not want it to become "Hooker City" or "Organized Crime Heaven." Therefore, they began to take measures to make certain that its streets were not cluttered with prostitutes and that organized crime figures would not be allowed to form a menacing presence within the ownership and management of its casinos.

Cleaning Up the Streets

Many male tourists who come to Las Vegas with the intent of buying the services of a prostitute are not aware that prostitution is illegal in Las Vegas. Although prostitution is legal in several counties in Nevada, it is not legal in Clark County, the county in which Las Vegas is located. The brothels that are legal are licensed and have specific ordinances established to safeguard the health and safety of the public (Brents and Hausbeck 2001).

Although prostitution is illegal in Las Vegas, this is not to say that prostitutes do not make themselves available in many of the bars located in the casinos or through services provided by enterprising hotel staff such as bell captains who, upon request from a guest, draw from a list of call girls who have agreed to make "outcalls" and make arrangements for the prostitute to discretely go to the guest's room. We emphasize the word "discretely" because it speaks to the ethos to which we made reference earlier: that the entire procedure is kept from public view. Thus, those prostitutes who work the bars, in their effort to procure customers, must exercise a certain manner and demeanor so as not to render their behavior offensive to those customers in the bar who may be offended by their presence. This takes skill on the part of the prostitute who, although she must employ tactics to entice customers, must do so in a subtle manner. Hence, she often relies on her pre-arranged agreement with certain bartenders who, for a fee, will let those customers seeking the services of a prostitute know that she is available.

One area in which prostitutes sometimes seem to make a random appearance (but not for long) is on the main streets of Las Vegas. Although the police do not tend to be as avid in their surveillance of street prostitutes in the remote and lower-class neighborhoods located away from tourist traffic, it is common practice for police to arrest those streetwalkers who tread into the areas where they run the risk of being viewed as a public nuisance. Las Vegas and its police department are particularly sensitive to its streets being cluttered with prostitutes. This sensitivity resulted from an era in the early 1970s and a mode of soliciting customers employed by street prostitutes which was bound to bring about an immediate reaction on the part of law enforcement, for this mode of soliciting simply went contrary to the Las Vegas penchant for keeping sinful activities out of the view of the visiting tourists. This sensitivity remains today as one observes how quickly streetwalkers who attempt to ply their trade on streets with high-tourist traffic are quickly told to move on or are simply apprehended by police.

The sensitivity, as we already have noted, has its origin in a practice on the part of streetwalkers that occurred several times in Las Vegas during the early 1970s when a mass of street-level prostitutes congregated on or near the Las Vegas Strip. After all, that is where the major source of potential clients could be found. Some of the prostitutes were dressed in stylish clothing while others used more provocative outfits to attract attention. They did attract attention, but not always the type that fostered a positive image for the city. According to informants, law enforcement at the time used various methods, including arrest, in an effort to persuade the women to move on and out of the area. It was not the sale of sex itself, although it was illegal, which created a stain upon the Las Vegas image. Instead, it was the uncouthness of the sight of hundreds of prostitutes lining the Strip and milling around in front of the casinos that simply did not make for comfort on the part of those tourists, both male and female, who had come to Las Vegas not to seek sexual adventure but to enjoy its many other forms of entertainment. Something had to be done.

Albini conducted an interview in Las Vegas in 1991 with three former prostitutes who were very young at the time when this phenomenon was occurring, and who themselves were among the masses of prostitutes on the Strip. This interview revealed how this "herding" practice was terminated. They noted that when law enforcement first attempted to use officers in efforts to verbally persuade individual prostitutes to move on, the women kept returning back to the street shortly after the warning. Next the police tried arresting them, which again resulted in their returning to the street. Law enforcement then, according to these women, began waiting until nightfall when the herding was most intense and, employing several buses, police officers went from one end of the Strip to the other, simply arresting the prostitutes and loading them onto the buses. When a bus was filled to capacity, it was driven several miles into a remote part of the desert. There, the busload of women were taken off the bus and told that they would now have to walk back to the city. They were warned that if they returned to work on the street, the same fate would await them. Needless to say, the walk back in the heat, particularly since many of the women typically wore high heels, was not a pleasant trip. The first trip on the bus evidently convinced the three women whom Albini interviewed to not return to the Strip. It seems that after several such roundups by law enforcement, the women dispersed. Although mild forms of this herding activity has reoccurred for decades, these have been limited to areas around individual casinos and have been successfully controlled by the security forces of these casinos along with the help of the city police. Cleaning up the Strip went a long way to cleaning up the image of Las Vegas so that it could now perhaps be better described as "Not So Sinful City."

We should note that this practice of herding prostitutes is not unique to Las Vegas, as Albini encountered it in his study of streetwalkers in Detroit that he conducted in the 1970s. In Detroit, like Las Vegas, this phenomenon occurred suddenly when several blocks of a major thoroughfare or main street became infested, almost overnight, with hundreds of prostitutes. This section of the street had for several years become known for its prevalence of porno shops, strip clubs, and other forms of sexual enticements which, the prostitutes knew, drew many adult males to the area. Normally, the customers would be solicited as they drove into the area in their cars and the cars were then driven into a secluded nearby neighborhood street where the sex act was performed. However, the peak disturbance — which finally brought about a public outcry on the part of the citizens living in the area — occurred when the prostitutes began entertaining customers who walked into the area on foot and thus could not use cars as the place where the sex act would be performed. The prostitutes now boldly began using the front porches or lawns of the neighborhood houses. Thus children were often subjected to witnessing sex acts as they left or returned to their homes. So, too, if the citizens protested or otherwise chastised the prostitutes, some of the prostitutes would respond with obscene language, disturbing the peace, or, in some cases, threats of violence. The public outcry soon created a massive police response resulting in arrests that brought the herding to an end for the targeted neighborhood.

The Creation of the Black Book

The greater concern regarding the safeguarding of the Las Vegas image, however, had to do with the state governmental forces making certain that the influence of syndicated organized crime itself was under control. To that end, in 1960, state regulators in Nevada created a list of excluded persons that came to be popularly known as "the Black Book." The regulators identified and listed in this book various functionaries of organized crime such as nationally known professional gamblers, bookies, sport fixers, casino owners, known gambling cheats and others who represented, in the eyes of these regulators, a menace to the legitimacy of the gaming industry and offer potentially a negative image to the city itself. There is no question that the inherent need for such a list was made functional by the fear created by the Kefauver hearings in 1950 that, as we have already noted, alluded to the presence of the Mafia in Las Vegas. Consequently, a list was created to assure the public that the government had control over the situation and citizens could be certain that no such organized criminal influence would be allowed to exist. Although, as we have already indicated, Las Vegas has managed, particularly after casinos became corporate entities, to shed this Mafia image, the list has served, it seems, the function of helping the public, particularly during the 1960s and '70s, to feel more confident that the Las Vegas regulators had things under control.

The list itself and the actual results that it has produced, however, has been a subject of controversy. Contributing to this controversy is the work of Farrell and Case (1995) who, in examining the hearings of the regulatory commission as well as examining official documents and media accounts, find a disturbing pattern regarding the actual effect and outcome which this listing process has come to create. Their findings serve to argue that the process of adding each name to the list was ritually conducted in an atmosphere of melodrama for which the media served as a source of calling public attention to the event. This served to inform the public that all was "well in Babylon"(Farrell and Case 1995:218).

Farrell and Case note further that by highlighting the listing itself, the process served to draw attention away from other threats to gaming and instead concentrated upon the act of assuring the public that another criminal influence in Las Vegas had been discovered, appropriately identified and now was being denied access to the gambling establishments. Farrell and Case further note (pp. 221–222) that almost two-thirds of those nominated into the Black Book were Italian, which of course helped feed into the Italian stereotype that had been generated by the widely accepted belief in the presence of the Mafia as a major organized crime force in Las

Vegas. This, in turn, kept non–Italian organized criminals (especially native-born Nevadans) largely out of the spotlight and free to carry out their activities. In conclusion, Farrell and Case (p. 230) note that some of the individuals who were the subjects of the Black Book listings, although they had notorious backgrounds, in reality did not constitute a serious threat to the industry. Thus, in its ultimate outcome and value, the listing process came to serve as a symbolic mechanism aimed at assuring America during Las Vegas' post–1960 historical development that the city was in fact free of organized criminal influence.

Beyond the Mafia

In reality, despite the negative and criminal stereotyping which the mafia image produced for Italians in Las Vegas during this era, the outcome has served to demonstrate that far from having contributed organized criminals to the city, the Italians instead had been a force that played a major role in the development of the legitimate enterprises that have come to make Las Vegas the unique city it has become. In setting his research focus to look "beyond the Mafia," political scientist and historian Alan Balboni (1996) has conducted an exhaustive survey of the contributions of the Italian Americans to Las Vegas. Based upon interviews with key individuals prominent within the Italian community, Balboni found evidence to show that the Italian presence in Las Vegas resulted in an experiment that allowed Italian Americans there to demonstrate that crime was not their most important product. Yes, argues Balboni (pp. 58–59), there were Italians with criminal backgrounds that made their way to Las Vegas, but, when comparing their influence to those Italian Americans who simply wanted to participate in the legitimate development of an exciting city, the legitimate ones have come to be those that are currently most admired for their work and efforts.

Balboni (1996) notes that Las Vegas offered unique opportunities for rapid economic and social advancement to Italians that allowed them to assimilate into the community at a rate much faster than in other parts of the country. Interestingly, Balboni observes that no Italian American neighborhoods ever came into existence in Las Vegas. Even for those with shady pasts, Las Vegas was generally forgiving and prone to quickly forget their transgressions and, particularly in those cases where these individuals managed to accumulate wealth, to allow them, irrespective of their past, to attain social prestige and political influence. During the 1950s and '60s, Balboni notes, over a quarter of the headliner entertainers and lounge performers in Las Vegas were Italian Americans like Frank Sinatra, Dean Martin, and Tony Bennett and that since that time Italian Americans have made their mark in the city as architects, contractors and developers. This is not to say that the Italian Americans were completely free of discriminatory practices; the mafia mythology did raise its ugly head against Italian Americans, particularly those who sought to venture into casino management positions. Yet, as Balboni (p. 134) concludes, even in such cases, the Italian Americans managed to successfully overcome this form of obstacle and achieve success.

And the Winner Is ... Las Vegas!

It appears that, after being battered by elements of organized crime itself and subjected to attempts on the part of journalists and government investigations that tried desperately to make Las Vegas appear to be the organized crime center of America, the city had its own agenda and forces spinning its web of fate. These forces succeeded. In its January 10, 1994, issue, *Time* magazine announced on its cover that Las Vegas was now "The New All-American City." The story itself, entitled "Las Vegas, U.S.A." (Andersen, 1994:42–51), revealed the observation that the hyper-eclectic dream city had now become mainstream and it had done so because the rest of America had become more like Las Vegas. And so now we can reveal the nature and drive of that sometime mysterious, sometime outright persistent force that insisted in shaping its outcome — it was America itself and Americans living in other cities outside Las Vegas that, themselves desiring to shed the shackles of an inconsistent Puritanism that had come to hover over their lives, looked to Las Vegas as their symbol of freedom to enjoy that which they were told was sinful.

And so Americans and visitors from around the globe keep coming to Las Vegas to gamble, ride roller coasters, attend conventions, shop in high-end malls, and enjoy expensive dining on the pseudo-streets of exotic replicas of Paris, Venice, New York City, and Treasure Island. After seeing the new, cleaned up Las Vegas, many visitors decided to move there and they brought their families with them. Las Vegas and surrounding communities like Henderson exploded, creating numerous master-planned suburban communities filled with soccer moms and Little League dads. These visitors and new residents kept Las Vegas alive with the money they spent to keep it afloat until the real estate bubble of the 2000s finally exploded. Organized crime benefited, and suffered, from this process as the evolving social system that was Las Vegas symbiotically affected the social system of organized crime in Las Vegas. Yes, the organized criminals helped, as did Howard Hughes and the many visionary corporate entrepreneurs that followed him. Ultimately, however, Las Vegas belongs to the Americans who made certain that the experiment was a success as well as to those from a globalized world who travel there every year for a bit of fun in the sun and tastes of the forbidden fruit of vice.

SEVEN

Globalization and
Organized Criminals

When we began researching this work, the World Trade Center, the Pentagon, and a field in Shanksville, Pennsylvania, were burning. As we end writing this work, the entire world seems to be aflame with war in Afghanistan; terrorists striking at random; governments suddenly experiencing unpredictable forms of revolution, flux, and chaos, newly formed democracies in danger; and increasing daily disturbances in financial markets. Since the end of the Cold War and the onset of the information age, borders that formerly served to impede, limit, or confine the location of the enterprises of specific organized crime groups no longer serve as boundaries for their operations. Just like in the legitimate world, these borders are rapidly disappearing as boundaries limiting the criminal ventures of such groups are opening up an arena within which both new and old ventures can generate profit for these criminals. The borders of countries themselves have rapidly begun to give way to a new phenomenon that will soon become part of the history of the world itself. This phenomenon, globalization, represents a sometimes subtle, sometimes chaotic set of changes that we are struggling to comprehend yet simultaneously are caught up within its vortex of change as these forces unleash their innovations at this moment in history.

We mention these concerns regarding globalization in order to emphasize that the social changes associated with and resulting from it are entwined with the mysterious elements of fear, misunderstanding and sometimes a complete lack of understanding regarding the current appearance of this phenomenon. These misgivings should not be viewed as unusual, for the world is indeed changing while its inhabitants are themselves experiencing and becoming the observers and inheritors of the changes taking place. Workers are being displaced as globalization requires that, in order for them to continue working in their current occupations, they must migrate to foreign countries which house the factories of the companies that employ them. This goes contrary to the lifestyles and life-goals of many of these workers who, unfortunately, up to the present time in history, were operating under the assumption that their jobs would allow them to stay in the countries where they originally chose to live and work for the entirety of their lives.

Globalization is disrupting the world as we know it for good and bad. It affects every element of social life. Since organized criminals are an integral part of the societies in which they exist, they, too, have come to experience the effects of this new form of social change. As such, we must understand the elements involved in the process of globalization itself so as to be able to discuss the effects it most probably will exert upon the future functioning of and the ventures developed and operated by organized criminals around the world. It should not come as a surprise, however, to note that the organized criminals have already become aware of the coming effects and changes resulting from the globalization process and are thereby making plans to adjust to its challenges because their livelihood depends upon it and thus requires continuous monitoring of the social changes taking place in the world. One can be certain that they will be watching for and finding ways of exploiting any opportunities created by the globalization process in order to better serve their self-interests.

Defining Globalization

Since globalization is an emerging process, it stands to reason that its definition is also part of that emerging process; thus, the literature extols a variety of definitions. For our purposes, we find the work of Held, McGrew, Goldblatt and Perraton (1999:16) to offer a strong treatment of the topic and thus draw from their work to define globalization as follows: "A process (or set of processes) which embodies a transformation in the spatial organization of social relations and transactions assessed in terms of their extensity, intensity, velocity and impact-generating transcontinental or interregional flows and networks of activity, interaction and the exercise of power."

These authors (Held et al. 1999:27–28) qualify their definition by explaining that globalization is better understood as a process rather than a condition and note further that the spatial reach of this global interconnectedness will result in the spawning of various networks of relationships between communities, states, international institutions, non-governmental organizations and multifunctional corporations. The authors emphasize an important feature of globalization by noting that the overlapping of these networks will produce both constraints on and an empowerment of states, communities and social forces such that it comes to represent a "structuration" resulting from the cumulative interactions between numerous agencies and institutions in interaction with one another throughout the world. Its development, they argue, will be profoundly uneven and will come to include some current existing patterns of inequality and hierarchy.

However, this development will also allow for the creation of new patterns, some of which will survive and win their place in the new order while others will lose and thus be excluded. Globalization, they note, will encompass all the major arenas of social life — the political, legal, economic, military and environmental. This will alter existing and current conceptions of territory in that globalization will cause local, national and continental political, economic and social space to be viewed as no longer necessarily being coterminous with established legal and territorial boundaries. As such, the authors maintain that the globalization process will involve a "deterritorialization" and "reterritorialization" of both political and economic power, resulting in the globalization process best being described as "aterritorial."

Above all, the authors emphasize that power is the most distinguishing feature of globalization. They note in the spatial innovations of its process, the sites of power and the exercise of power become increasingly distant from the subjects and locales that come to experience their consequences. Hence the ultimate effect of globalization will be manifested in the reality that the exercise of power as emanating from the decisions, actions or inactions of agencies located in one continent can have significant consequences for nations, communities and households on other continents. Thus, the authors note that globalization results in the structuring and restructuring of power at a distance.

Regarding basic characteristics of globalization, Held et al. (1999)

describe this process as new and its understanding cannot be properly derived by associating it with such existing concepts as interdependence, integration, convergence, or universalism as none of these concepts, in themselves, contain or express the complexities and uniqueness of globalization as a process. Thus, they note that whereas the concept of interdependence assumes symmetrical power relations between social or political actors, globalization leaves open the possibility of asymmetrical actions between such actors. Likewise, whereas integration implies a sense of community, shared fortunes and shared institutions resulting in a process of economic and political unification, to view globalization as a word that signifies one single world community or society as expressed within the concept of integration and/or universalism is flawed in that global interconnectedness is not experienced by all peoples and communities to the same extent or even in the same manner.

Finally, convergence is misleading as a synonym for globalization in that convergence implies that, within its process, the continued growth of homogeneity and harmony will occur. Quite the contrary, argue the authors, as they point out that growing interconnectedness may result in intense conflict rather than cooperation with the interconnectedness itself often resulting not from harmonious relationships, but, instead, from the shared fears and deeply ingrained animosities held by the members of the interconnected community. In terms of our discussion we note that Held et al. (1999:12) make note of the fact that not only will the changes brought on by the process of globalization affect the legal, political, ecological and military sectors of the societies of the world, they will also bring about changes among and between the criminal elements as well.

We cite a work that brings together the thoughts of an American literary theorist, Michael Hardt, and an Italian political theorist, Antonio Negri, to further illustrate the various conceptualizations of the term "globalization." They choose to use the term "empire" (Hardt and Negri 2000) to both as the title of their work and as the term they employ instead of "globalization" to explain this phenomenon in their work. Presenting a neo–Marxist conception of the process, they stress that empire must not be viewed as an erosion of sovereignty but, instead, as a process of transforming it into a system of diffused national and supranational organisms or institutions. Thus Hardt and Negri (2000:xii) maintain an increased decline in the sovereignty of nation-states in the modern era has resulted in their inability to regulate economic and cultural forms of exchanges.

The boundaries defined by these nation-states in the past became the basis for the development of European colonialism and expansion. Sovereignty over these colonized lands became the cornerstone for imperialism that, in essence, consisted of the process by which these European nation-states extended their sovereignty beyond their own boundaries to colonial holdings. In contrast to imperialism, argue Hardt and Negri, empire does not establish a territorial center of power and does not rely on fixed boundaries. Instead, it is an apparatus of rule that is "decentered" and "deterritorializing" which incorporates the entire world within its open and expanding frontiers. Thus, they conclude that sovereignty has taken on a new form consisting of a series of national and supranational organisms that are united under a single logic of rule. This new form of sovereignty they call empire.

Rather than focusing on the globalization process itself, Francis Fukuyama (1999) gives us insight into a phenomenon that is causing an upheaval in American society, an upheaval that he describes, as indicated by the title of his book, as *The Great Disruption*. Fukuyama (1999:1–3) attributes the origins of the current disruption in values, norms and morals in American society as emanating from the fact that our society, like those of many other economically advanced nations, has entered the new "Information Age," an era in which information and intelligence as manifested in the nature of the occupations of the modern worker and the creation of smart machines such as computers, mobile phones, and GPS systems have become pervasive. It is an era in which mental labor has substantially replaced physical labor. As a result, the United States and other economically advanced nations like the United Kingdom, Canada, Italy and Spain began witnessing the stress of the social changes in their societies as indicated by increases in the crime rate, the deterioration of the family as a social unit, a deterioration of the traditional relationship between the sexes and, ultimately, an erosion of trust as evidenced in the decline of such practices as the willingness of individuals to keep commitments, honor the norms of reciprocity, and to avoid behaviors which are opportunistic in intent and outcome (Fukuyama 1999). The main thesis of Fukuyama's work is that of describing the nature and content of a new form of social order, a great reconstruction that will replace the old order that has fallen apart. This will happen, Fukuyama argues, because "human beings are by nature social creatures" (1999:6).

Globalization constitutes a number of undefined paths like the dissolving of borders and new forms of sovereignty that govern from a distance. It is a process that is unfolding in a manner which prevents us from knowing how local communities will interact with the new forms of power that transcend boundaries and influence how and when current boundaries will dissolve. Furthermore, it prompts us to ask how exactly a world with a total absence of boundaries will function when its contemporary inhabitants residing in current territories break their established bonds of ethnic, religious, racial and social identities to become part of large, decentralized and heretofore unimagined systems. Globalization may be a nebulous term but the current descriptions of its process serve to foretell, as Fukuyama notes, of a disruption of the current social order. However, as Fukuyama also promises, this will result in a world that will ultimately come to order because humans intrinsically need a form of social order in order to survive.

The lesson learned from examining the gleaned meanings of globalization basically tells us that the present and future citizens of the world will become part of a social order that is not planned, but will develop through the innovations and adaptations on the part of governments, corporations, social networks and individuals who must strive to adjust to the new ways of a world without boundaries. There will obviously be tremendous amounts of conflict as history has shown that individuals typically do not quickly or willingly adapt to rapid and uncharted forms of change. The industrial revolution created a similar scenario. However, in that revolution, territorial boundaries were not lost as workers simply moved from working in their homes into the factories and assembly lines that became the most prominent features of that era.

What takes globalization into uncharted waters is the transcendence of boundaries. As contemporary citizens move into the new space that will become the locus of activity and interaction of the new order, they may have to adjust their patterns of interacting and adapt, along with other citizens, to this new course of action. As such, then, globalization will produce new ventures and may require those who engage in them to give up their customary modes of dealing with others. Old traditions will become meaningless as they may have no relevance within the new modality of relating. Networks will have to be altered to meet the requirements of interacting in settings where the boundaries of old no longer exist. Thus, new forms of networking will emerge with the networks that were formerly established within cities, states or nations, no doubt giving way to networks that also transcend boundaries. This will certainly have its effect upon the structure, role and function of organized crime.

One can envision, as mafia functionaries in Sicily continue to expand their enterprises outside the borders of Sicily, that they will lose the traditional protection of omerta as this power came from the value system inherent within Sicily's history and culture. Mafiosi operating outside Sicily, then, will have to find other means of providing legal protection for their enterprises, most likely bribing the governmental officials of the countries in which they operate. However, even in Sicily, as Letizia Paoli (1999:38–39) observes, mafia has come to be increasingly condemned by larger and larger sectors of the population of southern Italy since the 1960s. This has caused the mafia to become more secretive in the operation of its enterprises and has also served to weaken the historical bonding of the brokerage function between mafiosi and politicians. As a result, notes Paoli, the use of monetary rewards, rather than offering political favors, has become increasingly more common. Thus, mafia entrepreneurs are now increasingly making direct payments to politicians for favors received and the politicians are increasingly using the direct payment of bribes to secure the support of the mafia entrepreneurs during election campaigns.

All syndicate organized criminals will need to change tactics regarding the need to protect their interests as borders disappear and sovereignty changes the position of its power bases. This will require networking on the part of outsiders that involves the use of criminal insiders who are familiar with the conditions that exist within the region or locale where the enterprise takes place. This has already been taking place among those criminals involved in drug trafficking enterprises, but, with globalization, the process will become far more complex. So, too, globalization will bring into focus an area of study that has not yet been given the attention it deserves; mainly, the attitudes of organized criminals in terms of their willingness to work with and/cooperate with individuals from different ethnic and religious groups.

Current evidence, as we have already argued in the early chapters of this work, seems to indicate that when it comes to making money, most organized criminals are willing to shed ethnic and religious prejudices and cooperate with criminals from a variety of different social backgrounds (i.e., Block 1983; Bovenkerk, Siegel, and Zaitch 2003; McCoy 2003; McIllwain 1998, 1999, 2003 and 2004; Saviano 2008; Zaitch 2002). Will the complexities resulting from the new alliances spawned by the changes produced by the disappearance of boundaries change this practice? We may find that the alignment of groups resulting from the breakdown of borders and the creation of entirely different intermixing of races and cultures may create different preferences on the part of the various members of the global social system of organized crime.

The rapidly closing limitations of borders and the opening of the gates of the nations of the world to one another most certainly will produce new concerns or complications which organized criminals never had to face before. For example, terrorism, insurgency and other forms of irregular warfare will continue to produce all manner of new networking alliances among and between the various types of organized crime groups. But consequences resulting from a world in which the fate of nations has become more susceptible to a nightmare where chaos can quickly dart from one nation to another overnight will also have its effects upon the functioning of organized criminal ventures. Thus, the rapid outbreak of diseases like severe acute respiratory syndrome (SARS) and avian influenza (bird flu) in China had an effect upon the human smuggling trade as currently practiced by Chinese criminal syndicates. Since Hong Kong serves as a major base for routing illegal immigrants to various destinations, both the criminals involved in this enterprise and their clients, during this outbreak, were forced to deal with the possible consequences of becoming victims of these pandemics.

The problem was further exacerbated by the fact that China itself represents the major source for recruiting clients who become the customers of syndicates involved in the human smuggling enterprise. Yet Southern China was, during these crises, also plagued with the outbreak of SARS and avian influenza. Organized criminals were vulnerable and, given the rapidity of the viruses' transmission, it did not matter which segment of the trafficking enterprise they were responsible for or where they plied their trade as the viruses did not recognize such distinctions. It remains to be seen with certainty what affect the SARS and avian influenza epidemic had on the volume of illicit human trafficking in China. Yet there is no question that this epidemic served as one of the early indicators that global-ization has become a stark reality, with its borders giving way to a rapid transmission of plagues that, within a short period of time, had spread from China into numerous other countries.

Trafficking in Illicit Drugs

As we view the coming interactions and networking patterns of the world's organized crime groups as they become part of the globalization process, it becomes evident that one of the core enterprises that will expand in volume and spawn the development of new liaisons between groups around the world will be that of illicit drug trafficking. Not only is this probable because a variety of effective and protected international drug routes have been established over the years (i.e., Block 1989, Courtwright 2002, Jonnes 1999, McCoy 2003, McIllwain 1998, Meyer and Parssinen 1998), drug trafficking, as an enterprise in itself, has currently become a major source of funding for politically active groups such as rebel, terrorist, counterterrorist and guerrilla organizations and their leaders. Drugs and the political order or disorder have joined hands as we find that drug cul-tivation and sales have become a major enterprise for the funding of such groups.

As revealed in the works of Alfred McCoy (2003) and Brian Fremantle (1985), the region known as the Golden Triangle — the area where the bor-ders of Laos, Thailand and Burma meet — came under the rule of the famous warlord Khun Sa during the 1970s. It is generally conceded that this warlord served as an intelligence source to the CIA and he eventually came to establish ties with the Burmese Communists, who grew the opium poppy in the Chinese province of Yunnan. Khun Sa established a powerful and worldwide trafficking enterprise by gaining control over the growers, the manufacturers who processed the opium into heroin, and the smugglers who transported it into various countries.

The current and complex politics of heroin trafficking in this region, however, were revealed along the Thai-Burmese border when on May 22, 2002, Burma's foreign minister protested Thailand's alleged support of the Shan United Revolutionary Army (SURA) that is fighting for an inde-pendent homeland in Burma's Shan state. As Chakrit Tongsrichum

156

(2002:36) explains, the crisis began when Thai troops, as part of the Thai government's attempt to curb drug trafficking along the Thai-Burmese border, fired into Burmese territory, thus attacking the United Wa State Army (UWSA) whose soldiers were fighting against SURA. However, as Tongsrichum notes, UWSA, which is also involved in drug trafficking in Thailand, is allied with Burma's ruling junta, the WPR. The foreign minister protested the fact that the attacks rendered clear evidence of the belief that Thailand supports SURA. Ironically, the Thai army insisted that it had only fired warning shots. But, as Tongsrichum further notes, the issue became intensified when the movement of Thai troops to the border simply as part of routine military exercises was interpreted by the Burmese government as a movement in preparation for war despite Thai assurances that this was not the case. Evidently, the situation had been given impetus when the U.S. Assistant Secretary of State for International Narcotics and Law Enforcement had named UWSA as a terrorist organization with ties to drug trafficking in a visit to Burma in March 2002.

Immediately thereafter, the Burmese junta leaders called a meeting, which was held on March 22, 2002, with the five leading drug traffickers in Burma issuing an ultimatum that they cease all drug trafficking activity immediately or risk the threat of their enterprises being raided. The movement of the Thai army forces along the Burmese border, then, was simply viewed as an action in preparation for the conducting of such raids. And so, as Tongsrichum (2002:35) concludes, the logistics for the speedy Thai exercise along the Burmese border was, in the words of the deputy commander of the Thai Third Army, an action "linked to U.S. drug policy and international politics." Tongsrichum ends his discussion of this occurrence by emphasizing that the entire scheme was purposefully clouded in obscurity, which he notes was part of the Thai government's game plan.

It was not obscurity, however, when in February 2003, the Thai government authorized the use of extra-judicial killings of anyone in Thailand suspected of involvement in the drug trade. Six hundred people were reportedly killed in the first three weeks after the authorization was enacted. While the Prime Minister of Thailand lauded the actions of his government as honoring its pledge to rid the country of the greatest threat to Thai society, the human rights group Amnesty International protested the action, arguing that drug suspects should be brought to trial rather than being killed before having an opportunity to defend themselves (CNN 2003).

Such is the division in attitudes and judgments that has become part of the daily rhetoric regarding the various wars being fought in the many places where drugs are trafficked by syndicate criminals. Simultaneously, government agents and officials of these countries play a sometimes brutal but all too often futile game of politics that never solves the problem. Instead, the rhetoric serves to keep alive the hope that a solution is close at hand, thus making it appear as though everything is being done to solve the problem when, in fact, the problem becomes more devastating for the inhabitants of these countries every day. One can readily understand why major public officials like British Member of Parliament and head of the Labour Government's anti-drug campaign Mo Mowlam called for the international legalization of the drug trade in an effort to combat terrorism (Wintour 2002). Yet, in making her suggestion, Mowlam recognized that the trafficking of drugs, because it is an illegal enterprise, looms as one of the most lucrative enterprises for organized criminals around the world. If it indeed were legalized, she reasoned, it would shut down funding for many of the revolutionary groups and, in some cases, the governments that sponsor them. Hence, she argued, it is highly unlikely that drug trafficking will be legalized. There is just too much money involved and, in many cases, if governments themselves are the beneficiaries of the profits, they can use the profits to fund various types of covert enterprises, which can be camouflaged to appear as the activities generated by organized crime (McCoy 2003).

Central to the issue of the continued expansion of drug trafficking are the rapidly developing networks between terrorist groups and syndicate criminals dealing in this trade. One of many possible cases serves to illustrate the nature and extent of these types of liaisons. Anderson (2002) recounts a case in which U.S. agents secretly taped meetings between four individuals who were arranging a deal in which they would exchange cocaine and cash for twenty-five million dollars' worth of weapons, which would have included not only pistols and assault rifles but three hundred thousand grenades, grenade launchers and shoulder-fired anti-aircraft missiles, all of which were to be turned over to the Colombian United Self-Defense Forces, a Colombian (AUC) paramilitary group which the U.S. has classified as a terrorist organization. What is important to note in this case is that the four accomplices had held meetings during which they allegedly discussed their weapon-for-drugs plan in London, the Virgin

Islands and Panama City. This stresses our point that such groups select and use various locations remote from one another in an attempt to lessen their chances of being followed or apprehended. We also should note that the use of shoulder-launched anti-aircraft missiles that were to be made available as part of the deal, currently, represents one of the most serious threats posed by terrorists groups around the world. As Levine (2003:48) explains, the design of these missiles is such that terrorists can easily hide them in the trunks of cars. They weigh only thirty-five pounds, require relatively little training to use, yet can strike planes flying up to fifteen thousand feet. As such, theoretically, as Levine notes, they can be launched from inside a 150-square-mile zone surrounding a commercial airport. As terrorist groups expand their operations, the link between drug traffickers and terrorists will become ever more symbiotic.

Terrorists and Insurgents as Drug Traffickers

It should be understood that, although terrorist and insurgent groups link up with and exchange services and goods with members of drug syndicates, the terrorists or insurgents themselves often find it more expedient to oversee the growth of opium poppies, its refining into heroin, and the transporting and smuggling of the end product out onto the world market. This makes for a complex web of networking patterns as, in some cases, small segments of the terrorist or rebel groups oversee the cultivation and refining process and then dedicate themselves to the smuggling process as well. Thus, Cooley (2000:136) notes that in the late 1970s, rebels in Afghanistan were given time off from their fighting by their leaders so that they could help harvest the opium crops, recalling the "agricultural armies" that dominated warfare up to the days of Napoleon Bonaparte.

However, since the cost-benefit nature of terrorism and insurgent warfare seeks to place many trained fighters into roles where they are available to commit acts of terrorism or destruction, typically, those groups that use drug trafficking as a major source for their funding, are more prone to make their profits from the selling of the product in the original form, after it is harvested, of the opium poppy and leave the refining and distribution in the hands of those who purchase this original product. Thus, as Cooley notes (2000:133), during the late 1970s, syndicated organ-

159

ized crime groups in the United States were developing an effective system for distributing the heroin refined from the opium poppies grown in Afghanistan into American cities such as Chicago, Boston and Newark. This system involved the use of a chain of pizza parlors and thus became known as the "pizza connection." A similar network, composed largely of African American organized criminals like Frank Lucas (portrayed by Denzel Washington in the 2007 film *American Gangster*), smuggled heroin from Southeast Asia to the east coast using extensive U.S. military connections and logistics capacity (Griffin 2003, 2005; McCoy 2003).

Terrorists and insurgent groups find drug trafficking a very useful source for financing their enterprises and as a means of procuring weapons for their warfare. Afghanistan has become a major source for supplying drugs through which terrorist groups such as Al-Qaeda fund their enterprises. Although there is much dispute in the literature concerning this issue, Adam Robinson (2001:200) argues that Osama bin Laden, as of 1996, had made it known in private that opium production constitutes a major source of his funding. Robinson tells of a conversation between bin Laden and one of his relatives in which bin Laden disclosed that since the West was exporting its corrosive culture to Muslim countries, he was exporting illicit drugs to help, in turn, to corrode Western cultures. There is no question that, irrespective of the ambiguity regarding whether funds derived from Afghanistan poppy production directly funded bin Laden enterprises, they do constitute a major source of funding for rebel and other terrorist causes (McCoy 2003). Indeed, as reported by ABC News, one raid alone closed two opium production sites and seized eleven tons of opium in the Taliban-controlled town of Musa Qala in southern Afghanistan in December 2007 (Grey and Schecter 2007).

Yet, this is not just an Al Qaeda/Taliban issue. Indeed, opium is a fungible commodity of lucrative economic and political benefit to the many factions, tribes and alliances engaged in the Afghan conflict, including many of the warlords and powerbrokers of the central and provincial Afghan governments (Peters 2009, 2010). As Thomas Schweich bluntly reported in the *New York Times Magazine* in July 2008, "While it is true that [Afghan president Hamid] Karzai's Taliban enemies finance themselves from the drug trade, so do many of his supporters" (Schweich 2008). The illicit drug enterprise has served to create problems for the inhabitants of Afghanistan itself in that, as Cooley (2000:137) observes, the opium crop has become the preferred crop for cultivation among Afghan farmers to the point that it has resulted in a net deficit in food supplies. This, Cooley argues, is why there is so much unproductive land in Afghanistan and why Afghanistan had so many underfed people at the turn of the twentieth century. After harvesting the poppy, Cooley (2000:137) notes, the raw opium derived from the poppy is converted into morphine bricks, which make it easier to transport, as the raw opium is messy and gives off an ominous smell which can readily be detected by sniffer dogs and customs inspectors.

In this form and sometimes in the form of raw opium, Robinson (2001:202) explains, the drug is then sold to local traders, who, using donkeys, camels, trucks and sometimes transporting the loads on foot, employ a labyrinth of trade routes to smuggle it into neighboring Pakistan, Turkmenistan, Uzbekistan, and Iran. Although some of the refined heroin is used in these neighboring countries, most of the heroin is destined for use in Europe and North America. Britain has evidently been a major destination and former prime minister Tony Blair made obvious the connection between guns and drugs when he noted, in 2001, that the arms that the Taliban was buying at the time were being paid for with the lives of young British people buying these drugs on the streets of Great Britain (Robinson 2001:202).

The removal of the Taliban from Afghan governance resulting from the American military action taken against it after the September 11 attacks does not appear to have affected the volume of crop production and the supply of heroin currently coming out of Afghanistan and border provinces in Pakistan. Indeed, current estimates place this region as the major source of opium production in the world. As Hopkins and Taylor (2002) note, Great Britain has again become a major target for the traffickers. Thus, despite the fact that the interim government of Afghanistan, led by Hamid Karzai, in 2002, introduced a ban on the growing of the opium poppy, the crop produced in 2002 was the equivalent in size to that of the crop produced during the time the Home Office issued its warning in 1998. This resulted, as Hopkins and Taylor explain, in a serious concern on the part of law enforcement and customs agents in Great Britain regarding the challenges they face in their efforts to curb this flow.

Drugs and weapons then flow together or drugs become the collateral for procuring weapons. Such weapons continue to kill and maim even after

the conflicts come to an end. Hence, a February 2003 RAND report entitled "Alternatives for Landmine Detection" speaks to the most pervasive
obstacle confronting such countries in their efforts to put their conflict-
ridden pasts behind them; mainly, the nightmare produced by landmines
(*Foreign Policy* 2003:18–19). Afghanistan serves as an example of this nightmare as five to seven million landmines scattered throughout its countryside
currently continue to maim children, kill livestock and otherwise make
vast stretches of territory unfit for human habitation. It is estimated that
at the current rate of detecting and removing these landmines, using mine-
detecting dogs and metal detectors, it will take those specialists who seek
out the mines (de-miners) about 450 to 500 years to find them all, assum-
ing no new mines are laid during that time period. (*Foreign Policy* 2003:
18–19).

The bonding of weapons and drugs has been, within the past decade,
a vital part of the conflicts that have taken place in Central Asia. As Ahmed
Rashid (2002) documents in his work dealing with the various conflicts
during this period and continue to take place and involve militant Islamist
movements, these movements have continuously presented threats to the
stability of the region. Thus, Juma Namangani created the Islamic Movement of Uzbekistan (IMU) in 1997, a guerrilla movement which, as Rashid
(pp. 164–165) reports, succeeded in creating all manner of consternation
within and further widening the rifts that existed between Uzbekistan,
Tajikistan, and Kyrgyzstan, whose governments kept repeatedly pledging
cooperation with one another. The tactics of the IMU included, among
others, the staging of surprise attacks of military bases, attempts at the
public assassination of government leaders through the use of car bombs,
and the kidnapping of foreign tourists and mountain climbers for the purpose of holding them for ransom. It is important to note here for the sake
of its relevance to our discussion that, according to Rashid (2002:165),
Namangami received his weapons, ammunition and money to continue
these acts of terror from Osama bin Laden and Mullah Omar, who were
then located in Afghanistan. Equally important to our discussion here is
the noting by Rashid (2002:165) that this funding for IMU was derived
from the lucrative opium trade in Afghanistan and that Namangami himself was involved in smuggling opium through Tajikistan.

In another work, Ahmed Rashid (2001:119) makes note of the fact
that, since the 1980s, all the warlords in Afghanistan involved in the Muja-

heddin conflict against the former Soviet Union were using drug money to fund their military operations as well as to buy houses, businesses, and new off-road vehicles and to make deposits into foreign bank accounts. Rashid (2002:229), who joins the ranks of those who assert that bin Laden received funding for his Al-Qaeda operations from the Afghanistan drug trade, maintains that the threat to the stability of Central Asia as a region comes from the ongoing civil war in Afghanistan and the growth of Islamic extremism and the growing menace spawned by the terrorist activity under the leadership of Osama bin Laden. The mainstay to such further conflicts, however, he concludes, lies in the reality that, as he puts it, "drugs fund political activism and drugs pay for weapons." As such, he further notes, drugs currently are the mainstay of the IMU and other militant Islamist movements, thus adding to the uncertain future of the Central Asian nations.

It is no wonder, then, that when analyzing a conflict like the current war in Afghanistan that the lines between tribal and insurgent warfare are readily blurred with warfare over criminal enterprises and turf. Gretchen Peters (2010:ii–iii) provides a first-rate analysis of three of the main actors in the insurgency. She finds that the Afghan Taliban (Quetta Shurra Taliban or QST) behaves like a traditional drug cartel, moving from taxing farmers to more profitable processing and exporting with proceeds from extortion and narcotics going to central coffers, not district-level commanders. The Haqqani Network (HQN), she explains, works closely with the Pakistani Taliban and Al-Qaeda in diverse enterprises such as kidnapping, protection rackets directed towards smugglers, and the extortion of businesses, while Hezb-e-Islami (HIG) protects the looting and smuggling of resources and opium and competes against local groups tied to Al-Qaeda. Peters concludes all three syndicates compete for funds and fight over illicit and licit revenue streams to the extent their financial motives "are behind their tactics." These tactics are not just directed toward each other but toward the Afghan government. After all, its ruling coalition is filled with competitors in the underworld marketplace (Norton-Taylor 2010). Drawing comparisons to similar behaviors found in the history of organized crime in the West, Peters concludes (2010:90):

> Within this complex adaptive system, criminal profits fund the insurgency and terrorist violence helps militants to coerce and exert a level of control over local communities. Insurgents find ways to justify criminal behavior

as part of their jihad, claiming, for example, that they live off the alms of the people, or that they deal in drugs in order to make addicts of infidels. As with Mafia families and street gangs operating in the West, criminal insurgent behavior can be simultaneously protective and predatory towards the communities where insurgent entities operate.

Civil Wars: The Markets of Conflict

Since September 11, an evolving theme concerning the conflicts taking place in the Middle East have given rise to the thesis that these conflicts are basically grounded in the historical past and thus embedded in the ethnic hatreds which history and ethnic identity have brought upon the inhabitants of this region. This may be true of the Middle East. However, a recent study draws attention to factors other than history and ethnicity as forces manifested in the many civil war conflicts that are increasingly becoming common, yet so often attract little or no attention.

Paul Collier (2003:38–45) questions this belief that such conflicts are embedded in ethnic roots and history. Drawing data from fifty-two major civil wars fought between 1960 and 1999, he notes that these conflicts, which often lasted for about seven years, resulted in the devastation of the countries involved and left their inhabitants ridden with disease and in a state of poverty. Collier, along with his co-researcher, economist Anke Hoeffler, examined the data in an effort to define and identify those factors that would serve to predict the outbreak of such conflicts. They found that ethnicity is often at the core of such conflicts because the media tends to emphasize this as a significant variable in its reporting of the events and the rebel leaders of such conflicts, themselves, tend to make this a major theme of their discourse. Collier concludes that although conflicts in such countries can be ethnically patterned, they are not, in their origin, ethnically caused. Contrary to the current belief that democracy helps reduce the risk of such conflicts, Collier finds that politically repressive societies run no greater risk of civil war than do those that have full-fledged democratic systems. It is not past history, but, rather, recent history, he argues, that has a bearing on this form of conflict. Thus Collier observes that a country that has experienced a recent civil war will be more likely to experience another one. The longer peace endures, the less the chance for conflict.

Above all, Collier points to the fact that his examination of the most predictable factors involved in the creation of civil war lies in the economy of the country. Thus, the risk for war was shown to increase at an alarming rate in those countries in which the economy was poor, declining and dependent upon natural resources. In those cases, however, where a country's per capita income doubles, the risk of a conflict occurring drops roughly by half. The reason for this is simple, argues Collier, in that economic growth is vital to the youth who are typically the combatants in these conflicts. Hence, economic growth becomes significant because opportunities for youth are dependent upon the existence of a robust economy (2003:41). One of the other major factors that Collier found to be a contributing cause for the emergence of civil conflict revolved around natural resources. That is, if a population of a country depended heavily upon the exporting of its natural resources for its earnings, the potential for conflict was shown to be much higher. In this respect, diamonds, as Collier puts it, can become "a rebel's best friend."

This brings us to the relevance that Collier's study has to our discussion concerning the involvement of organized crime in procuring weapons for the combatants in such revolutionary enterprises. Natural resources can and do, as Collier notes, serve as means for funding such operations. Hence, "conflict diamonds" funded the rebel group — the National Union for Total Independence of Angola (UNITA) — in its war in Angola as well as the efforts of the Revolutionary United Front (RUT) in Sierra Leone, and the Al-Qaeda network's global insurgency and terrorism agendas thanks to the alliance between it and Liberia's infamous former president Charles Taylor (Farah 2004). Timber became the major source for providing funds for the Khmer Rouge in Cambodia. Such enterprises give birth to the practice of extortion when the multinational corporations involved in the extracting of natural resources in these countries are forced to pay huge sums of money to ransom workers who are kidnapped by the rebels and/or to pay these rebels extortion fees in order to safeguard the company's people, property and infrastructure from potential acts of sabotage (Collier 2003:41).

Above all, Collier concludes, the motivations for rebellion matter less than the financial and military conditions that make it viable. Civil wars occur only if rebel organizations have the ability to create private armies. Armies, however, are expensive to maintain. Hence, of optimum importance to the formation and success of civil war conflicts is the ability for those groups fighting the war to build and maintain such armies. If they manage to do so, then, as Collier notes, they are likely to promote whatever political agenda their leaders happen to support (2003:42).

Civil Conflict, Anomie and the Emergence of Organized Crime

Decades ago, sociologist Emile Durkheim (1997) noted the existence of a condition within the moral order of societies in which a point is reached where the individual living in such societies finds it difficult to be guided by its norms. This occurs when such norms become weak, unclear or conflicting. The result, he argued, was the creation of a state of "anomie," otherwise translated as "a state of normlessness." The brutality and chaotic conditions that have followed many of the recent civil wars and ethnic conflicts occurring in the world have produced a form of organized crime where the only proper classification that can be employed to describe it is what we have come to call "anomic organized crime."

The genesis for defining this type of crime emerges from the work of Chris Hedges (2002), whose treatment of the subject of war itself awakens a reality that begs to view war in terms of the scathing horrors that it produces. Within this horror emerges a form of organized criminality whose major purpose is that of venting savage anger and revenge. War, Hedges argues (2002:103–104), perpetuates a state of anomie in that it serves to break down long-established prohibitions against violence, destruction and murder. The result is that the brutality of the battlefield finds its way into personal life and comes to be manifested in rape, mutilation, and other offenses in which force is the rule of law and human beings become objects for the sole expression of anger and rage. The infection becomes pervasive and society becomes atomized.

Hedges (2002:104–105) describes how the wars in the Balkans gave rise to the creation of rape camps where women kept under guard were continuously abused by Serbian paramilitary forces. Of course this was based on a well-established practice of rape being used as a systematized instrument of war (Leatherman 2011), perhaps most prominently by the Japanese (Hicks 1997; Chang 1998; Soh 2009) during the second World

166

War. Similar sex camps existed during Argentina's Dirty War and the sex slaves from these camps were later murdered and, like garbage, some were dumped from helicopters into the sea (Taylor 1997; Feitlowitz 1999). Likewise, militias in Africa, often consisting of various mixtures of ideologues, criminals, misfits, and children, engaged in killings and torture based upon their changing whims and moods in places such as the Sudan, Sierra Leone, Uganda, and the Congo (Stearns 2011). Such militia forces use routinized sexual violence and slavery that serve to release a lifetime of bitterness against those whom they had come to hate through victimization and/or indoctrination (Singer 2006; Eichstaedt 2009; Leatherman 2011). Along with the deaths and physical and psychological wounds resulting from such criminal outrages come the displacement and dislocation of people whose property is confiscated by those who force them from their land, commonly referred to as ethnic cleansing. Regarding such displacements, Hedges (2002:106) reminds us that such devastating dislocations create a population of stateless people who become refugees within their own countries. Forced into refugee camps or dispersed into squalid urban slums, these refugees simultaneously become both a pool of victims ripe for further exploitation and a recruiting pool from which future predators and criminal entrepreneurs evolve. Such is the crisis that accompanies the many civil wars and other forms of social conflict that have become commonplace in the modern world. As such, they have given rise to anomic organized crime.

The Convergence of Political-Social and Syndicated Crime

Political-social forms of organized crime will constitute a major form of criminal ventures in the coming decades. As globalization erupts the tranquility of given countries or serves to exacerbate conditions of poverty into armed conflict in others, the syndicated organized criminals of the world will make certain that they profit from the sale of weapons that make the continuation of such conflicts possible. However, the work of Alfred Schulte-Bockholt serves to remind us that organized crime has historically been a vital force in the political movements both in the past and around the world.

Schulte-Bockholt (2001) illustrates this point by noting the fact that in 1927, the Shanghai Green Gang, which consisted of a powerful organized crime group in China, executed a coup that led to the establishment of the dictatorship of Chiang Kai-shek and the Kuomintang (KMT). In return for their support in accomplishing this coup and for their help in ridding Shanghai of Communists and unions, Chiang Kai-shek gave the Green Gang and its leader, Du Yue-sheng, free reign in Shanghai's underworld enterprises, which included dealing in prostitution, protection rackets and the narcotics trade. These gang members, Schulte-Bockholt notes, soon became members of the Nationalist Army. Chiang Kai-shek came to rely on these "troops," composed of local organized crime forces, to maintain order under his regime. Schulte-Bockholt (2001:232) points out that, after the coup, prominent business groups praised both Chiang Kai-shek and the efforts of the Green Gang by lauding both as being the saviors of the country. Basking in this glory and the impunity afforded to them by Chiang Kai-shek, these Green Gang gangsters not only performed tasks similar to those performed by members of repressive agencies in Europe's Fascist regimes, they also reorganized and managed the labor forces in Shanghai during Chiang Kai-shek's reign of power.

In the early 1990s in Peru, Schulte-Bockholt (2001:233) points out, the cash-starved Peruvian army allied itself with drug traffickers in order to finance a civil war against the Maoist rebel movement, "el Sendero Luminoso" (the Shining Path). Once again, we see the military forces of Peru participating in the drug trade, the profits of which served as its method for obtaining funds to procure weapons, equipment and food that helped them carry on their operations. Along with their emergence in Peru, Schulte-Bockholt (p. 233) shows a sudden explosion of organized crime groups in Latin America had presented a further menace in that the demand for cocaine jolted regional economics because of the introduction of a new force in Latin American politics: the drug-trafficking political Right. In Bolivia, Schulte-Bockholt notes, corrupt military personnel joined forces with that country's major drug dealers and their paramilitaries to topple the government in 1980. A major menace, however, was taking place in Colombia. Here, as Schulte-Bockholt (p. 233) makes clear, organized criminals and their allies drawn from agrarian elites and military and police officials set up "Mafia Republics," no-go territories inside which the state has little presence and the inability to defend and enforce its sovereignty.

The Case of Colombia

Organized crime in Colombia presents a unique case in terms of its persistence over time and its ability to play a menacing role in the globalization of drug trafficking itself. This menace originates within a reality, beginning with Pablo Escobar in the 1980s, which places organized criminality itself in a unique situation. Primarily, its forces in Colombia have become intricately webbed within the government itself. Thus we are dealing with a situation where crime and political power have become bonded together as part of the history of Colombia itself. Any attempt to extricate organized criminal forces from the government agencies in Colombia would necessitate a simultaneous extrication of the forces of the government from organized crime. In other words, the government of Colombia, like that of contemporary Russia, has been primarily under the control of organized criminals.

Colombian syndicates also control the growth, refinement and distribution of the world's largest supply of cocaine. This in itself represents power in a world that is daily morphing into one where borders are shrinking due to the forces of globalization. The growth in recent years of transnational criminal organizations related to the narcotics trade and the expansion of criminal ventures in general have become a major concern for governments and police forces around the globe. As with the nations of Central Asia, Colombia presents a specific threat within the world in that it has, within the past thirty years, become a powerful dual force in the arena of international organized criminality. Not only have its criminal syndicates become the world's largest producers and traffickers of cocaine, some of their members have become major players in global terrorism, thus forcing the U.S. and other governments to now view the war on drugs as a matter of national security.

Patricia Bibes (2001:243–258) brings to the immediate foreground the issues that make Colombia stand out as a case study used to evaluate similar occurrences taking place throughout the world. For example, the "Fuerzas Armadas Revolucionarias de Colombia" (FARC) translated as the Revolutionary Armed Forces of Colombia, and the "Sendero Luminoso," translated as the Shining Path, have bonded the criminal operations of drug trafficking with the political aspirations of guerrilla warfare and have produced a movement that seeks to replace the state in the name of an egalitarian social revolution. As such, Bibes argues, these narco-terrorists have come to view themselves as leaders of a movement in which they determine the best interests of the state and, as a revolutionary tactic, use the competing nationalism existent in Colombian society to their own advantage. These syndicate criminals, in our usage of the terms, have blended syndicate organized crime with the social-political form of organized crime.

As Bibes (p. 245) makes clear, they not only wish to make profits from drug trafficking, they seek to change and, if necessary, overthrow the government. Their syndicate features include the bribing of government officials who allow them to operate their criminal enterprises without any interference from the legal authorities and their social-political goals are realized through the effective execution of terrorist acts. These forces have killed those judges who have dared to impede the attainment of their goals and, in many cases, the drug traffickers have succeeded in having themselves elected to city councils and national legislatures.

Above all, as Bibes (245, 249) notes, these criminals view themselves as the defenders of national sovereignty and the promoters and providers of economic progress. Violence is their stock and trade. Two major syndicates or cartels, the Medellin and the Cali, waged an inter-cartel war from 1988 to 1993 that involved raids and massacres that killed hundreds of people. As Bibes (p. 248) explains, the FARC draws its funds not only from the trafficking of cocaine itself, but also from taxing both the peasants that cultivate the coca plant and those working in the cocaine-production laboratories. The international expanse of the cartel drug enterprise is evidenced by the networks operating in Chile, Brazil, Venezuela, Bolivia, Argentina, Italy, Spain and other parts of Europe and the Far East. Bibes (2001:547) also observes that the trade has come to include numerous independent traffickers and a host of high-tech traffickers who subcontract work to specialists and use the Internet in order to protect and conduct their business dealings.

This case study serves to illustrate that in the coming globalization of the world, nations will need to give attention to the reality which the Colombian case study makes clear: organized criminal forces, particularly when they can draw funds from the narcotics trade, can become the sovereigns of governments themselves. The Colombian narco-traffickers wield a political force that is normally confined to the state. Indeed, in Colombia, these criminals are capable of using violence and bribery to basically run significant portions of the country. They can force the enactment of laws favoring their goals and interests. They can sabotage electoral campaigns, kidnap foreign nationals, raise prices, cause the loss of foreign investments based upon a lack of faith and trust in the Colombian government itself, displace large segments of the population, extort the owners of legitimate businesses, negotiate with sympathetic heads of state (like President Hugo Chavez of Venezuela) and cause the citizens themselves to lose faith in their government and its leaders.

As Rensselaer Lee III and Francisco Thoumi (1999:60) reveal in their analysis of this issue, democracy in Colombia was subverted by a vast array of conditions that made for the development, production and export of illicit drugs. Among these were a weakness in civil society, the widespread use of violence to resolve disputes, the geography of the country, various obstacles that thwarted the achievement of upward mobility, the structure of the political parties, the vast volume of illegal economic activity that took place within its society, the social acceptance of contraband and the practice of money laundering. As many countries are currently struggling to develop and/or retain democratic systems of government, the fate of such democracies, like that of Colombia, could be seriously influenced by organized criminal forces which would seek to gain or retain control of unstable democracies. Even given recent significant gains by the Colombian government (thanks in part to major assistance from the U.S. via Plan Colombia) against the cartels, it would do well to pay close attention to what has happened in Colombia for it is a lesson from which the entire world can learn (Preston 2009).

The case of the Colombian narcotics trade takes on further significance in the field research of Damien Zaitch (2002), which not only serves to offer an inside look at how the trade functions in The Netherlands but impresses upon us an understanding of the nature of the structure of the syndicates that operate it. A sense of urgency develops as this structure and functioning becomes the norm for syndicate operations as the world continues to go global. Zaitch employed the method of ethnographic research that allowed him to interview informants and observe their behavior by spending time in salsa bars, churches, prisons and prostitution streets, empowering his results and giving the study further significance by being studied both in its country of origin (Colombia) and in The Netherlands, where the drugs are distributed to the users themselves.

In his description of the structure of drug syndicates in Colombia, Zaitch (2002:59–63) argues that the use of the term "cartel" is misleading in that, in Colombia, the requirements necessary for a successful operation of the narcotics trade would not be served by the presence of a large, hierarchically structured, centrally managed, and easily identifiable organization. Instead, the structure is a fluid one in which the membership is constantly changing. Hence, there is no "Mr. Big" who controls everything and certainly no board of directors or other functionaries who are typically associated with the concept of "cartel." The risks involved and the very nature of the enterprise, argues Zaitch, have given rise to a structure of differentiated networks, basically small dyadic (two individuals viewed as belonging to one unit) groupings where trust is established not through the reciting of secret oaths by its participants, but instead, by participants placing their trust in the friends, relatives and neighbors whom they select as partners in their enterprises.

As such, functionaries do not know anything about the roles of those above them and lack a general picture of the overall business itself. This form of relating is not meant to imply that clashes between competing groups do not occur as differences between groups and changing situations can and do produce conflicts. However, here again, these clashes occur between and within the small networks of the groups involved. Another feature that differentiates the Colombian syndicate structure from that of other organized crime groups where secrecy is viewed as a mandatory requirement, Zaitch (2002:66–67) notes, is found in the fact that the Colombian organizations are characterized by their very public and "open" nature. So, too, these organizations function with a loose and constantly changing set of rules and the enterprises themselves are too short-lived to be "inherited."

Zaitch (p. 67) makes note of another difference between the operators of syndicates in Colombia and those of other countries, such as the U.S., where the public views organized criminals in negative terms. Rather, the Colombian organized criminals are judged by their surrounding social groups primarily as being more or less legitimate entrepreneurs. Interestingly, Zaitch (p. 65) points out that territory for the Colombian drug organizations is not a primary importance as it is with organized crime groups in other countries. The reason for this, he argues, is that the Colombian organizations have emerged and grown out of a demand for cocaine that originated in foreign countries beyond Colombia's shores and therefore these organizations live from and for a market that is international rather than local in scope. As such, then, the activities of these organizations derive meaning only from within the dynamics of the international drug market itself. Although the paramilitary groups were not created by the drug entrepreneurs, as Zaitch (pp. 69–70) points out, their drug money helped improve the quality of the equipment, training and resources of these groups and by supporting the paramilitary groups; these entrepreneurs cemented their ties with two important groups in Colombian society: the land-owning classes and the right-wing military factions.

As for cocaine distribution in Europe, Zaitch (p. 86) once again notes that, like those in Colombia, the syndicates operating the ventures supplying and distributing cocaine in Europe do not consist of large, bureaucratic, centralized organizations, but, instead are best characterized as consisting of decentralized networks. These networks are very flexible in structure and levels of organization and their memberships include a variety of ethnic and/or national groups. Although the membership of some groups is attached to larger criminal organizations that have been in existence for a long time and thus have refined their skills over time, the cocaine traffic in Europe is basically organized and conducted by independent groups that have managed to establish links with exporters in South America. Zaitch (p. 87) emphasizes that large multinational, hierarchical enterprises are extremely rare and notes that these, when they have been in existence, were prone to fall prey to regular detection by law enforcement agencies, indicating that largeness and bureaucratic structuring is indicative of a weakness inherent to such an organizational structure.

Once again, Zaitch stresses a point that we, in turn, agree with and emphasize: organized syndicate criminals groups tend not to form as large, formal structures. Contrary to the typical portrayal of such groups by the media, the nature of the structuring of these groups and the attaining of their membership tends to originate from within a setting where small numbers of individuals using the trust developed over time through friendship and/or blood relationships take further steps to link into a variety of networks through which they can then ply their trade.

This naturally leads to Zaitch's (2002:87) observation that such networks vary from country to country. Thus, in Spain, a major center for importing cocaine into Europe, this network includes Colombian and local Spanish functionaries from the Galician region, as this region is geographically suited to sea smuggling. This illustrates that criminals will take advantage of geographical areas where they can stealthfully enter illicit goods into a country and form relationships with syndicate members in those regions. This serves to contradict the popular conception that large, powerful criminal organizations, purposefully and with advanced forms of intuition, select given areas and then turn these areas into regions for importing their goods. Organized crime does not work that way. Instead, its functionaries allow for opportunity and feasibility to guide their networking relationships.

In Italy, Zaitch (p. 88) points out that importing cocaine involves interaction between Colombians and Italian organized groups such as the Camorra. As Tom Behan (2002) detailed in his analysis of the rise of this organization during the 1800s, although its origins are obscure, evidence seems to point to the fact that the Camorra emerged within the prison system of Naples, Italy, around 1820. In this system, prisoners were forced to give part of any money they received from friends and relatives to the head or boss of the Camorra group operating in that prison. Along with controlling virtually every aspect of the lives of the prisoners, these bosses also took money from the prison authorities as a payment for keeping order among the prisoners. Later, the organization was structured into groups or gangs that began engaging in criminal activities in the city of Naples itself. Early in their development, major enterprises included protection rackets, illegal gambling and usury. Today, these activities have come to include illegal drug and cigarette trafficking.

Once again, geography becomes an important factor, a point evident when Behan (p. 20) notes that Naples has historically served as a major Italian port, with three-quarters of all Italian trade passing through, and hosted a large population of workers employed at its docks. Lydia Rosner (2000:143) makes an interesting observation in this regard when she notes that port cities possess a culture of their own and, historically, their diverse internationalism has held an appeal to roving criminal elements long before the use of airplanes for travel and the phenomenon of open borders. It is not surprising that, once again, Neapolitan criminals would join forces with Colombian distributors to become a major importer of cocaine to be distributed in Italy and Europe.

However, Zaitch (2002:89) emphasizes that even within the structuring of the Italian syndicates currently working with Colombian exporters of cocaine, many of the Italian criminal groups involved in this trade today consist of a membership which does not belong to a large criminal organization but, instead, is drawn from the local underworlds of Rome and other northern Italian cities. According to Zaitch, the import and distribution cocaine trade in Europe has made room for the involvement of Lebanese, Israelis, Portuguese, Croats, Serbs, Kosovars, Argentineans, Peruvians and numerous other groups who work within ethnic or national networks or function as individuals belonging to internationally integrated local groups. Since the early 1990s, Zaitch points out, South American exporters have established ties with criminal groups in Eastern Europe and Russia.

In conclusion, Zaitch (2002:298–299) speaks to the variation that is so frequently found in the behavior and tactics employed among and between syndicate criminals, by observing that, although violence does play a major role in the cocaine business, it is not employed, as is true in many other organized crime operations or among other types of organized crime groups, as a commodity for its own sake. This is so because the cocaine enterprise itself imposes its own structural limitations on its use; as such, the transactions that take place are primarily contractual in nature rather than being motivated by threats. Illustrating that there is a rational mode of thinking found among criminals operating certain types of organized criminal activities, these criminals recognize that violence only mars their ability to operate their enterprises in an atmosphere characterized more by cooperation than conflict, the cocaine enterprise in The Netherlands reveals that the actors there recognize the competitive nature of the drug business itself, and thereby, act accordingly.

The Effects of Globalization and the Changing Nature of Organized Crime

In their very comprehensive work on the topic, Adamoli, Di Nicola, Savona and Zoffi (1998) describe various changes that organized groups have undergone in order to meet the challenges to their operations brought about by globalization. In Europe, these changes have caused organized crime groups to recruit specialists with technological and other skills that will make it possible for such groups to infiltrate and make profits from new markets. This has resulted, as we have noted earlier in our discussion, in the development of transnational organizations. Once again, as we noted in reference to the structure of cocaine-trafficking groups in The Netherlands, as these authors highlight, because large monolithic criminal organizations have proved to be easy targets of law enforcement agencies, the modern trend continues to develop small, decentralized networks whose activities are guided and structured through mutual understandings and agreements. These groups have the flexibility to adjust to changing demands in the illicit marketplace and to the changes brought about by competition in the markets of the goods and products that they provide. Adamoli et al. (1998:12) reinforce our point made earlier that globalization would necessitate the use of varying styles of entering markets in foreign countries. Thus, in some cases, force may be employed to do so, while, in others, the criminal groups seeking entry into a market in a foreign country may choose instead to cooperate with local groups who know the territory and have provided the means of assuring themselves protection from the legal authorities.

What emerges as a clear pattern resulting from globalization is that crime groups are increasingly becoming interdependent. Also emerging is a pattern that the authors (Adamoli et al. 1998:16–18) describe as "vertical interdependency," a process where, in order for a syndicate to perpetuate its ultimate or final form of crime, it must first perpetuate intermediate offenses. We can here illustrate this phenomenon by noting that the money made by those operating Nigerian e-mail scams may appear to be motivated solely for making a final profit for those who operate such scams. In reality, as Jeffrey Robinson (2002) points out, these funds are acquired for the purpose of ultimately making larger profits from investing in illicit drug-trafficking operations. Robinson shows that the money made from the scams is used first to buy heroin from Thailand. This heroin is then imported into the United States where further profit is made by trading it for cocaine obtained from Dominican and Colombian street gangs. The cocaine is then shipped to Britain, where it is sold to Jamaican street gangs, thus doubling their money a second time.

"Horizontal interdependency," on the other hand, is described by Adamoli, et al. (1998:17–18) as a pattern of criminality where the same organization itself goes through the process of perpetuating several crimes in order to accomplish its goal of perpetuating its main criminal enterprise. Thus they offer as an example of this form of interdependency, the operation of Turkish crime groups which now make use of the networks of corruption that they established in the past through enterprises such as drug trafficking and the sale of falsified documents, to engage in their relatively new venture of trafficking aliens from Eastern and Central Asia into Western Europe (Zhang 2007:17).

These patterns are reflected in a multitude of interweaving criminal networks on an international level and the future can be expected to spawn even more networks. We can be certain that current networks will constantly adapt and change in order to meet the requirements of new markets and adjust to changes occurring in the older markets. It seems to us that organized criminals have made major headway in seizing opportunities created by, and in meeting the challenges of, globalization. This does not mean that all of their ventures will be met with undisturbed passages along the new landscape of the global map (Varese 2011). Indeed, the violent disruptions in the global social system of organized crime will be a replay in the international arena of what took place in the cities of the United States during the Prohibition Era. Battles will be fought along the various fault lines of the world stage, caused in no small part by the complex types of criminal ventures that may result in gangs, syndicates and their upperworld partners vying for control of given territories and/or markets.

It will be hard to predict where and when they will take place, but they will take place because that is the nature of organized criminal activity. Just as some syndicate leaders in the cities of the United States during the first decades of the twentieth century managed to secure the protection of corruption and managed to stifle the growth and development of other competitive syndicates, so, too, on the world stage, certain leaders and syndicates, because of timing and location, will forge partnerships to secure advantages over competitors. However, like in the cities of the United States during the past several decades, syndicates have also shown that they understand that cooperation allows for better business relations among criminals and they may choose that route, whenever possible, in future international ventures.

Violence between international criminal networks is already marked by killings in places that view themselves as historically immune. Consider the example of Madrid, Spain. An editorial in Madrid's daily newspaper, *El Mundo* (April 11, 2003:13) called attention to the gangs of Colombian drug dealers turning Madrid into a killing field over the previous few years. These Colombian gangs have partnered with criminal gangs from Central Europe who entered Spain illegally. The turf wars became ferocious as machine guns were used by assassins in the killing of two men who were changing a tire by the roadside. The victims, it turned out, were Bulgarian car thieves and the attack, it seems, was meant to settle a score. The magnitude of this conflict was evidenced by the exponential increase in such killings. The editorial ended by describing Madrid as a sophisticated city that therefore should not be the setting for such brutal disputes. We agree. However, this conflict serves to illustrate the point that we have just made: no city is immune from becoming the latest battleground for syndicates vying for power in an increasingly globalized world.

EIGHT

The Organized Crime Matrix: A Transnational System of Social Networks of Organized Criminal Activity

There is seemingly nowhere on Earth where organized crime does not exist in some form and the available evidence leads us to the inescapable conclusion that the criminal groups involved in this activity have in many cases formed vast, complex and intricate types of linkages with one another, forming what we call the "organized crime matrix." It is a matrix guided by the elements found in organized crime as a method rather than organized crime as an organization. As such, the organized crime matrix represents an interlocking of networks and relationships that involve a vast number of individuals and groups from around the world who weave in and out of criminal ventures as they also weave in and out of the group structures themselves. As a result, any "structure" assessed by the media, government, or scholars is inherently transitioning as internal and external forces are constantly shaping it. Although hierarchy is a mode of structuring for some groups, it appears that the evolution of transnational criminality has found that the survival of the fittest in the coming evolutionary process of globalization will become evident among those groups which are structured as decentralized organized crime groups and allow both the group and its members to quickly adjust to the rapid social changes which globalization will surely produce.

As borders continue to erode and provide a serious challenge to the traditional conception of territorial sovereignty, new laws mingle with the old and technology changes daily, giving both criminals and law enforcement agencies new devises to expand communication and operating procedures. As this occurs, the new criminal groups simply will not put their trust in the reciting of secret oaths or the other traditional methods that have been used to profess loyalty to a group. Instead, the new groups will put their trust in the stealth created within the networking process itself. Criminals have learned that trust is best served by the element of time; the time they have spent with those whom they have come to trust. Close friendships, close family ties, and the trust created within the bonds of a clan will continue to produce secrecy and trust among future organized crime groups, their reputations for such preceding them into new ventures.

Conflicts will continue as markets, leadership and opportunities for involvement in new enterprises evolve. It will be a time of flux and modern criminal groups have learned from terrorist and insurgent organizations that operating as small "cells" which do not require immediate instructions or orders from a leader allow both groups and members an independence of movement. Once the goal and strategy has been set, these small groups can be extremely effective. The demise of one cell does not have a serious deterrent effect upon the functioning of all the other cells. Such small groups can also be effective intelligence gathering sources as their creative and varied roles allow them to more easily blend into legitimate society.

It is a new world of criminality. Unlike the larger structuring created by some syndicate leaders in the past, and the Mafia mystique they engendered, this new world is one where the new groups have adapted to the use of decentralizing and developing entities. One can argue that large structures may have been functional in operations by crime syndicates in the past; however, experience has taught the modern criminal that large organizations are more readily targeted and made dysfunctional by law enforcement efforts. Hence, small, interweaving networks have become the mode. As a result, the organized crime matrix has come of age.

The More Things Change...

The coming changes in organized criminal activities will ultimately consist of blending old enterprises and creating new ones. A feature that is increasingly becoming evident as a result of the intricate web woven by the organized crime matrix is the frequent blending in business enterprises of the legal with the illegal. The lines have become so blurred at times that it is increasingly difficult to distinguish the criminal from the non-criminal actor. Adamoli et al. (1998:21) put the issue into clear perspective when they note that criminals are increasingly making use of legitimate businesses as a means of diversifying their investments and as a means for obtaining legitimate incomes. However, criminals also do this in order to reduce the risk of detection and seizure of their capital. As a result, these authors argue, the traditional distinction between the illicit and legitimate methods of operation employed by the organized criminal is becoming less distinguishable, resulting in the blurring of the thin line between what is legal and what is criminal.

But, as Adamoli et al. (1998) point out, there is another reason why criminals are infiltrating the licit economy; they are seeking respectability. Hence, by infiltrating the world of legitimate business, they have more opportunity to climb the social ladder of legitimate success. These authors note, as we have in our discussions of Russian organized crime throughout this work, that by increasingly engaging in legitimate enterprises, criminals from the countries that were part of the former Soviet Union have slowly managed to gain respectability and have already begun to merge with the ruling classes of these countries.

As further evidenced by Amy Chua (2003:24–31), the proliferation of free markets are blurring the line between legal and illegal commercial activity in many developing countries. For example, currently in Burma, many of the country's most influential businessmen come from backgrounds in which they engaged in black market activity and in the trafficking of heroin. Additionally, there are hundreds of businesses stacked up next to the Mexican border in San Diego. Many are owned by drug cartels without any knowledge of the employees, but that does not stop the traffickers from shipping or storing their product through the company, laundering their illicit proceeds through company transaction, or even, in a few cases, constructing a smuggling tunnel entrance in the floor of the back office for use after hours. Indeed, the global social system of organized crime binds local social systems of organized crime from around the world via tens of thousands of such relationships, the organized crime matrix. The networks of underworld and upperworld actors that compose the organized crime matrix create global catchment zones linking, for instance, neighborhoods in the urban slums of Karachi and Caracas to cartel-backed political power brokers in Mexico and to the gilded halls of multinational financial institutions in Hong Kong, London, and Dubai. What illicit goods and services occur within these catchment zones depends on the whims of the opportunity, the market, and individual and collective initiative.

Organized Crime and the Theft of Antiques and Works of Art

Perhaps a good way to picture this process is to examine a case study of art and antiquities theft and the trafficking and fencing of both once stolen. The looting of the Baghdad Museum which followed the Coalition's invasion of Iraq in 2003 brought to light criminal enterprises occurring in various parts of the world over the past three decades, art theft and art trafficking. As an article pertaining to the looting of the Baghdad Museum in *Business Week* (2003, April 28) noted, it was believed at the time that the reason the thievery was thought to be so well organized was due to the fact that shady art dealers had ordered the theft of the most important pieces well in advance. This belief would certainly have been in keeping with a venture of organized criminals that involves a global network of art thieves who use sophisticated methods of stealing the goods themselves and an equally sophisticated system of fencing or selling the goods to private collectors desiring to own them.

Trafficking in stolen art goods by syndicated criminals has presented a major threat to museums which house the world's great art treasures and to archeologists who excavate sites that unlock the mysteries of ancient civilizations. The work of many of these archeologists is disrupted, and in some cases brought to a halt, because of thieves patiently waiting for these archeological teams to leave their sites unattended. The thieves then unearth pottery, jewelry, artifacts and fossils while leaving the sites themselves in shambles. Whereas the archeologist uses careful techniques that include a delicate brushing of the soil covering the artifacts at such sites so as to be able to examine these items in their original placement relative to other items at the site, these thieves use shovels, picks and other objects to quickly unearth these artifacts, taking enough care only to preserve the artifact enough to bring them the profits that they hope to gain by selling them to traders in the world of art theft. As a result, the validity of the historical data unearthed at these sites stands to be destroyed forever.

Albini (1986) first researched antiquities and art theft during his study of organized crime in Great Britain in 1972–73. His contacts at New Scotland Yard indicated to him that art theft was becoming a major problem in England, a problem magnified by the fact that many owners of valuable paintings that were being stolen could not offer adequate descriptions of these paintings to the police, thus making the recovery of such artworks difficult. As a result, owners of paintings were instructed to take very clear photographs of the paintings they had in their possession. In this manner, if they were stolen, detectives would have an actual photo of the painting that would help in the process of attempting to recover it. In any respect, as Laurie Adams (1974:12–15) observed, the art teams at New Scotland Yard in the early 1970s became very serious in their efforts to combat this escalating form of theft. Meanwhile, in New York City, Robert Volpe, a detective who considered himself both an artist and detective, a combination of roles that earned him the title of the "Art Cop," served as a major force among the art theft teams of the New York Police Department. London and New York became centers for the investigation of this form of theft in that, as Adams notes (p. 13), both London and New York are key financial centers in the international art market.

The thieves who specialize in this form of theft, as Middlemas (1975:85) described them, are habitual criminals who have turned their skills toward this form of robbery and possess the organizational traits of intelligence and discipline that allow them to organize efficient teams to carry out their art-theft ventures. The membership, as Albini learned from informants in his study in Great Britain, is flexible, as each theft presents a different set of obstacles and thus requires the use of different functionaries with particular specialties in the art and science of thievery. These "rings," as they are commonly referred to by the criminals themselves, are led by one boss who chooses the artwork or works to be stolen and then develops the logistics for executing the plan for the theft.

Needless to say, since artworks are generally protected by guards in museums and by sophisticated electronic surveillance equipment found both in these museums and in the homes of those who own valuable works of art, the leader of these rings must find methods to circumvent such security obstacles in order to accomplish the feat. Thus, careful planning and rehearsals on the part of the team members involved precedes the actual robbery attempt itself. Like commandos, these teams practice precision drills that must be accurate to the second in their timing. Stealth and imagination are also employed in devising plans that will catch security forces off guard and are aimed at the dismantling of the high-tech alarm systems employed to protect these valuable works of art. In some cases, as Esterow (1973:8) relates, artworks are stolen from churches by bribing the caretakers, after which, in some cases, the original is simply replaced by a copy and the theft itself is never noticed.

There are different motivations for stealing art goods. In some cases, the theft results from an order from an art lover who seeks a particular painting or sculpture. This is the type of theft that generally does not result in the recovery of the stolen art as the new owner does not reveal his or her knowledge of the possession of such works. These owners simply want the joy of having these works in their personal possession for viewing by their eyes only. In other cases, the paintings or works of art are stolen and held for ransom from the insurance company that has insured the work. This results in an intricate interplay between shady negotiators who serve as arbitrators between the thieves and the representatives of the insurance company. Such deals are, by their very nature, secretive, as the insurance company, all too often, would rather pay the ransom since this would ultimately be a lesser sum than the amount that would be paid within the terms set by the insurance policy itself. The thieves must be careful to keep the stolen artwork in excellent physical condition in such cases so as to be able to barter its safe return, unharmed, to the insurance company.

In other cases, artworks are stolen and sold to art dealers who then sell them to customers through their art dealerships. This form of dealing, however, requires a sophisticated process of fencing. At this point, the ring of thieves that stole the art simply sells it to another ring that now specializes in making the work available on the art market itself. This function requires different sets of skills on the part of the members of these "fencing rings" and necessitates previously established contacts with shady traders in the art world market.

Although most art dealers are honest business people, there are a small number who are willing to participate in the process of buying and selling stolen art goods. Paramount to the success of these illegal enterprises or shady sales transactions is the process known as "cleaning," when the stolen work gets put on the buyer's market. In some cases, this cleaning consists merely of an art dealer, who when offered a particular work which the seller claims to have been given to him as a gift and whose financial conditions now force him to part with it, simply writes up a sales slip showing that he or she has purchased the artwork and then can readily sell it to a customer interested in buying it. In other cases, a fence approaches the art dealer with a work of art that has been stolen and, using forged forms of personal identification and a false name, presents the dealer with a forged bill of sale with which he claims ownership of the artwork. Based upon the document provided, the dealer now purchases the artwork and everything has a semblance of legitimacy; the dealer has paid for a work and now he or she can sell it to an interested customer.

The cleaning of a major work of art usually involves a more elaborate process, one requiring several steps. First, a fence places an advertisement in the local paper stating that a given individual is interested in selling a painting. A confederate, usually a little old lady, is hired by the fence to play the role as the owner of the painting and an apartment is rented with the address listed in the advertisement. When a prospective customer answers the ad and goes to the apartment to view the work, with tears in her eyes, the little old lady describes her financial difficulties since the death of her husband and how she is now forced to sell a "family heirloom" for half the price it is worth on the market. The buyer now has a painting for which he or she can produce a sales receipt and the little old lady makes ready to pose as a sorrowful widow sitting in another apartment waiting to sell yet another family heirloom.

Auction houses are one of the best outlets for fencing stolen art since the house is in possession of the seller's sales receipt and no one is interested in the provenance of the work of art. This is also a good avenue for criminals not involved in the world of art theft itself but in that of the laundering of illicit funds. By bidding on and paying in cash for a work of art, they now have the work itself and a sales slip proving legitimate ownership. They can now sell the painting either at the price they paid for it or, in some cases, at a profit above what they paid for it. Above all, in this transaction, they have succeeded in hiding the illicit origins of the funds that they used to purchase it.

Although most art thieves know the value of the works they steal, in some cases, petty thieves venture into these kinds of thefts. As Rochelle

Steinhaus (2003:79–83) notes in her discussion of the 1990 heist that took place at the Isabella Stewart Gardner Museum in Boston, many of these thieves, like the ones that participated in this theft, knew nothing about art. Instead they merely knew how to steal. As a result, during the theft that took place at this museum, in those cases where frames enclosed valuable paintings could not readily be removed from the museum walls because they were firmly attached, the thieves crudely and savagely cut the paintings out of the frames. They compromised both the beauty and the value of those paintings by doing so. Such is the nature of both the sophistication and crudity of the techniques employed in contemporary art theft.

In the world of the organized crime matrix, stolen art works are also bartered for weapons. Thus, the well-known Irish criminal Martin Cahill (better known as "the General") stole valuable paintings from the collection of Sir Alfred Beit, a collection housed in his stately home in the South of Ireland. The fencing process involving these paintings, as Paul Williams (2003:106) notes, unfolded on the international stage within a web of organized crime groups in Holland where Irish criminals have established extensive contacts through their dealings with cannabis and heroin smugglers in Amsterdam and Rotterdam. Ultimately, according to Jim McDowell (2001:32), the paintings were fenced in exchange for guns through the loyalist Ulster Volunteer Force (UVF) terrorist group operating in Portadown in Northern Ireland.

The Future of Organized Crime

As we view the organized crime matrix at this time in history, we foresee that most enterprises that we have described in this work will continue to thrive and new ones will continue to originate and evolve. For example, identity theft will take on greater proportions. As Chellis Glendinning (2002:1–8) observed, one of the consequences of globalization is the loss of everything that is encompassed within the meaning of the term "roots." With the rapid uprooting of individuals, caused either by their dislocation due to war or by the relocation into new countries necessitated by the demands brought about by the transnational nature of the future workforce, individual roots will be torn from their traditional sources and tradition will become increasingly difficult to cultivate. Whereas in the past, identities were commonly associated with community and neighborhood, the future will increasingly rely on the use of paper and plastic forms of identity. Since these can be forged, identity theft is bound to continue its rapid increase, especially when one's information can be accessed by any number of individuals working for the multinationals in numerous countries we use for banking, investing, telecommunications, information technology, travel, and shopping around the globe.

Then consider another structural vulnerability inherent to the world of big business. Although businesses are taking major steps to protect the privacy of the personal information of their clients, banks and other lenders seem reluctant to expose incidents of victimization by identity thieves as such exposure may have a negative effect on their business. Hence, as Hawkins (2003) notes, they are willing simply to write losses off as a business expense. As such, we believe the problem of identity theft will get worse before (and if) it gets better. After all, sometimes one's identity continues to live on after one's death on a massive scale. Consider what happened in Myanmar. Tens of thousands of poor but enterprising immigrants from China swept down from nearby Yunnan and purchased the identity papers of dead Burmese for as little as three hundred dollars, thus making them nationals overnight (Chua 2003:14). Such wholesale swapping of identities in a globalized world has profound implications for those who call the organized crime matrix home and the countless victims they will exploit.

As we leave our discussion of the organized crime matrix, we do so with the final observation that the matrix will continue its existence while expanding its enterprises and frontiers as the frontiers of the regions of the world break down in the process of globalization. Organized crime, as we have noted, is a component of societies everywhere. Its matrix transcends the world through the multiple forms it takes and the different strategies it employs. Organized crime is an inherent part of the world's human dynamics and social systems and will remain such so long as there are individuals in societies who seek goods and services that the governments of those societies deem illegal or that are regulated or taxed too severely.

Our most productive means of combating organized crime is to continue research that seeks to discover why certain individuals are willing to risk death and/or imprisonment to make the profits that lure them into such enterprises. Understanding these incentives will provide for society a proper target for prosecution and harm-reduction strategies. The study of organized crime is indeed fascinating in that it involves the investigation of virtually every area of life itself. Yet it can be frustrating as the complexity of the organized crime matrix hides its intricate features all too well. This is so because the study of organized crime necessitates not only discerning the motivations of the individuals who participate in its ventures, but those of representatives of government agencies and governments themselves which, through their willingness to be corrupted or themselves directly engaging in the committing of such offenses, make this enigma even more complex.

We wish we could predict that organized crime will disappear, but that would be an exercise in folly. Organized crime will continue to exist. For the sake of debating the issue, we call on history as our expert witness and ask if there has ever been a period in which organized crime has not been present as a component of its social structure? As far as we can discern, the answer is no. Although the past cannot always be used accurately to forecast the future, it seems that if organized crime, as a phenomenon, is to disappear, that will occur only when there is a complete restructuring of the opportunity-generating social institutions, reflective of social values and personal, group, and national interests, that compose the current structures of the societies of the world. Thus, ultimately, the study of organized crime is really the study of human behavior in context of the structures, roles and functions of the institutions that compose society.

Perhaps when we understand these subjects more completely, and such understanding is followed by an absolute, united and determined desire on the part of all citizens and governments toward eliminating the factors that breed it and make it more harmful, then we can create a successful strategy to end its existence forever. But given nation-states cannot agree on issues like monetary, trade, and defense policies, or even where to host the next Olympics, we are naturally pessimistic. However, our view of the pain and suffering that organized crime in its various forms has caused and continues to cause the people of the world urges us to strive ever forward in mitigating the harms organized crime creates.

For here we arrive at the essence of the organized crime matrix as a philosophical system itself; that is, we have the choice of taking the allegorical blue pill or the red pill, just like the character Neo in the film *The Matrix*. There is no question that the ingestion of the figurative blue pill has caused many Americans and citizens of other nations to view organized crime in terms of the illusions that have been offered to explain its existence. Whether or not these illusions existed in the form of the mythologies created (such as the belief in the existence of Italian criminal secret societies such as Mafia or Cosa Nostra), or whether or not they were based upon a desperate need on the part of the public to deny personal or societal responsibility and culpability (such as corruption in college and professional athletics wedded to billions in fan dollars and desires to win on the field and in the sports book), the fact remains that people seek to look beyond their own communities and their own borders to find those which they believe have brought organized crime to their communities and countries. Yet history is too powerful a witness to allow this belief to stand unchallenged. Hence, we must look for other explanations.

Ingesting the figurative red pill brings forth just too many realities that simply cannot be hidden. Therefore, we must accept certain conclusions. One major reality is found in the fact that, despite all the efforts on the part of law enforcement agencies over the past several decades, organized crime remains, both in the United States and the world, an entity that is currently alive and prospering. As Michael Woodiwiss (2001:227) so aptly observes, when we compare the status of the presence of organized crime in the United States today with that of its developing and thriving era during the 1920s and 30s, we find that police, politicians, judges, lawyers and legitimate businessmen are still as actively involved in organized crime today as they were during that era. We have, as a society, not managed over the past century to make a dent into its activities or the volume of such activities. Illusions, in the form of high-profile arrests or new "tough-on-crime" laws, have been created that have served to allow the public to temporarily obtain relief from this reality.

Thus, Lyman and Potter (1997:433–436) use the appropriate term to describe the strategy employed in such efforts: "head-hunting." The basic aim and tactic of this strategy is for the government and federal law enforcement agencies to target and prosecute the group leaders and members of organized crime syndicates. Lyman and Potter note that one of the results of this tactic is that by targeting the easiest cases and successfully prosecuting syndicate leaders who are highly visible in the eyes of the public, "good press" results for the law enforcement agencies involved. Also, the tactic serves to give the public the message that organized crime has been severely and effectively attacked and that these syndicates have been rendered ineffective. That is the illusion created by the head-hunting strategy.

This strategy goes along with taking the blue pill that offers the consoling belief that all is well. But, as Lyman and Potter go on to evaluate the reality of this strategy, they note that, ultimately, it has little impact on eliminating organized crime. The reason for this, they note, is that the head-hunting strategy is based upon a misunderstanding of the structure of the organized crime groups themselves. These structures, they argue, are such that they allow for syndicate members to adapt to a threatening legal environment. Indeed, as Lyman and Potter note, the more successful federal investigators and prosecutors are at incarcerating organized crime leaders, the more the criminal networks respond by decentralizing their structures and enterprises.

Thus, ironically, the head-hunting strategy serves to strengthen and reward some organized crime groups by helping weed out their careless, slothful, less efficient and less trustworthy competitors. Organized crime will be eliminated entirely only when all the individuals and segments of societies everywhere in the world purposefully decide that it should no longer exist. Do we believe that this will happen soon or ever? No. However, there will be those who for a variety of reasons desire or need to take the blue pill. Among these will be those political leaders or others in positions of power who in the future will continue to develop programs that further serve to give the illusion that organized crime will, with the introduction of these new programs, be forced to disappear from the earth. To those who currently maintain, or in the future come to maintain, this belief, we offer best wishes for success. However, our heartfelt advice to them would be stolen from a classic crime film: "Forget it, Jake, it's Chinatown."

Works Cited

Abadinsky, H. 1981. *The Mafia in America: An Oral History.* New York: Praeger.

Abyanker, J. 1997. "Phantom Ships." *Trends in Organized Crime* 3(4): 86–89.

Adamoli, S., A. Di Nicola, E. Savona, and P. Zoffi. 1998. *Organized Crime Around the World.* Helsinki: European Institute for Crime Prevention and Control.

Adams, D. 1999. "Drive Against the People Smugglers." *Jane's International Police Review* 14:31.

Adams, L. 1974. *Art Cop: Robert Volpe, Art Crime Detective.* New York: Dodd, Mead.

Albanese, Jay. 1991a. "Organized Crime and the Oldest Vice." Paper presented at the Annual meetings of the American Society of Criminology, San Francisco.

_____. 1991b. "Organized Crime: The Mafia Mystique." In *Criminology: A Contemporary Handbook,* edited by J. F. Sheley. Belmont, CA: Wadsworth. 201–217.

_____. 1996. *Organized Crime in America.* 3rd ed. Cincinnati: Anderson.

Albini, J. L. 1971. *The American Mafia: Genesis of a Legend.* New York: Appleton-Century-Crofts.

_____. 1986. "Organized Crime in Great Britain and the Caribbean." In *Organized Crime: A Global Perspective,* edited by R. J. Kelly. Totowa, NJ: Rowman and Littlefield. 95–112.

_____, and J. Anderson. 1998. "Whatever Happened to the KGB?" *International Journal of Intelligence and Counterintelligence* 11(1): 26–56.

_____, and R. E. Rogers. 1998. "Proposed Solutions to the Organized Crime Problem in Russia." *Demokratizatsiya* 6(1): 103–117.

_____, R. E. Rogers, V. Shabalin, V. Kutushev, V. Moiseev, J. Anderson. (1995). "Russian Organized Crime: Its History, Structure and Function." *Journal of Contemporary Criminal Justice* 11(4): 213–243.

Alexander, G. 2008. "The U.S. on Tilt: Why the Unlawful Internet Gambling Enforcement Act Is a Bad Bet." *Duke Law & Technology Review* 0006.

Andersen, K. 1994. "Las Vegas, U.S.A." *Time,* January 10, 42–51.

Anderson, A. G. 1979. *The Business of Organized Crime.* Stanford, CA: Hoover Institution Press.

Anderson, C. 2002. "U.S. Charges 4 in Drugs-Weapons Plot." *Yahoo! News.* Retrieved from http://story.news.yahoo.com/news?tmpl=story&u=asp/20021106/ap_go_ca_st_pe/drug...

Asbury, H. 1942. *Gem of the Prairie: An Informal History of the Chicago Underworld.* Garden City, NY: Garden City.

Balboni, A. 1996. *Beyond the Mafia: Italian Americans and the Development of Las Vegas.* Reno: University of Nevada Press.

Barck, O. T., and H. T. Lefler. 1968. *Colonial America.* London: Macmillan.

Barnes, H. E., and N. K. Teeters. 1959. *New Horizons in Criminology.* 3d ed. Englewood Cliffs, N.J.: Prentice Hall.

Barnes, M. A. 1999. *The Tragedy and Triumph of Phenix City, Alabama*. Macon, GA: Mercer University Press.

Bell, D. 1962. *The End of Ideology: On the Exhaustion of Political Ideas in the Fifties*. New York: Collier Books.

Bibes, P. 2001. "Transnational Organized Crime and Terrorism: Colombia, a Case Study." *Journal of Contemporary Criminal Justice* 17(3): 243–258.

Block, A. 1978. "History and the Study of Organized Crime." *Urban Life* 6: 455–474.

_____. 1979. "The Snowman Cometh: Coke in Progressive New York." *Criminology* 17, May: 75–99.

_____. 1983. *East Side-West Side: Organizing Crime in New York, 1930–1950*. New Brunswick, NJ: Transaction.

_____. 1989. "European Drug Traffic and Traffickers between the Wars: The Policy of Suppression and Its Consequences." *Journal of Social History* 23(2): 315–337.

_____. 2002. "The National Intelligence Service-Murder and Mayhem: A Historical Account." *Crime, Law and Social Change* 38(2): 89–135.

_____, and W. Chambliss. 1981. *Organizing Crime*. New York: Elsevier.

_____, and F. R. Scarpitti. 1985. *Poisoning for Profit: The Mafia and Toxic Waste in America*. New York: William Morrow.

Blok, A. 1969. "Peasants, Patrons and Brokers in Western Sicily." *Anthropological Quarterly* XLIII: 159–170.

_____. 1988. *The Mafia of a Sicilian Village 1860–1960: A Study of Violent Peasant Entrepreneurs*. Long Grove, IL: Waveland Press.

Boissevain, J. 1966. "Patronage in Sicily." *Man* I: 18–33.

Bonanno, J. 1983. *A Man of Honor: The Autobiography of a Godfather*. London: Unwin Paperbacks.

Bovenkerk, F., D. Siegel, and D. Zaitch. 2003. "Organized Crime and Ethnic Reputation Manipulation." *Crime, Law & Social Change: An International Journal* 39(1): 23–38.

Breen, T. H. 2010. *American Insurgents, American Patriots: The Revolution of the People*. New York: Hill & Wang.

Brents, B. G., and K. Hausbeck. 2001. "State-Sanctioned Sex: Negotiating Formal and Informal Regulatory Practices in Nevada Brothels." *Sociological Perspectives* 44(3): 307–332.

Brin, D. 1998. *The Transparent Society*. Reading, MA: Perseus Books.

Brink, S. 2000. "Sleepless Society." *U.S. News & World Report*, October 16, 62–72.

Bruno, C. 1900. *La Sicilia e la Mafia*. Roma: Ermanno Loeschere Co.

Business Week. 2003. "A Nation's Past Wiped Out in a Flash: Why the Looting of Baghdad's Museum Seems Premeditated." April 28, 35.

Caldwell, R. G. 1965. *Criminology*. 3d ed. New York: The Ronald Press.

Candida, R. 1964. *Questa Mafia*. 3d ed. Roma: Salvatore Sciascia, Editore.

Carr, C. 2002. *The Lessons of Terror: A History of Warfare against Civilians—Why It Has Always Failed and Why It Will Fail Again*. New York: Random House.

Casino Advisor. 2008. "An Analysis of the UIGEA: Legal and Practical Repercussions." January 5. Retrieved from http://www.casinoadvisor.com/uigea-article.html.

_____. (n.d.). "USA Online Casinos." Retrieved from http://www.casinoadvisor.com/usa-online-casinos.html.

CBS News. 2009. "Following the Trail of Toxic E-Waste." August 27. Retrieved from http://www.cbsnews.com/stories/2008/11/06/60minutes/main4579229.shtml.

Chan, A. B. 2010. *Arming the Chinese: The Western Armaments Trade in Warlord China, 1920–1928*. 2d ed. Vancouver: University of British Colombia Press.

Chang, I. 1998. *The Rape of Nanking: The Forgotten Holocaust of World War II*. New York: Penguin.

Chua, A. 2003. *World on Fire: How Exporting Free Market Democracy Breeds Ethnic Hatred and Global Instability.* New York: Doubleday.

CNN. 2003. "'Shoot-to-Kill' in Thai Drugs War." February 21. Retrieved from http://article s.cnn.com/2003-02-21/world/thailand.drugs_1_suspicious-death-human-rights-drug s?_s=PM:asiapcf.

Cohen, R. 1998. *Tough Jews: Fathers, Sons, and Gangster Dreams*. New York: Simon & Schuster.

Cohen, S. F. 2000. *Failed Crusade: America and the Tragedy Of Post-Communist Russia*. New York: W. W. Norton.

Collier, P. 2003. "The Market for Civil War." *Foreign Policy*, May/June, 38–45.

Collins Mondadori Nuovo Dizionario Inglese. 1997. New York: HarperCollins.

Combating Organized Crime. 1966. Report of the 1965 Oyster Bay, New York, Conferences on Combating Organized Crime. Albany: Office of the Counsel to the Governor.

Cook, F. F. 1910. *Bygone Days in Chicago: Recollections of the "Garden City" of the Sixties*. Chicago: A. C. McClung.

Cooley, J. K. 2000. *Unholy Wars: Afghanistan, America and International Terrorism*. 2d ed. London: Pluto Press.

Coontz, P. 2001. "Managing the Action: Sports Bookmakers as Entrepreneurs." *Deviant Behavior* 22(3): 239–266.

Cordingly, D. 1995. *Under The Black Flag: The Romance and the Reality of Life Among the Pirates*. San Diego: Harcourt Brace.

Cowan, R., and D. Century. 2002. *Takedown: The Fall of the Last Mafia Empire*. New York: G.P. Putnam's Sons.

Cressey, D. 1969. *Theft of the Nation: The Structure and Operations of Organized Crime in America*. New York: Harper and Row.

Dallaire, R., and I. Beah. 2011. *They Fight Like Soldiers, They Die Like Children: The Global Quest to Eradicate the Use of Child Soldiers*. New York: Walker & Company.

D'Allessandro, E. 1959. *Brigandaggio e Mafia in Sicilia*. Firenza: Casa Editrice G. D'Anna.

Demaris, O. 1981. *The Last Mafioso: The Treacherous World of Jimmy Fratianno*. New York: Times Books.

Denton, S., and R. Morris. 2001. *The Money and the Power: The Making of Las Vegas and Its Hold on America, 1947–2000*. New York: Alfred A. Knopf.

Department of Health and Human Services. (n.d.). "Labor Trafficking Fact Sheet." Retrieved from http://www.acf.hhs.gov/trafficking/about/fact_labor.pdf.

Dettmer, J. 2002. "Cash Combat." *Insight* 18(12), April 1–8, 12–14.

Dickey, C. 2002. "Fears in the 'Un-America.'" *Newsweek*, February 11, 30–35.

Dillon, R. H. 1962. *The Hatchet Men: The Story of the Tong Wars in San Francisco's Chinatown*. New York: Coward-McCann.

Duffy, W. J. 1967. "Organized Crime-Illegal Activities." *Law Enforcement Science and Technology*. Washington, DC: Thompson Book Company.

Durkheim, E. 1997. *Suicide: A Study in Sociology*. New York: Free Press.

Eichstaedt, P. 2009. *First Kill Your Family: Child Soldiers of Uganda and the Lord's Resistance Army*. Chicago: Lawrence Hill Books.

El Mundo. 2003. "Gangs of Madrid Are at War." 3(100), April 11, 13.

Elliot, M. 1953. *Crime in Modern Society*. New York: Harper and Brothers.

Esterow, M. 1973. *The Art Stealers*. Rev. ed. New York: Macmillan.

Farrah, D. 2004. *Blood from Stones: The Secret Financial Network of Terror*. New York: Broadway.

Farrell, R., and C. Case. 1995. *The Black Book and the Mob: The Untold Story of the Control of Nevada's Casinos*. Madison: University of Wisconsin Press.

Feitlowitz, M. 1999. *A Lexicon of Terror: Argentina and the Legacies of Torture*. New York: Oxford University Press.

Fong, S. H. 1898. "Letter from Soo How Fong to Chan Mi Puing." As found in U.S. Senate, *Testimony Taken before the Committee on Immigration*, 1902.

Foreign Policy. 2002. "The People Trade." March/April, 31–35.

Frasca, D. 1963. *Vito Genovese: King of Crime*. New York: Avon Books.

Fremantle, B. 1985. *The Fix: Inside the World Drug Trade*. New York: Tom Doherty Associates.

Froehlich, L. 2002. "Al Qaeda at Home, Our Home: A Conversation with Rohan Gunaratna." *Playboy*, November, 72–74, 147–150.

Fukuyama, F. 1999. *The Great Disruption: Human Nature and the Reconstitution of Social Order*. New York: Touchstone.

Galliher, J., and J. Cain. 1974. "Citation Support for the Mafia Myth in Criminology Textbooks." *The American Sociologist* 9(2), May, 68–74.

Gambetta, D. 1993. *The Sicilian Mafia: The Business of Private Protection*. Cambridge, MA: Harvard University Press.

Glendinning, C. 2002. *Off the Map: An Expedition Deep into Empire and the Global Economy*. Gabriola Island, BC, Canada: New Society Publishers.

Gong, E. Y., and B. Grant. 1930. *Tong War! The First Complete History of the Tongs in America, Details of the Tong Wars and Their Causes, Lives of Famous Hatchetmen and Gunmen, and Inside Information as to the Workings of the Tongs, Their Aims and Achievements*. New York: Nicolas L. Brown.

Gosch, M. A., and R. Hammer. 1976. *The Last Testament of Lucky Luciano*. New York: Dell.

Greenpeace. 2007. "Toxic Tea Party." July 23. Retrieved from http://www.greenpeace.org/international/en/news/features/e-waste-china-toxic-pollution-230707/.

Grey, S., and A. Schecter. 2007. "Exclusive: 11 Tons of Opium Discovered in Taliban Town." *ABC News*. December 20. Retrieved from http://abcnews.go.com/blogs/headlines/2007/12/exclusive-11-to/.

Griffin, S.P. 2003. *Philadelphia's Black Mafia: A Social and Political History*. New York: Springer.

_____. 2005. *Black Brothers, Inc.: The Violent Rise and Fall of Philadelphia's Black Mafia*. Wrea Green, UK: Milo Books.

_____. 2011. *Gaming the Game: The Story Behind the NBA Betting Scandal and the Gambler Who Made It Happen*. Fort Lee, NJ: Barricade Books.

Gwynne, S.C. 2010. *Empire of the Summer Moon: Quanah Parker and the Rise and Fall of the Comanches, the Most Powerful Indian Tribe in American History*. New York: Scribner.

Hack, R. 2001. *Hughes: The Private Diaries, Memos, Letters; The Definitive Biography of the First American Billionaire*. Beverly Hills, CA: New Millennium Press.

Haller, M. 1985. "Bootleggers as Businessmen: From City Slums to City Builders." Pp. In *Law, Alcohol, and Order: Perspectives on National Prohibition*, edited by D. E. Kyvig. Westport, CT: Greenwood Press. 139–157.

Handelman, S. 1997. *Comrade Criminal: Russia's New Mafiya*. New Haven: Yale University Press.

Hardt, M., and A. Negri. 2000. *Empire*. Cambridge, MA: Harvard University Press.

Hawkins, D. 2003. "Hide and They Can't Seek." *U.S. News & World Report*, May 19, 39.

Hawkins, G. 1969. "God and the Mafia." *The Public Interest* 14, Winter, 24–51.

Hedges, C. 2002. *War Is a Force That Gives Us Meaning*. New York: Public Affairs.

Held, D., A. McGrew, D. Goldblatt and J. Perraton. 1999. *Global Transformations: Politics, Economics, Culture*. Stanford, CA: Stanford University Press.

Henderson, M. A. 1986. *Rip-Offs, Cons and Swindles: Money for Nothing*. Fort Lee, NJ: Barricade Books.

Heppner, K. 2002. *"My Gun Was as Tall as Me: Child Soldiers in Burma."* New York: Human Rights Watch.

Hess, H. 1973. *Mafia and Mafioso: The Structure of Power*. Lexington, MA: Lexington Books.

Hicks, G. 1997. *The Comfort Women: Japan's Brutal Regime of Enforced Prostitution in the Second World War*. New York: W.W. Norton.

Hirata, L. C. 1979. "Free, Indentured, Enslaved: Chinese Prostitutes in 19th-Century America." *Signs: Journal of Women in Culture and Society* 5(1): 3–29.

Homeland Security Newswire. 2011. "China Plans to Build Alternative to Panama Canal." March 2. Retrieved from http://www.homelandsecuritynewswire.com/china-plans-build-alternative-panama-canal.

Hopkins, N. and R. N. Taylor. 2002. "Heroin: MI5 Fears Flood of Heroin." *The Guardian*, February 21. Retrieved from http://www.guardian.co.uk/uk/2002/feb/21/drugsandalcohol.afghanistan1.

Hosenball, M. 2002. "Islamic Cyberterror." *Newsweek*, May 20, 10.

Huston, P. 1995. *Tongs, Gangs and Triads: Chinese Crime Groups in North America*. Boulder, CO: Paladin Press.

Jackman, I., ed. 2003. *Con Men: Fascinating Profiles of Swindlers and Rogues from the Files of the Most Successful Broadcast in Television History*. New York: Simon & Schuster.

Jacobs, J. B., C. Friel, and R. Radick. 1998. *Gotham Unbound: How New York Was Liberated from the Grip of Organized Crime*. New York: New York University Press.

Jonnes, Jill. 1999. *Hep Cats, Narcs, and Pipe Dreams: A History of America's Romance with Illegal Drugs*. Baltimore: Johns Hopkins University Press.

Kempton, M. 1969. "Crime Does Not Pay." *New York Review of Books*, 13, September 11: 25–39.

Kennedy, R. F. 1994. *The Enemy Within: The Mcclellan Committee's Crusade Against Jimmy Hoffa and Corrupt Labor Unions*. New York: Da Capo Press.

Kilby, J., and J. Fox. 1998. *Casino Operations Management*. New York: John Wiley & Sons.

Klebnikov, P. 2000. *Godfather of the Kremlin: Boris Berezovsky and the Looting of Russia*. New York: Harcourt.

Lasswell, H. D., and J. McKenna. 1971. *The Impact of Organized Crime on an Inner — City Community*. New York: Policy Sciences Center.

Leatherman, J. L. 2011. *Sexual Violence and Armed Conflict*. Cambridge, UK: Polity.

Lee III, R., and F. E. Thoumi. 1999. "The Political-Criminal Nexus in Colombia." *Trends in Organized Crime* 5(2), Winter, 59–84.

Lestingi, F. 1884. "L'Associazione della Fratellanza nella provincial di Gergenti." *Archivo di psichiatria*, ed. Scienze Penali, *Antropologia Criminale*, IV, 452–463.

Levine, S. 2003. "Unfriendly Skies." *U.S. News & World Report*, April, 48.

Liddick, D. 1999. *The Mob's Daily Number: Organized Crime and the Numbers Gambling Industry*. New York: University Press of America.

Lorenz, A. 2005. "Choking on Chemicals in China." *Spiegel Online*, November 28. Retrieved from http://www.spiegel.de/international/spiegel/0,1518,387392,00.html.

Lowry, T. P. 1994. *The Story the Soldiers Wouldn't Tell*. Mechanicsburg, PA: Stackpole.

Lyman, M. D., and G. W. Potter. 1997. *Organized Crime.* Upper Saddle River, NJ: Prentice Hall.

Maas, P. 1968. *The Valachi Papers.* New York: Putnam.

Maheu, R., and R. Hack. 1992. *Next to Hughes: Behind the Power and Tragic Downfall of Howard Hughes by His Closest Advisor.* New York: HarperCollins.

Maltz, M. D. 1994. "Defining Organized Crime." In *Handbook of Organized Crime in the United States,* edited by R. J. Kelly, Ko-Lin Chin, and R. Schatzberg. Westport, CT: Greenwood Press. 21–37.

Martens, F. T. 1991. "Transnational Enterprise Crime: A Comparative Perspective." In *Illicit Drugs And Organized Crime: Issues for a United Europe,* edited by S. Flood. Chicago: The Office of International Criminal Justice. 1–12.

McCoy, A. 2003. *The Politics of Heroin in Southeast Asia: CIA Complicity in the Global Drug Trade.* Chicago: Lawrence Hill Books.

McDowell, J. 2001. *Godfathers: Inside North Ireland's Drugs Racket.* Dublin: Gill and Macmillan.

McGraw, D. 1997. "The National Bet." *U.S. News & World Report,* April 7, 50–55.

McIllwain, J. S. 1997. "From Tong War to Organized Crime: Revising the Historical Perception of Violence in Chinatown." *Justice Quarterly* 14(1), March, 25–51.

_____. 1998. "An Equal Opportunity Employer: Chinese Opium Smuggling Networks in and around San Diego during the 1910s." *Transnational Organized Crime* 4(2): 31–54.

_____. 1999. "Organizing Crime: A Social Network Approach." *Crime, Law & Social Change: An International Journal* 32(4): 301–323.

_____. 2003. *Organizing Crime in Chinatown: Race, and Racketeering in New York City, 1890–1910.* Jefferson, NC: McFarland.

_____. 2004. "Bureaucratic Rivalry, Corruption and Organized Crime: Enforcing Exclusion in San Diego, 1897–1902." *Western Legal History* 17(1): 83–128.

_____, and Leisz, C. 2006. "California Dreams and Gangster Schemes: The Standley Commission, the Guarantee Finance Company, and the Social System of Organized Crime in post-World War II Southern California." In *The Organized Crime Community: Essays in Honor of Alan Block,* edited by Frank Bovenkerk, and Michael Levi. New York: Springer. 31–44.

McMahon, C. 2001. "Russia Oks Nuclear Waste Plan." *Las Vegas Review-Journal,* June 7: 1A, 17A.

Merzer, M. 2009. "New Internet Gambling Regulations Go into Effect." *Credit Cards.com,* January 9. Retrieved from http://www.creditcards.com/credit-card-news/unlawful-intern et-gambling-enforcement-act-credit-card-1282.php.

Meyer, K., and T. Parssinen. 1998. *Web of Smoke: Smugglers, Warlords, Spies, and the History of the International Drug Trade.* New York: Rowman and Littlefield.

Michalowski, R. J. 1985. *Order, Law and Crime: An Introduction to Criminology.* New York: Random House.

Middlemas, K. 1975. *Double Market: Art Theft and Art Thieves.* Farnborough, England: Saxon House DC Heath, Ltd.

Mieczkowski, T., and J. L. Albini. 1987. "The War on Crime: Are Social Scientists Effective in Changing Conceptions of Organized Crime?" *Law Enforcement Intelligence Analysis Digest* 2, February, 45–56.

Migliorini, B., and T. G. Griffith. 1966. *The Italian Language.* London: Faber and Faber.

Milmo, C. 2009. "Dumped in Africa: Britain's Toxic Waste." *The Independent,* February

18. Retrieved from http://www.independent.co.uk/news/world/africa/dumped-in-africa-britain8217s-toxic-waste-1624869.html.

Moehring, E. 1989. *Resort City in the Sunbelt*. Reno: University of Nevada Press.

Montalbano, G. 1953. "La Mafia." *Nuovi Argumenti* V, November–December, 168–182.

Moore, W. H. 1974. *The Kefauver Committee and the Politics of Crime, 1950–1952*. Colombia: University of Missouri Press.

Myers, D. G. 2002. *Intuition: Its Powers and Perils*. New Haven: Yale University Press.

Nelli, H. S. 1976. *The Business of Crime: Italian Syndicate Crime in the United States*. New York: Oxford University Press.

Norton-Taylor, R. 2010. "Leaked Afghanistan Files Reveal Corruption and Drug-Dealing." *The Guardian*, July 26. Retrieved from http://www.guardian.co.uk/world/2010/jul/26/leaked-afghanistan-files-corruption-drug-dealing.

Pantaleone, M. 1966. *The Mafia and Politics*. New York: Coward-McCann.

Paoli, L. 1999. "The Political-Criminal Nexus in Italy." *Trends in Organized Crime* 5(2), Winter, 15–58.

_____. 2003. *Mafia Brotherhoods: Organized Crime, Italian Style*. New York: Oxford University Press.

Paulsen, G. E. 1971. "The Yellow Peril at Nogales: The Ordeal of Collector William M. Hoey." *Arizona and the West* 13: 113–28.

Peters, G. 2009. *Seeds of Terror: How Heroin Is Bankrolling the Taliban and Al Qaeda*. New York: St. Martin's Press.

_____. 2010. *Crime and Insurgency in the Tribal Areas of Afghanistan and Pakistan*. West Point, NY: Combatting Terrorism Center.

Pileggi, N. 1995. *Casino: Love and Honor in Las Vegas*. New York: Simon & Schuster.

Pitre, G. 1904. *Bibliotecha della Tradizioni Populari Siciliane, XXII, Studi di Leggende (Populari) in Sicilia*. Torino: Carlo Clausen.

_____. 1889. *Bibliotecha della Tradizioni Populari Siciliane, XV, Usi e Costumi, Credenze e Preguidici*. Palermo: Lauriel di Carlo Clausen.

Potter, G. 1994. *Criminal Organizations: Vice, Racketeering and Politics in an American City*. Prospect Heights, IL: Waveland Press.

President's Commission on Law Enforcement and Administration of Justice. Task Force on Organized Crime. 1967. *Task Force Report: Organized Crime*. Washington, DC: Government Printing Office.

Preston, C. 2009. *Drugs and Conflict in Colombia: A Policy Analysis of Plan Colombia*. Saarbrücken, Germany: VDM Verlag.

Puzo, M. 1969. *The Godfather*. New York: G. P. Putnam and Sons.

Rashid, A. 2001. *Taliban: Militant Islam, Oil and Fundamentalism in Central Asia*. New Haven: Yale Note Bene Books.

Reid, E. 1954. *Mafia*. 2d ed. New York: Signet.

Reuter, P. 1983. *Disorganized Crime: Illegal Markets and the Mafia*. Cambridge: MIT Press.

_____, and Rubinstein, J. 1982. *Illegal Gambling in New York: A Case Study in the Operation, Structure and Regulation of an Illegal Market*. Washington, DC: Government Printing Office.

Robinson, A. 2000. *Bin Laden*. New York: Arcade.

Robinson, J. 2002. *The Merger: The International Conglomerate of Organized Crime*. New York: The Overlook Press.

Roemer, W. F. 1990. *War of The Godfathers*. New York: Ivy Books.

_____. 1994. *The Enforcer*. New York: Ivy Books.

Rogovin, C. H., and F. T. Martens. 1989. "Albini on Cressey." *Criminal Organizations*, 4(4): 11–14.

Rose, I. N. 2006. "Congress Makes Sausages." *Gambling and the Law*. Retrieved from http://www.gamblingandthelaw.com/columns/209-congress-makes-sausages.html.

Rosen, C. 1999. *The Scandals of '51: How the Gamblers Almost Killed College Basketball*. New York: Seven Stories Press.

Ruth, D. E. 1996. *Inventing the Public Enemy: The Gangster in American Culture, 1918–1934*. Chicago: University of Chicago Press.

Safe and Secure Internet Gambling Initiative. 2011. "Congressional Hearing Focuses on Need for Internet Gambling Regulation to Protect Consumers." *PR Newswire*, October 25.

Salgo, L. 1999. "Challenge of Organized Crime." Paper presented at a conference sponsored by the George C. Marshall European Center for Security Studies and The Federal Bureau of Investigation, Garmisch-Partenkirchen, Germany. August 29–September 2.

Sasuly, R. 1982. *Bookies and Bettors: Two Hundred Years of Gambling*. New York: Holt, Rinehart and Winston.

Satter, D. 2004. *Darkness at Dawn: The Rise of the Russian Criminal State*. New Haven: Yale University Press.

Saviano, R. 2008. *Gomorrah: A Personal Journey into the Violent International Empire of Naples' Organized Crime System*. New York: Picador.

Scarne, J. 1949. *Scarne on Cards*. New York: Signet.

_____. 1961. *Scarne's Complete Guide to Gambling*. New York: Simon & Schuster.

_____. 1976. *The Mafia Conspiracy*. North Bergen, NJ: Scarne Enterprises.

Scarpitti, F. R., and A. Block. 1987. "America's Toxic Waste Racket: Dimensions of the Environmental Crisis." In *Organized Crime in America: Concepts and Controversies*, edited by T. S. Bynum. Monsey, NY: Criminal Justice Press. 115–128.

Schulte-Bockholt, A. 2001. "A Neo-Marxist Explanation of Organized Crime." *Critical Criminology* 10(3): 225–242.

Science Daily. 2010. "Hazardous E-Waste Surging in Developing Countries," February 22. Retrieved from http://www.sciencedaily.com/releases/2010/02/100222081911.htm.

Scientific American. 2000. "Special Report: Waging a New Kind of War." June, 48–65.

Shannon, E. 2002. "Who Built Reid's Shoes?" *Time*, February 25, 50.

Sifakis, C. 1999. *The Mafia Encyclopedia*. 2d ed. New York: Checkmark Books.

Singer, P. W. *Children at War*. Berkeley: University of California Press.

Sladen, D. 1907. *Sicily*. New York: E. P. Dutton.

Smith, D. C. 1990. *The Mafia Mystique*. New York: University Press of America.

Soh, C. S. 2009. *The Comfort Women: Sexual Violence and Postcolonial Memory in Korea and Japan*. Chicago: University of Chicago Press.

Sprigle, R. 1950. "Numbers Take $50,000,000 Yearly in City." *Pittsburgh Post-Gazette*, July 10, 1.

Steinhaus, R. 2003. "Raiders of the Lost Art." *Razor* 3(8), July/August, 79–83.

Strumpf, K. 2003. "Illegal Sports Bookmakers." Unpublished paper. Located at http://rgco.org/articles/illegal_sports_bookmakers.pdf.

Surette, Ray 2006. *Media, Crime, and Criminal Justice: Images, Realities and Policies*. Beverly, MA: Wadsworth.

Sylos-Labini, P. 1961. "Problems of Sicilian Economic Development Changes in Rural-Urban Relations in Eastern Sicily." Mediterranean Social Sciences Research Council, General Assembly. Catania. October 30–November 4.

Taft, D. R. and R. W. England. 1964. *Criminology*. 4th ed. New York: Macmillan.

Talbot, S. 2002. *The Russia Hand: A Memoir of Presidential Diplomacy.* New York: Random House.

Taylor, D. 1997. *Disappearing Acts: Spectacles of Gender and Nationalism in Argentina's "Dirty War."* Durham: Duke University Press.

Teresa, V. 1973. "A Mafioso Cases the Mafia Craze." *The Saturday Review,* February 23–29.

_____, and T. C. Renner. 1973b. *My Life in the Mafia.* Greenwich, CT: Fawcett.

Tongsrichum, C. 2002. "Psychological Warfare Along the Thai-Burmese Border." *World Press Review* 49(8), August, 35.

Transparency International. 2010. "Corruption Perception Index 2010 Results." Retrieved from http://www.transparency.org/policy_research/surveys_indices/cpi/2010/results.

U. S. Senate. 1963. Committee on Government Operations. "Organized Crime and Illicit Traffic in Narcotics." Hearings before the Permanent Subcommittee on Investigations. 88th Cong., 1st sess.

Varese, F. 2001. *The Russian Mafia: Private Protection in a New Market Economy.* New York: Oxford University Press.

_____. 2011. *Mafias on the Move: How Organized Crime Conquers New Territory.* Princeton, NJ: Princeton University Press.

Wessells, M. 2009. *Child Soldiers: From Violence to Protection.* Cambridge, MA: Harvard University Press.

Williams, P. 1997. "Human Commodity Trafficking: An Overview." *Transnational Organized Crime,* 3(4), Winter, 1–10.

Wintour, P. 2002. "Legalize All Drugs Worldwide, Says Britain's Former Cabinet Minister." *The Guardian,* September 22. Retrieved from http://www.disinfo.com/pages/article/id 2736/pgl/.

Wired Magazine. 2000. "Caught in the Act." November, 110.

_____. 2002. "Radioactive Leak: Tracking the Trade in Runaway Nuke Materials Worldwide." August, 44–45.

Wolf, E. 1966. "Kinship, Friendship and Patron-Client Relations in Complex Societies." In *The Social Anthropology of Complex Societies,* edited by M. Banton. London, Routledge. 1–22.

Woodiwiss, M. 2001. *Organized Crime and American Power: A History.* Toronto: University of Toronto Press.

Yergin, D., and T. Gustafson. 1995. *Russia 2010: And What It Means to the World.* New York: Vintage Press.

Zaitch, D. 2002. *Trafficking Cocaine.* The Hague, the Netherlands: Kluwer Law International.

Zhang, S. 2007. *Smuggling and Trafficking in Human Beings: All Roads Lead to America.* Westport, CT: Praeger.

_____, and Ko-Lin Chin. 2002. "Enter the Dragon: Inside Chinese Human Smuggling Organizations." *Criminology* 40(4): 737–768.

Index